Contents

Preface

This book contains several cases illustrating psychological consultation and collaboration. Written by authorities in the field for undergraduate and graduate students in the helping professions, it is designed to fill the gap between knowing what consultation and collaboration are and knowing how to conduct them. Psychological Consultation and Collaboration: A Casebook is the result of my increasing concern that, in order to be effective in their efforts to engage in consultation and collaboration, students in the helping professions need a firm and realistic grasp of what occurs during these two unique helping relationships.

My own experience and the discussions I have had over the years with others who teach courses in consultation and collaboration have led me to conclude that the most difficult aspect of teaching these subjects is "bringing them alive"; that is, helping the student better understand, in interesting ways, the links between theory and practice. To this end, in my course I have students engage in consultation and collaboration in the field, make extensive use of role-play involving practice of consultative and collaborative skills, provide instructional videos from my own practice of consultation, and discuss case examples illustrating the primary elements of the processes of consultation and collaboration.

Cases, such as those included throughout this text, can provide an added dimension in the attempt to help students understand not only what consultation and collaboration are but also how to engage in them effectively. In my opinion, the study of cases creates unique learning opportunities that teach students to blend theory and practice. This blending likely assists students to develop the best methods when they provide consultation and collaboration services in their professional lives. Through the cases in this text, I have tried to present a cross section of real-life consultation and collaboration as they exist today. One distinguishing element of this book is its emphasis on providing services in a variety of community and school settings. By understanding the wide applicability of consultation and collaboration, students may well be better able to provide effective services in a variety of settings.

FEATURES OF THE FOURTH EDITION

This fourth edition of the text retains the name Psychological Consultation and Collaboration: A Casebook to more accurately reflect its expanded content. It has been extensively revised and updated. Since the previous edition was published, collaboration has continued to become increasingly important to the helping professions. Consequently, in this edition I have maintained two cases involving collaboration, each written by a recognized authority in that area. Cases from the previous edition have been both updated and revised. Each chapter contains a new section entitled "Tips for Practice." Important aspects for each case include a description of the model used in the case and a set of questions for discussion and reflection. Following the cases, the penultimate chapter focuses on the key themes brought out in the cases. The final chapter, which includes several practice cases, has been expanded with a practice case on positive behavior support.

BENEFITS OF USING CASES

Why use cases as a tool for teaching consultation and collaboration? First, cases allow for some of the complex variables that impact the consultative and collaborative processes (such as their organizational context) to be analyzed and related to effective practice. Second, cases bring novice helpers closer to real-life consultation and collaboration. Cases provide a nice interface between content and practice. Third, cases offer specific situations that call for analysis and specific application. By analyzing such situations, students will develop habits that they then will generalize to real-life practice. Fourth, the cases reflect my view that the organizational context in which consultation or collaboration occurs strongly influences their processes. For example, how a consultant would go about process consultation in a health care setting will vary from how process consultation is performed in a university counseling center. The cases used in this text represent a variety of settings to help the novice gain insight into organizational dynamics as they affect consultation and collaboration.

Cases make the reader an active participant. By being involved intellectually and emotionally with a case, the reader will most likely benefit more than by hearing a lecture about some aspect of consultation or collaboration. Cases allow readers to test their knowledge of theories with practice. They do this by raising questions in the mind of the reader that encourage problem solving and reflection. Finally, the analysis of cases in the classroom provides an exciting approach to teaching. The cases in this book and the questions that follow them foster learning that is marked by the opportunity for thoughtful and lively discussions.

I am of the opinion that the use of cases has a more powerful impact when small group instruction and discussion are employed.

THE ORGANIZATION OF THIS BOOK

Psychological Consultation and Collaboration: A Casebook is divided into five parts. Chapter 1 gives the reader a brief overview of psychological consultation and collaboration.

The reader may then proceed to read and analyze cases in consultation or collaboration in each of the next nine chapters. Each of the cases is written in the following format: a description of the model used; setting and background issues; goals; functions and roles taken on by the helper; the experiences of the people receiving assistance; techniques and procedures employed throughout the stages of entry, diagnosis, implementation, and disengagement; implications for practice; tips for practice, questions for discussion and reflection; and references and suggested readings. Such a format should facilitate, across the cases, the identification of the major concepts and procedural dilemmas common to the practice of consultation and collaboration.

In Part 2 of the text, three case studies illustrate different forms of case consultation. In Chapter 2, Carrington Rotto shares a behavioral case consultation involving a teacher. Tack and Morrow describe in Chapter 3 a prototype mental health consultation case revolving around a client with AIDS. Kottman, in Chapter 4, presents an illustration of Adlerian case consultation in a school setting.

Part 3 of this book provides four cases studies that describe different types of organizational and group consultation. In Chapter 5, Deck and Isenhour discuss an innovative education/training consultation with school personnel. James, Addy and Crews, in Chapter 6, relate an example of a systems model of program consultation with a police department. In Chapter 7, Tack, Morrow and I describe a case of process consultation with a university counseling center. In Chapter 8, Becker-Reems discusses a case of process consultation in a health care setting.

Part 4 presents two case studies on collaboration. In Chapter 9, DeEsch and Murphy present a case using collaboration in a university reading and writing center. Boat and Boat, in Chapter 10, write about a case of collaborative teaming in special education.

Finally, in Part 5, I discuss conclusions suggested by the case studies and provide some practice case studies. In Chapter 11, I discuss the implications of these cases for the effective practice of consultation and collaboration. I provide nine more cases for practice in Chapter 12. These cases are open ended and each contains extenuating circumstances that challenge the reader to determine how to proceed with the case.

Psychological Consultation and Collaboration: A Casebook is intended as a supplement to Psychological Consultation and Collaboration in School and Community Settings (Fourth Edition, 2005) or any other basic consultation text. I make the assumption in Psychological Consultation and Collaboration: A Casebook that the reader is becoming, or is already, familiar with the literature on consultation and collaboration. This text can be used alone with advanced students in seminars, practica, and internship courses. It is my hope that this book will contribute to the student's professional development by providing a real-life sense of the enterprises we call consultation and collaboration.

Acknowledgments

I would like to thank Dr. Larry Golden who years ago provided his ideas on getting a book such as this off the ground. I am grateful to all of the contributors for taking time from their busy schedules and for helping to produce a quality text. My many graduate students over the years have contributed to this text by providing their input into how they learn best, with many pointing out the value of studying real-life cases as instrumental to their learning how to engage in consultation and collaboration effectively. Many thanks to all of the clients, consultees, and fellow collaborators with whom I have had the privilege of working over the years. I can only hope that they have received as much enhancement in the quality of their lives from our work together as I have received in mine. I am indebted to my family for all of the love and support they provided me during the term of this project. Finally, to the fine people at Brooks/Cole and Wadsworth, my sincerest thanks for all of the support and professional assistance in this endeavor.

**To my family: Leslie, Matt, and Ashley;
and in memory of my wonderful parents**

PART I

The Basics of Consultation and Collaboration

Before you start reading the case studies, I would like to suggest that you read Chapter 1, which reviews the basics of consultation and collaboration. This review will help you approach the cases with some concepts and ideas that allow for greater depth of understanding and analysis. I hope you'll consider referring back to Chapter 1 while reading the cases to supplement your thoughts about what you are reading.

Introduction

A. MICHAEL DOUGHERTY

OVERVIEW OF THIS BOOK

One of the most difficult things to learn in any of the helping professions is how to get down to the basics, or "nitty-gritty," and actually help someone. This is certainly true for mental health professionals when they engage in the services of consultation and collaboration. It is one thing to know theories and concepts related to consultation and collaboration and another to be able to effectively apply them. One way to attempt to link theories and concepts with effective practice is to study actual cases in consultation and collaboration.

The use of cases can help answer the question, What do experienced and effective practitioners "know" about consultation and collaboration when they conduct these activities? One thing effective practitioners know is the practical wisdom about common circumstances encountered in their work. By reading and analyzing cases, prospective consultants and collaborators can tap that practical wisdom. Another thing such experienced and effective practitioners know is that they carry their own "personal baggage" to the consultation and collaboration process. By reading the cases of experienced consultants and collaborators, perhaps prospective helpers will become more aware of some of their own personal issues and will better understand how these issues may impact their practice.

The main purposes of this text are to provide you, through exposure to consultation and collaboration cases, with a view of real-life consultation and collaboration and to assist you in beginning to develop your own personalized style of providing these services. By reading how practicing professionals actually consult and collaborate, you can obtain a better grasp of the mechanics or "nuts and bolts" of these activities in real-life situations. By being asked to analyze and discuss these cases, you will be able to identify a sense of "who you are" as a consultant and collaborator and thus begin to forge a personalized approach to these activities.

In this first chapter, I present an overview of consultation and collaboration. In each of the following nine chapters (Chapters 2–10), one or more practicing professionals present a case illustrating consultation or collaboration. Each case shows how a certain approach to consultation or collaboration is applied in a given setting. At the end of each case, you are asked to critically analyze it using the questions for discussion and reflection as a guide.

Following the case study chapters, Chapter 11 pulls together the ideas of the case contributors and focuses on implications for effective practice. In Chapter 12, I provide nine additional practice cases for your consideration. For each case in this final chapter there is a brief description of the case itself along with some extenuating circumstances I have chosen to add. Given that information, you are asked how you would proceed as the consultant or collaborator in the case.

It is important to review the basics of psychological consultation and collaboration to provide a common ground for exploring the cases. Consultation and collaboration are becoming even more important in the practice of many professionals and are becoming increasing scientifically based (Zins, 2002). The next section of this chapter provides you with a brief overview of consultation and collaboration. First, I define consultation and list its characteristics. Next, I note the skills consultants need to be effective, the roles they frequently assume, and some popular models of consultation. I then discuss the recent emergence of collaboration as a viable service that practitioners in the helping professions can provide.

You should not be misled by the proportion of space allocated to consultation relative to collaboration in the discussion that follows. In fact, the knowledge base, skills, and attitudes required in collaboration are essentially the same as those employed in consultation (West & Idol, 1993). Finally, I briefly discuss ethical behavior in consultation and collaboration.

CONSULTATION

Human service professionals such as counselors, psychologists, social workers, and human resource specialists practice consultation in a variety of settings.

For example, a counselor educator assists the staff of a counseling center in identifying its major work concerns and in making plans to solve them. Or a school psychologist consults with a team of teachers concerning the classroom behavior of certain children. Consultation is one of many roles human service professionals can take on when providing assistance to others.

Throughout this text the term consultant is used interchangeably with human service professional all the while understanding that consultation is only one of the roles the professional might assume.

When human service professionals consult, their primary purpose is to help their consultees to work more effectively with the concerns that led to the request for consultation. Consultation can be defined as a process in which a human service professional assists a consultee with a work-related (or caretaking-related) problem with a client system, with the goal of helping both the consultee and the client system in some specified way (Dougherty, 2005). When they consult, human service professionals assist other professionals (consultees) as well as parents of children. The client system can consist of an individual, group, organization, or the entire community.

CHARACTERISTICS OF CONSULTATION

Consultation has many agreed-upon characteristics. Here is a list of some of the more common ones: _ Consultation is one of a variety of professional roles taken on by human service professionals.

- Consultation is a problem-solving process with the term problem defined in the broad sense as something needing consideration.

- Consultation is triadic in nature: the three parties are the consultant, the consultee and the client system. The consultant delivers direct service to the consultee who delivers direct service to the client system. The consultant provides indirect service to the client system by providing direct service to the consultee.

- The goal of consultation is to help both the client system and the consultee in some way. That is, consultation can have both a remedial and preventive focus.

- The consultant can be either internal or external to the system in which consultation is to occur.

- Participation in consultation is voluntary for all of the parties involved, although there is the danger that consultees can be subtly coaxed to participate by superiors.

- The relationship between the consultant and consultee is one of peers and tends to be collaborative whenever possible.

- The consultative relationship is a temporary one. Consultation deals exclusively with work-related (or caretaking-related) problems. The consultant does not deal with the personal problems of the consultee.

- Consultation can be either remedial (i.e., solving a defined problem) or developmental (i.e., assisting in the realization of potential).

COMMON CONSULTANT ROLES

If modes of consultation represent the approach taken, roles reflect the functions taken on by consultants in the various modes. Consultants can assume a variety of roles in any given consultation relationship. The primary role a consultant engages in depends upon a variety of factors such as the consultant's abilities, values, and frame of reference; the consultee's expectations and skill level; the nature of the consultation problem; and the environmental context in which consultation is occurring. It is important to note that the consultant can take on a variety of roles during the consultation process.

Consultant roles are often described as running on a continuum from directive to nondirective (Lippitt & Lippitt, 1986). The following are six common roles taken on by consultants:

- Advocacy. This most directive of consultant roles has the consultant persuading a consultee to take some course of action.
- Expert. This is the most common role consultants take on and consists of the consultant providing the consultee with some knowledge, advice, or service.
- Trainer/Educator. In this role, the consultant facilitates skill and/or knowledge acquisition in the consultee.
- Collaborator. Consultants frequently attempt to involve consultees as joint problem solvers in all steps of the consultation process with the exception of the implementation phase. Collaborative efforts in consultation should not be confused with the service of collaboration discussed later.
- Fact Finder. In this role, the consultant typically gathers information, analyzes it, and feeds it back to the consultee.
- Process Specialist. In this least directive role, the consultant focuses on the process events; that is, on how things are being done instead of on what is being done.

There are a large number of other roles consultants can assume, such as planner, motivator, or facilitator. Part of the art of becoming an effective consultant is knowing when to engage in a given role at any given point in the consultative process.

SKILLS NECESSARY FOR EFFECTIVE CONSULTATION

To be effective in the various modes and roles of consultation, human service professionals need to have a personal and professional growth orientation, knowledge of consultation and human behavior, and skills in consulting. Many skills are required to function effectively as a consultant. The importance of communication and interpersonal skills is increasingly being pointed out. Competence in problem-solving skills is essential since consultation is problem solving by its very nature. Skills in working with organizations are becoming increasingly important as more human service professionals conduct organizational consultation. Effective skills in group work can be important components of successful consultation because psychologists, counselors, and social workers are more commonly being called upon to consult with groups of consultees. Because we live in a culturally diverse society, skills in dealing with cultural diversity are essential so that the consultants can discern the complex role of diversity in their work. In order to be professionally responsible, consultants need skills that allow them to behave ethically and professionally.

A GENERIC MODEL OF CONSULTATION

Whatever skills consultants use, whatever roles they assume, they typically have a model of consultation that guides their practice. I present here an overview of a generic model of consultation (Dougherty, 2005) to help you develop a framework for analyzing the cases that follow in the later chapters of this book. All consultation involves building relationships, defining problems, implementing and evaluating plans, and disengaging. I have chosen four stages each with four corresponding phases to make up the generic model. As you will note in the cases you read, no real-life consultation experience will parallel each and every stage and phase of this model. In real-life consultation, the stages of the generic model will overlap. For example, the consultation process commonly reverts back to the problem definition stage when a new aspect of the problem arises. Or a consultant may be called in after the problem has been defined. There is nothing magical about having four stages each with four phases to make up this generic model of consultation; this simply reflects how I view the process of consultation. I have tried to put together a model that describes the process of consultation in general enough terms to include most of the cases you will be reading later on in this text.

Stage One, entry, consists of the phases of exploring organizational needs, contracting, physically entering the system, and psychologically entering the system. During the entry stage, the consultant attempts to get a general feel for the problem(s) to be dealt with in the relationship, develops some form of working agreement with the parties involved, sets up a physical presence within the organization and starts building relationships with those involved in consultation. A key point about entry is that consultants must "enter" with each consultee with whom they come into contact.

Stage Two, diagnosis, involves the phases of gathering information, defining the problem, setting goals, and generating possible interventions. The consultant and/or consultee can gather data to shed further light on the problem through the use of observations, surveys and questionnaires, examination of records, and interviews. The consultant and consultee define the problem by analyzing and interpreting the information that has been gathered. They then set goals to solve or cope with the defined problem. The diagnosis stage concludes with the consultant and consultee generating a series of possible interventions, some of which can be put into a plan for resolving the problem.

Stage Three, implementation, consists of the phases of choosing an intervention, formulating a plan, implementing the plan, and evaluating the plan. The stage begins when the consultant and consultee select activities they believe have a strong chance of positively affecting the problem. With these interventions in mind, the consultant and consultee carefully develop a plan that is tailored to the unique aspects of the problem. The consultee then implements that plan while the consultant remains "on call" to provide any needed assistance. After the plan has been implemented, it is evaluated. Based on the results of the evaluation, the consultative process either moves to developing another plan or on to the disengagement stage.

Stage Four, disengagement, consists of the phases of evaluating the process of consultation, planning postconsultation matters, reducing involvement and following up, and terminating. This stage is the "winding down" of the consultative relationship. Evaluation of the consultation process is a planned event and can be accomplished in a variety of ways, ranging from a face-to-face meeting with the consultee to the use of consultee satisfaction surveys. Postconsultation planning involves determining how the consultee is going to take care of the "business" of maintaining the effects of consultation. The consultant then reduces involvement by increasingly becoming less active in dealing with the situation for which consultation was sought. However, the consultant engages in agreed-upon follow-up activities. Terminating involves the formal ending of the relationship.

MODELS OF CONSULTATION

There are three theoretical models of consultation that are very popular. These models include organizational, mental health, and behavioral consultation. The name associated with a given model serves to identify that model's given focus.

Organizational consultation tends to consider the entire organization to be the client system; that is, the goal is to enhance the overall effectiveness of the organization in some way, even if the consultant is dealing with only some part of the organization. Mental health consultation focuses on the mental health implications for organizations and consultees' clients; it attempts to enhance the psychological well-being of the parties involved. Behavioral consultation focuses on specific changes in the client, client system, and/or consultee. You will want to remember that these models are more alike than different. They vary more in what they emphasize than in their nature. All of these models can be practiced in a variety of settings ranging from business and industry to schools.

Organizational Consultation Organizational consultation tends to define the problem in terms of an organization's structure or processes. For example, a consultant may help an organization reorganize (i.e., change structure) or help members make changes in the way they communicate (i.e., change processes). The goal of organizational consultation is to help alleviate a problem through carefully designed interventions that affect the organization's system. There is no one set model of organizational consultation, but rather a series of approaches. The most popular approaches are the purchase of expertise model, the doctor/patient model, and the process model (Schein, 1988).

When consultees request help from consultants, they frequently seek some form of expertise. Expertise can take the form of knowledge and/or skill. The consultants provide some combination of information, methods, tools, and support to the consultee. By its nature this model is very content oriented. The purchase of expertise model is most appropriate when the problem has been well defined, such as when a consultant provides specific information or training, or when a glitch arises in a human service program. Two common forms of the purchase of expertise model are education/training consultation and program consultation. Consultants provide education/training consultation in a variety of settings, often in the form of workshops. In Chapter 5, you will read a unique case of education/ training consultation written by Deck and Isenhour. In program consultation, the organization might use a consultant to assist in planning a new program, revise an existing program, or deal with factors that affect a current program. In Chapter 6, James, Addy, and Crews provide a complex case that describes a systems approach to program consultation.

In the doctor/patient model, a consultant is called in because the organization knows something is wrong but doesn't know what that "something" is. The consultant is given the power to make a diagnosis and prescribe a solution. For example, a consultant from a community counseling center is hired to assist a university counseling center deliver services more effectively by examining the center and making a series of recommendations based on that examination.

In process consultation, the consultant usually works with a small group of consultees for the purpose of focusing on their interactions. The interactions of the consultees, such as the way they hold meetings, are assumed to be the source of the problem. By helping consultees examine their own interactions, process consultation attempts to create organizational change by changing the ways consultees interact with one another. In Chapter 7, Tack, Dougherty, and Morrow present a form of process consultation that was used with the staff of a university counseling center. Becker-Reems describes, in Chapter 8, a case in which process consultation was used in a hospital setting.

Mental Health Consultation Mental health consultation is based on the idea that the overall mental health of individuals in our society can be promoted through the efforts of consultants who work with human service professionals, teachers, parents, and other community members. Originally, mental health consultation was heavily influenced by psychodynamic theory (Caplan & Caplan, 1993; 1999). This type of consultation frequently takes the form of either case consultation or program consultation.

Consultees have problems with work-related or caregiving-related tasks due to the unique characteristics of the client or program or due to one or more of the following reasons: lack of knowledge, lack of skill, lack of confidence, or lack of objectivity. A major goal of this model is to improve the consultee's ability to function in the future. In Chapter 3, Tack and Morrow present an example of mental health case consultation.

Behavioral Consultation Behavioral consultation uses social learning theory and applies behavioral technology in an attempt to resolve the consultation problem. Behavioral consultants aim for specific changes and employ specific goals in their work (Bergan & Kratochwill, 1990). In behavioral consultation, the consultant and consultee use a problem-solving sequence that first uses behavioral terminology to describe the problem. Next, a functional analysis of the problem examines what happened before and after the problem occurred. The consultant and consultee choose a target behavior and then define behavioral objectives in terms of desired changes. Finally, they design a behavior change program to achieve those objectives and then implement and rigorously evaluate the program.

Behavioral consultation commonly takes on one of three forms: behavioral case consultation, behavioral system consultation, and behavioral technology training. In Chapter 2, Carrington Rotto presents a case of behavioral consultation with a teacher.

In behavioral case consultation a consultant provides direct, behavior based service to a consultee concerning the management of a client or group of clients assigned to the consultee. In behavioral system consultation, behavioral technology principles are applied to a social system such as an organization. Behavioral system consultants use behavior technology principles to analyze and change interactions among the various subsystems of the larger social system. In behavioral technology training, consultants provide consultees with training to increase their general usage of behavioral technology when working with clients. The principles and methods of the education/training model discussed earlier apply to behavioral technology training.

GRASPING THE ESSENCE OF CONSULTATION

As you have probably noticed, consultation can be a fairly complex process. One way to grasp the essence of consultation is to think of it in terms of its various dimensions. It may be helpful first to consider what model the consultant employs as a theoretical orientation. What roles are likely to be assumed in this mode or approach to the model employed? For instance, a school-based professional may "come from" a behavioral consultation model and take on a fact finder role the majority of the time during a consultative relationship working with a classroom teacher to cope with a child with attention-deficit hyperactivity disorder. In another example, a counseling psychologist may use a mental health model and function in a primarily collaborative role while consulting with a variety of therapists at a community mental health center.

COLLABORATION

Collaboration has become an increasingly important and popular service provided by practitioners in the helping professions. Because the concept of collaboration is relatively new as a professional relationship distinct from consultation a great deal of ambiguity surrounds it. There are two strands in the literature that describe collaboration; one is related to mental health (Caplan & Caplan, 1993; 1999), and the other is related to education (West & Idol, 1993).

One way to conceptualize collaboration is by contrasting it with consultation. Consultation is a "hands off," helping-the-helpers-help, indirect process, whereas collaboration is a "hands on," helpers-helping-one-another process in which the professionals involved provide both indirect and direct service to the client system. The collaborating specialist participates as a member of a team in which all team members reciprocally consult with one another in addition to treating the client system directly in some way (Caplan & Caplan, 1993; 1999). Collaboration is an inter-professional activity in which all of the professionals involved are responsible for some aspect of the outcome of the case. In consultation, the consultee retains responsibility for the outcome of the case. Furthermore, in collaboration, the team decides the critical issues to pursue in a case, while in consultation the consultant's expertise usually dictates the decision of topics to be pursued.

Mental Health Collaboration As a service, mental health collaboration can be described as an "interprofessional method in which a mental health specialist establishes a partnership with another professional worker, network, group, or team of professionals in a community field or human services institution" (Caplan & Caplan, 1993, p. 295). In this method, teams are used, and the collaborating specialist takes responsibility for the mental health outcomes related to the case or program. Whereas in consultation the consultee selects the case, in collaboration any team member can suggest a particular case, but the team makes the final decision.

Collaboration is called for when the specialist determines that the client system's problems are so severe that the indirect service of consultation is not indicated (Erchul & Schulte, 1993). The collaborating specialist also attempts to influence changes in the client system's institution in order to improve the mental health outcomes for its clients. These attempts include enhancing the skills and understandings of the other collaborators so that they can perform more effectively in the future (Caplan & Caplan, 1993; 1999).

Consider the following example of mental health collaboration. A senior psychologist who works in a mental health center and possesses expertise in family therapy presents a case involving a family to his colleagues at a staff meeting. Based on the details of the case, some of the members of the center agree to work together as a treatment team that will be involved directly with the family. A substance abuse counselor, school-community liaison, child development specialist, and the senior psychologist all put together and implement a treatment plan. The child development specialist agrees to serve as team leader. The senior psychologist not only provides and receives consultation services but also directly treats the family. Note the preventive element in collaboration: the professional provides consultative services within the framework of collaboration.

Contrast the previous example with the following one, which describes mental health consultation. A senior psychologist in a mental health center provides consultation upon request to one of the staff therapists regarding a family with which the therapist is working. The therapist retains responsibility for the case, and the staff psychologist provides expertise in family therapy procedures to the therapist so that a more effective treatment plan can be developed.

Educational Collaboration Educational collaboration is "an interactive planning, decision-making, or problem- solving process involving two or more team members. . . .Team interactions throughout the process are characterized by: mutual respect, trust, open communication; consideration of each issue or problem from an ecological perspective; consensual decision making; pooling of personal resources and expertise; and joint ownership of the issue or problem being addressed. The outcomes of educational collaboration may focus on changes in knowledge, skills, attitudes, or behaviors at one or more of three levels: child, adult, or system" (West, 1990, p. 29).

Consider this example of collaboration in which a school counselor and administrator work together to develop a dropout prevention program that incorporates the unique characteristics of the school. Each party brings his or her own expertise to the problem of developing a relevant and effective program.

The counselor brings knowledge and expertise related to students and their psychosocial concerns, and the administrator brings expertise in program development and school culture. Together, they pool their expertise and take mutual responsibility for developing a realistic and viable program for keeping the students who are at risk in school.

Notice how the previous example contrasts with the following example of program consultation. A school counselor is asked by a school administrator for assistance in developing a dropout prevention program for at risk students. The counselor works together with the administrator, and they develop a feasible plan. The administrator, however, takes the responsibility for getting the dropout prevention program up and running, while the counselor remains available for additional consultation as the program unfolds.

Although the knowledge base, skills, and attitudes necessary for effective collaboration are very similar to those needed for effective consultation (West & Idol, 1993), there are some basic differences between these two types of relationships.

In consultation the consultee retains responsibility for the outcome of the problem brought to consultation, while in collaboration the collaborator, along with other team members, retains responsibility for one or more aspects related to the outcome of the case. In consultation consultants do not treat the client system directly; that is, they are not directly involved in the implementation of the intervention. In collaboration the collaborator is involved directly in the intervention. In consultation the consultant is considered the ultimate expert in the relationship, whereas in collaboration there is no designated, final authority. In consultation the consultee retains ownership of the problem, while in collaboration there is a mutual ownership of the problem by the team. The concept of teamwork is inherent in collaboration, but in consultation the approach taken determines whether teamwork will be used.

The differences between consultation and collaboration may be clarified by Caplan and Caplan's (1993) continuum, which contrasts therapy, collaboration, and consultation on the basis of the degree of direct service. The most indirect form of service is consultation, in that the consultant does not provide any direct service, such as treatment, to the client system. Collaboration is in the middle of the continuum because it combines direct intervention with the client system in addition to providing and receiving consultation relative to the case within the team. Therapy with the client system would be the most direct form of intervention.

Perhaps collaboration can be best understood by thinking of it as a team-based service in which the specialist provides both direct treatment to the client system and consultation services to others involved in the case or program, while at the same time receiving consultation from other members of the team. One example would be a school psychologist providing counseling to a student and at the same time engaging in a reciprocal consulting relationship with the student's teacher about the student's behavior. In this example the teacher may also become a consultant to the counselor by providing suggestions for how the counselor might proceed with the child. The basic differences between mental health collaboration and educational collaboration revolve around their emphases. Mental health collaboration emphasizes the mental health perspectives of a case and provides the collaborating specialist with 'authority' over the mental health aspects of the case. As Caplan and Caplan (1993; 1999) discuss collaboration, there is minimal consultation by other team members with the mental health specialist. Educational collaboration can take on a much broader scope, including mental health aspects of a case or program. It emphasizes teamwork and reciprocal influence among the professionals involved. In Chapters 9 and 10, DeEsch and Murphy as well as Boat and Boat present cases involving collaboration.

ETHICAL BEHAVIOR

Ethics refers to principles established to provide direction for proper behavior.

Throughout their careers all human service professionals must make decisions about ethical dilemmas they will encounter. What kinds of ethical dilemmas might you face when you engage in consultation and collaboration? The following list provides many of the areas in which ethical dilemmas can arise for practitioners: _ the influence of one's values _ professional competence _ training _ the complexity of the consultant-consultee-client system relationship and the interrelationships among collaborators

_ the rights of consultees and fellow collaborators _ selection of interventions _ working with groups _ dealing with multicultural aspects _ service delivery via the Internet Professional codes of ethics can provide only general guidelines for ethical practice. The bottom line is that, within these broad guidelines, consultants and collaborators need to make informed, sound, and responsible judgments based on ethical decision making.

TIPS FOR PRACTICE

- Create a functional definition of consultation and collaboration.
- Develop the skills areas identified as related to effective consultation and collaboration.
- Study the various approaches to consultation and collaboration to develop a cognitive map to guide your practice.
- Follow the ethical code adapted by the professional organizations in your profession.

WHERE WE ARE GOING FROM HERE

Having read an overview of consultation and collaboration, you are now ready to consider some specific cases. As noted earlier, each of the next nine chapters presents you with a consultation or collaboration case. As you read these chapters, think about what it must have been like to be a professional involved with the case. At the end of each chapter you are asked to apply your own personal view of the case by responding to questions designed to help you reflect on what you have just read.

REFERENCES AND SUGGESTED READINGS

Bergan, J. R., & Kratochwill, T. R. (1990). Behavioral consultation and therapy. New York: Plenum Press.

Caplan, G. (1993).Mental health consultation, community mental health, and population-oriented psychiatry. In W. P. Erchul (Ed.), Consultation in community, school, and organizational practice: Gerald Caplan's contributions to professional psychology (pp. 41–56).Washington, DC: Hemisphere.

Caplan, G., & Caplan, R. B. (1993). Mental health consultation and collaboration. San Francisco, CA: Jossey-Bass.

Caplan, G., & Caplan, R. B. (1999). Mental health consultation and collaboration. Prospect Heights, IL: Waveland. (Original work published in 1993).

Curtis, M. J., & Stollar, S.A. (2002). Best practices in system-level change. In A. Thomas and J. Grimes (Eds.), Best Practices in School Psychology (4th ed., pp. 223–243).Washington, DC: National Association of School Psychologists.

Dougherty, A. M. (2005). Psychological consultation and collaboration in school and community settings. (4th ed.). Belmont, CA: Wadsworth.

Dougherty, A. M., Tack, F. E., Fullam, C. B., & Hammer, L.A. (1996). Disengagement: A neglected aspect of the consultation process. Journal of Educational and Psychological Consultation, 7, 259–274.

Erchul, W. P., & Schulte, A. C. (1993). Gerald Caplan's contributions to professional psychology: Conceptual underpinnings. In W. P. Erchul (Ed.), Consultation in community, school, and organizational practice: Gerald Caplan's contributions to professional psychology (pp. 3–40).Washington, DC: Hemisphere.

Kratochwill, T. R., & Pittman, P. H. (2002). Expanding Problem-solving consultation training: Prospects and frameworks. Journal of Educational and Psychological Consultation, 13(1&2), 69-95.

Kratochwill, T. R., Elliott, S.N., & Callan-Stoiber, K. (2002). Best practices in school-based problem-solving consultation. In A. Thomas and J. Grimes (Eds.), Best practices in school psychology (4th ed., pp. 583–608). Washington, DC: National Association of School Psychologists.

Kurpius, D. J. (1978).Consultation theory and process: An integrated model. Personnel and Guidance Journal, 56, 335–338.

Kurpius, D. J., & Fuqua, D.R. (1993). Fundamental issues in defining consultation. Journal of Counseling and Development, 71, 598–600.

Lippitt, G., & Lippitt, R. (1986). The consulting process in action. (2nd ed.). La Jolla, CA: University Associates.

Schein, E. H. (1988). Process consultation: Its role in organization development. (Vol. I). Reading, MA: Addison-Wesley.

Schein, E. H. (1999). Process consultation revisited: Building the helping relationship. Reading, MA: Addison-Wesley.

West, J. F. (1990). Educational collaboration in the restructuring of schools. Journal of Educational and Psychological Consultation, 1, 23–40.

West, J. F., & Idol, L. (1993).The counselor as consultant in the collaborative school. Journal of Counseling and Development, 71, 678–683.

Zins, J. E. (2002). Building a strong future for educational and psychological consultation. Journal of Educational and Psychological Consultation, 13(1&2), 5-6.

PARTII

Case Consultation

Now that you have reviewed the basics of consultation and collaboration, you are ready to approach the case studies in this book. The next three chapters discuss some popular approaches to case consultation. Case consultation refers to a type of consultation in which a consultant provides assistance to a consultee about a particular case. For example, a psychologist consults with a therapist concerning one of the therapist's clients. In another example, a school counselor assists a parent with some difficulties the parent's child is having at home. You will note from your reading of these case studies that they differ in terms of what approach is emphasized during consultation but are quite similar in terms of process they follow.

Behavioral consultation applies behavioral technology to the consultative process. For instance, a consultant and consultee may devise a plan using an operant conditioning approach to help the consultee's client. In Chapter 2, Carrington Rotto describes a case in which a school psychologist uses behavioral consultation to assist a teacher.

Mental health case consultation is a form of consultation in which a consultant assists with a mental-health-related problem that the consultee is experiencing with a client. Although it has been heavily influenced by psychodynamic theory, mental health consultation is increasingly eclectic in its approach. In Chapter 3, Tack and Morrow present a case in which one counselor assists another counselor using an eclectic approach to mental health consultation. Among other things, this case illustrates the sometimes fine line between consultation and counseling.

Adlerian consultation is based upon Alfred Adler's individual psychology. In this model, the lifestyle of both the consultee and the client are significant elements of the consultation process. In Chapter 4, Kottman presents a case in which a school counselor uses an Adlerian approach to consulting with a teacher.

2

Behavioral Case Consultation with a Teacher

PAMELA CARRINGTON ROTTO

DESCRIPTION OF THE MODEL USED

Behavioral consultation is rooted in the models and methods of behavioral psychology and cognitive psychology. Considered one of at least three major models of consultation, behavioral consultation emerged in the 1970s as an alternative to traditional service-delivery approaches in applied settings (Bergan, 1995). Behavioral consultation has three widely recognized features that enhance its use in applied settings. First, it is a model of **indirect service delivery**, wherein a consultant assists a consultee in identifying one or more problems and then implementing one or more strategies to solve the problems. Thus, direct care providers, such as parents and teachers, are involved as principal change agents. A second characteristic of behavioral consultation involves its use of a **problem-solving orientation** to solve academic, behavioral, and social difficulties. This problem-solving process is operationalized through the use of a series of structured interviews, which prompt integration of the consultant's problem-solving skills with the consultee's situation-specific expertise.

Consultant-consultee effectiveness is then maximized by a third important feature of behavioral consultation: the development of a **collegial relationship**. Characteristics such as acceptance through nonjudgmental statements, openness, nondefensiveness, and flexibility are thought to positively affect the interaction between the consultant and consultee (Kratochwill, Elliott, & Carrington Rotto, 1995).

Behavioral consultation has two primary goals. It provides methods for solving the behavioral, academic, and social problems of children. It also expands the knowledge and skill repertoire of the consultee, making future problems or similar difficulties in other children easier to prevent or respond to effectively.

Acquisition of these desired outcomes is augmented by use of behavioral assessment techniques, reliance on behavioral intervention strategies, and evaluation of outcomes based on behavioral analysis and related methodologies. A four stage model of problem identification, problem analysis, plan implementation, and plan evaluation serves as a framework to guide and focus the problem-solving activities of consultants and consultees (Bergan & Kratochwill, 1990; Kratochwill & Bergan, 1990).With the exception of the plan implemer........on phase, these stages are procedurally operationalized through three interviews that tend to overlap in a dynamic, reciprocal fashion. Although the problem-solving structure is sequential and overt, it should not be interpreted as inflexible or irreversible. These stages parallel the generic consultation process of entry, diagnosis, implementation, and disengagement (Dougherty, 2005).

Problem identification is the initial and perhaps most critical stage because it determines the goal(s) of consultation and subsequently drives the design and implementation of an effective plan. Appropriate selection of a behavior of concern ensures that a successful intervention will result in socially meaningful outcomes. Also, precise definition of the target behavior facilitates common understanding of the behavior among all involved persons. When data collected during problem identification indicate the existence of a problem in need of attention, the **problem analysis** stage of behavioral consultation begins. The consultant and consultee carefully examine the behavior across different situations and consider factors that may influence performance such as where, when, and under what conditions or contingencies the behavior occurs. During development of an appropriate intervention plan, the consultant and consultee consider the results of these analyses. The intervention plan specifies who will do what, when they will do it, where the plan will be implemented, how the steps will be completed, and with whom the plan will be implemented. During the **plan implementation** stage, the intervention is carried out with the child while being evaluated through frequent and repeated assessments to determine the need for modification. **Plan evaluation**, the final major stage of consultation, determines whether the goals of consultation have been attained, whether the plan has been effective at producing the desired behavioral change, and whether consultation and the intervention will be continued, terminated, or modified.

SETTING AND BACKGROUND ISSUES

Setting

While working as a school psychologist in a suburban elementary school, I was contacted for assistance by Ms. Keller, a third-grade teacher, regarding the deficient academic performance and problematic behavior of one of her students.

Michael, an 8-year-old child, was one of 23 students in Ms. Keller's classroom.

Ms. Keller sought help with Michael due to a number of concerns, including

poor classroom participation, difficulty initiating and completing assignments, failure following directions, and off-task behaviors that occasionally disrupted the classroom setting.

The elementary school in which this consultation took place had an enrollment of approximately 600 students in kindergarten through fifth grade. It was one of three elementary schools in a district serving approximately 3,000 students.

There was a combined racial and ethnic makeup of 11 percent of the student population in this particular school. Approximately 38 percent of the student population qualified for the free or reduced lunch program. Along with a fulltime school counselor, I provided support services three days per week at this school.

Background

Michael lived with his birth parents and 5-year-old brother. His father and mother had attained bachelor's degrees and were employed professionally in the community. According to his mother, Michael's developmental and medical histories were unremarkable. He was diagnosed with allergies that were managed using antihistamines.

Review of Michael's school records revealed a history of school-related concerns that dated from the first grade and included difficulties with completing assignments and following directions. His former teachers described Michael as a poorly motivated child who required significant adult attention in the classroom to address his inappropriate behaviors and lack of work production. However, Michael's teachers also noted that he displayed creativity and well-developed interests in specific, nonacademic subject areas (e.g., boxing, karate, baseball).

Michael previously had been evaluated for special education services but was determined ineligible. Results of intellectual assessment indicated average abilities.

Michael's parents historically had been supportive of school-based interventions to address their son's academic and behavioral difficulties and had been involved in regular communication with Michael's teachers.

Prior to consultation services, Ms. Keller had initiated several strategies, with the cooperation of Michael's parents, in an effort to decrease his problematic classroom behaviors and improve his work habits. For example, Ms. Keller increased the frequency of home-school communication by notifying Michael's parents of his problematic behaviors at school and urging them to provide consequences for these behaviors at home. She also offered Michael a weekly reward of free time for good behavior and timely completion of all classroom assignments.

Incomplete assignments were sent home for completion. Michael also was given a daily assignment sheet and was required to record assignments from each subject area and to obtain the signature of his parents indicating that his work had been completed at home.

These strategies were judged ineffective by Michael's teacher and parents and were gradually discontinued. Michael never earned the free time his teacher had offered. He frequently failed to bring his assignment sheet and school materials home, and his mother would drive him back to school almost daily to retrieve the needed materials. Michael's parents quickly became frustrated by the burden of assisting him in transporting his materials to and from school, providing consequences at home for inappropriate school behaviors, and working for lengthy periods of time each evening to ensure that Michael completed his homework. Michael's resistance and refusal to begin and/or complete his homework in a timely manner were highly disruptive at home and negatively impacted family interactions. Ms. Keller eventually stopped giving Michael homework because he so rarely completed it.

GOALS OF CONSULTATION

Behavioral consultation is a goal-oriented method of service delivery that focuses on developing and implementing solutions to identified issues. The goals of this behavioral consultation were to generate a method for changing Michael's academic and behavioral problems and to provide Ms. Keller with strategies that would enhance her response to Michael's difficulties as well as to similar problems in other children. Behavioral consultation provided a direct link between assessment and intervention activities in response to this teacher's request for functional and effective classroom-based services.

Specific objectives were met and various strategies were used during each stage of consultation to facilitate accurate problem specification and effective problem resolution. During the first stage of consultation, problem identification, my primary goal was to specify Michael's problem behaviors in clear, objective terms. The principal goal during the second problem analysis stage was to link the assessment data directly to a treatment plan. The treatment implementation stage followed clear identification and specification of the target behavior, systematic analysis of the baseline assessment data, verification of the nature of Michael's difficulty, and agreement on a treatment plan. The primary goal during this stage of behavioral consultation was implementation of a systematic plan by the teacher.

The fourth stage of treatment evaluation was accompanied by the consultation goals of evaluating treatment effectiveness and programming for generalization and maintenance (Bergan & Kratochwill, 1990; Kratochwill & Bergan, 1990).

CONSULTANT FUNCTION AND ROLE

Behavioral consultation involves a collaborative relationship in which the consultant functions as a facilitator and coordinator. As such, behavioral consultants require knowledge and competence in at least three broad areas:

- the process of consultative problem solving (i.e., procedural knowledge of the stages and objectives of behavioral consultation)
- the content of consultation interactions (i.e., knowledge regarding assessment, intervention, child development and learning processes, and child or population specific considerations)
- the dimensions of the consultation relationship

Although consultant competence in coordinating the problem-solving process and generating behavior change methods are necessary conditions of behavioral consultation, they are not sufficient to facilitate effective consultation interactions. Integration of positive interpersonal skills and understanding with technical expertise are equally important to maximize consultant-consultee effectiveness (Sheridan, Salmon, Kratochwill, & Carrington Rotto, 1992).

During the present consultation case, I conceptualized my role as consultant using this framework of procedural and content knowledge and relationship considerations.

My role as consultant was enhanced by procedural knowledge of the stages and objectives of behavioral consultation, which I used to elicit a description of the problem, assist in analyzing the problem, devise a plan for intervention, and monitor the program once it was implemented. Knowledge and expertise regarding child and population considerations were applied to assess broad dimensions of the problem accurately; identify potentially important intervening variables; generate and examine case-related hypotheses; identify factors that could impact problem solution; and develop an appropriate, as well as effective, intervention. Basic relationship-building and communication skills, including sensitivity to issues of importance to the teacher, were essential at every stage of consultation in order to develop a positive consulting relationship and to facilitate movement toward problem management. This interpersonal relationship played a major role in the use and effectiveness of behavioral consultation. Issues of trust, genuineness, and openness were important qualities within the relationship, particularly due to the predominant use of an interview mode of information gathering and sharing (Conoley & Conoley, 1992). Thus, personal characteristics, professional competencies, and behavioral principles all were important elements in establishing and maintaining constructive and professional interactions.

CONSULTEE EXPERIENCE IN CONSULTATION

The consultee, Ms. Keller, had no prior experience with the behavioral consultation model. During three years of teaching the third grade, Ms. Keller typically had sought direct psychological services such as assessment and counseling in response to academic and behavioral difficulties displayed by students in her classroom.

This pattern of referral was consistent with observations of the substantial variability among teachers in their use of consultation and with their significantly greater frequency of requests for direct psychological services than for consultative assistance from the school psychologist (Piersel & Gutkin, 1983). Although additional research is needed to more specifically identify the variables that contribute positively toward a teacher's decision to engage in behavioral consultation, recent findings have indicated that teachers are more likely to engage in consultation services when school psychologists offer help on a regular basis instead of waiting for teachers to request assistance (Stenger, Tollefson, & Fine, 1992).

Since Ms. Keller had no prior experience in behavioral consultation, I spent time overviewing this model of service delivery and explaining what might be accomplished through consultation. We discussed her role as consultee, which was defined as someone who would provide a clear description of the problem, assist with data collection, and work with Michael to implement the intervention program, observe progress, periodically evaluate the plan's effectiveness, supervise Michael's actions, and generalize the problem-solving objectives. Discussion of these issues at the time of referral also provided an opportunity to inquire and gain preliminary insight into important classroom systems variables, such as physical and environmental factors, academic and curricular issues, behavior management strategies, child and family characteristics, and the relationship between home and school. Since systems variables may at times transcend individual variables, it was important for me to understand the realities of the classroom in order to better understand the individuals within that setting (Conoley & Conoley, 1992).

APPLICATION: CONSULTANT TECHNIQUES AND PROCEDURES

Entry

The **problem identification** stage involved specifying and defining the problems to be targeted in consultation. My primary objective during this stage was to attain clarification of the referral concern, which then would lead to designation of the goals to be achieved through consultation, measurement of current child performance with respect to these goals, and assessment of the discrepancy between current and desired performance. This sequence of problem- solving activities involved identification of:

- target behaviors
- problem frequency, duration, and intensity
- conditions under which the target behaviors occurred
- the required level of performance
- the student's strengths
- behavioral assessment procedures
- consultee effectiveness (Bergan & Kratochwill, 1990; Kratochwill & Bergan, 1990)

A variety of assessment strategies (i.e., teacher rating scale, behavioral interviews, and direct observations) were used during the problem identification stage to obtain a comprehensive evaluation of Michael's problematic behaviors.

These strategies provided continuous opportunities to refine specification of the target behaviors, identify salient factors and conditions surrounding the occurrence of these behaviors, and test hypotheses regarding potential factors that may have enhanced or impeded intervention, implementation, and effectiveness.

Completion of the *Teacher Report Form* (TRF) (Achenbach, 1991) by Ms. Keller provided broad assessment of problem behaviors and objective data regarding the severity of these behaviors relative to a standardized population.

This measure is a multidimensional scale designed to record behavioral problems of children between the ages of 4 and 16. It also provides useful information regarding global changes in child behaviors and covariational effects (i.e., generalization to collateral behaviors). Results from this teacher rating scale yielded clinically significant T-scores on the uncommunicative, hyperactive, aggressive, and delinquent subscales.

Ms. Keller's concerns were described and defined in detail during the Problem Identification Interview (PII). She identified problem behaviors, such as Michael's poor participation, difficulty initiating and completing assignments, failure to follow directions, and disorganized and off-task behaviors. Two primary areas of difficulty emerged as Ms. Keller detailed her observations and impressions of Michael. First, Ms. Keller described deficits in Michael's academic performance. At this point, it was important to determine whether Michael's academic difficulties resulted primarily from performance deficits or from skill deficits (Elliott & Shapiro, 1990). Therefore, classroom work samples and results of past testing were reviewed; they revealed that the problems and questions Michael completed generally were accurate, and they documented acquisition of the skills necessary to perform grade-level work. Review of classroom progress to date indicated that while Michael's assignment completion difficulties were pervasive across subject areas, he demonstrated an inconsistent performance pattern within each academic subject. Thus, Michael's academic difficulties appeared to be the result of performance deficits rather than skill deficits.

Ms. Keller also described concerns regarding Michael's demonstration of problematic behaviors at school. Further discussion suggested that many of these behaviors (e.g., off-task behaviors, daydreaming, distractibility) were likely to be related to sporadic difficulties with task accuracy and consistent failures in task completion. As it became clear that Ms. Keller was primarily concerned with Michael's work production difficulties, this area was targeted for intervention.

Work completion also was selected as a target area because its occurrence was incompatible with Michael's other problematic behaviors. It was anticipated that improvement in Michael's work production might be accompanied by collateral improvement in his inappropriate behaviors.

Ms. Keller estimated that Michael typically completed less than 40 percent of his classroom assignments when given individual attention and frequent reminders to remain on task. Without prompts, his daily average productivity decreased to less than 20 percent. Although Ms. Keller reported that Michael's daily productivity was problematic across subject areas, it was decided that a single subject (in this case mathematics) would be targeted first for treatment purposes.

Work completion initially was operationally defined as completing assignments during classroom time, following directions, and coming to class with the appropriate materials (e.g., book, paper, and pencil). Later, this operational definition was revised to include four behavioral components (materials ready, start working immediately, work until the job is finished, and place completed work in the assignment basket).

During the problem identification stage, it was important to determine how much Michael actually was working compared to his teacher's expectations. At first, it seemed desirable for Michael to work nonstop for the entire academic subject period. However, this expectation later was believed to be both unrealistic and unnecessary. Ms. Keller indicated that it would be acceptable for Michael to work at a pace similar to that of another student who worked at a reasonable rate. It was decided that data would be collected to determine how long it took another student of average ability to finish an identical assignment and that Michael's performance would subsequently be compared to this time estimate.

Ms. Keller kept track of both students' performance in the selected subject area of mathematics for one week. Teacher prompts and individual attention were not provided for either student during this time. Data indicated that Michael's performance varied; with 20 percent assignment completion during the time it took the other student to finish the math assignment on the first day.

On the remaining days, Michael completed 40 percent, 10 percent, 25 percent, and 0 percent of the assignments, while the comparison student finished each assignment. Overall, Michael completed 19 percent of the math assignments for the week during the classroom work period. On one of the days, Ms. Keller noted that Michael seemed to work slightly faster when he noticed the teacher keeping track of his progress. However, he did not maintain this increase in production consistently across days.

Diagnosis

During the problem analysis stage of consultation, we focused on further exploring the problem through the evaluation of baseline data, identification of variables that might contribute to problem solution, and development of a specific plan to implement during the treatment stage. The process of problem analysis was completed in two phases. First, we identified factors that might influence the attainment of a solution to the identified problem (i.e., the analysis phase). Second, we used these factors in the design of a plan to solve the problem (i.e., the plan design phase). Specific steps included (Bergan & Kratochwill, 1990; Kratochwill & Bergan, 1990):

- evaluating the initial assessment data
- conducting a functional analysis of conditions that might impact the target behavior
- further identifying the nature of the target behavior
- developing plan strategies and tactics
- establishing procedures to assess performance during plan implementation

Following completion of the PII, two weeks elapsed before Ms. Keller and I were able to schedule a second meeting. Ms. Keller continued to collect baseline data on the rate and accuracy of Michael's math assignment completion during this time, although she did not document the rate of assignment completion for the comparison student. The baseline data initially collected on Michael and his classmate indicated that the other student had successfully completed each of his assignments in the allotted time. Ms. Keller believed that math was easy for Michael and that he should be able to complete his assignments within a similar time frame. However, baseline data revealed that Michael's performance continued to vary, with an overall rate of 19 percent completion during the second week and 14 percent completion during the third week. As we reviewed the available assessment data during the Problem Analysis Interview (PAI), we developed a more complete problem formulation that included etiological factors as well as the influence of ecological factors in the development and maintenance of the problem.

We also devoted time during the problem analysis to generating alternative strategies for resolving the problem, selecting strategies for implementation, and planning the implementation steps. The primary goal of consultation was to devise a plan to increase Michael's academic production (with an initial focus on completion of math assignments). However, it was difficult to determine what factors might motivate him to work more diligently. Since it was important to identify desirable reinforcers, a reinforcement survey was provided.

While administering this questionnaire to Michael, Ms. Keller discussed her concerns regarding his assignment completion as well as some of his responses to the survey. Following this interaction, Ms. Keller noted that Michael seemed to enjoy the individual attention he had received from her. Survey results revealed interests in activities such as playing board games and Nintendo, reading books, collecting baseball cards, playing basketball, playing with favorite toys, and making and fixing things. As we completed the objectives of the problem analysis stage, a threefold plan was devised to help Michael accomplish the goal of increasing his work production by building on his demonstrated strengths. I describe this intervention plan in the following implementation section. Procedural details, such as determining the roles and responsibilities of all involved individuals, were also discussed within the context of plan development; it was agreed that Michael's parents should be invited to participate in the intervention.

Since one of the main objectives of problem analysis was to develop an intervention to address the identified problem, it was important to obtain information regarding the preferences of the treatment agent (Ms. Keller) in order to facilitate development of a feasible and manageable plan. Ms. Keller's perceptions and opinions regarding the treatment procedures were critical in that implementation of the program likely would be impacted by whether she found the procedures practical, feasible, and otherwise acceptable. A number of factors impact a teacher's acceptability of an intervention. These include time required to implement the intervention, risk to the target child, potential side effects for other non-target students, and perceived fairness (Elliott, 1988). In the present case, treatment acceptability was assessed during the PAI using interview strategies.

However, a number of rating scales are available for formal, data-based assessment of pretreatment acceptability, and readers are encouraged to consult this material (Witt & Elliott, 1985).

Implementation

Treatment implementation involved the introduction of the plan, or treatment program, which had been designed during the problem analysis stage. Although there was no formal interview during this stage, the goal of consultation at this point was to maximize the likelihood that the plan would result in desired outcomes. For this reason, it was important to attend to the three major tasks of plan implementation, which included facilitating skill development of the consultee (if necessary), monitoring the implementation process, and assisting with plan revisions.

The treatment plan consisted of three components. First, a chart that contained a square for every day of the week was placed on Michael's desk. Michael could earn up to two stars in each square daily. At the beginning of each math period, the number of problems on the daily assignment was divided by two.

The resulting figure was the number of problems Michael had to complete during each half of the math period in order to earn a star. For example, if the math assignment consisted of 24 problems on Monday and the period was 40 minutes long, Michael would need to complete 12 problems in the first 20 minutes to receive one star. Similarly, he would need to complete 12 problems during the second 20 minutes to earn a second star. Each half of the period was independent of the other so that even if Michael failed to earn the first star, he still could earn a star during the second half of the class period. Dividing the assignments in half allowed Michael to receive reinforcement and feedback regarding his progress at briefer intervals. It also may have served to make the assignments appear less formidable.

The second part of the plan involved long-term reinforcement for weekly attainment of a target number of stars. Because Michael seemed to value individualized attention from his teacher, it seemed likely that he would be motivated to work for this reinforcement, particularly when it involved desirable activities.

However, it was neither feasible nor practical for Ms. Keller to set aside a block of time to spend with Michael each week. Since Michael had expressed an interest in "making and fixing things," the school custodian was approached, and he subsequently agreed to allow Michael to accompany and assist him for 30 minutes each Friday following successful attainment of the target number of stars.

The third component of the plan consisted of Ms. Keller meeting with Michael and his parents prior to implementation to discuss the intervention. The primary purpose of this strategy was to promote more positive home-school communication, since prior contacts between Ms. Keller and Michael's parents had become increasingly focused on his negative behaviors at school. In addition, Ms. Keller wanted to involve Michael and to encourage him to accept appropriate ownership for the plan, which was considered critical for his success.

During this meeting, Michael's parents expressed frustration regarding previous school expectations that they address and provide consequences for Michael's negative school behaviors. It was decided that Michael's parents would be involved only in the positive aspects of his treatment program. More specifically, information regarding Michael's success would be communicated to his parents regularly via a "note home" system; in this way they could reward progress instead of providing consequences for deficiencies. In addition, Michael no longer would be expected to take his incomplete assignments home for completion, although he would continue to receive routine homework assignments that were consistent with those of his classmates (e.g., studying for spelling tests, social studies and science projects).

Since Ms. Keller clearly demonstrated the skills and competencies necessary for plan implementation, it was not necessary to provide additional training to develop important skills for executing the treatment plan. As Ms. Keller implemented the program, I continued to maintain contact with her for purposes of monitoring the implementation process, assisting in plan revision, and scheduling subsequent meetings. Monitoring plan implementation was completed in two ways. First, Ms. Keller maintained an ongoing record of Michael's progress (i.e., production and accuracy). This monitoring was a continuation of the problem identification and problem analysis phases of consultation and remained consistent with baseline data collection procedures. A second type of monitoring activity involved evaluating the strategies associated with the treatment plan. Together, Ms. Keller and I monitored plan implementation and integrity by discussing the intervention plan periodically. This strategy was complemented by occasional classroom observations that provided an opportunity for me to observe child and consultee behaviors and to assist in determining the need for revisions in the plan. Another method for monitoring treatment integrity, which was not used in the present case, involves asking the consultee to report integrity data periodically (Gresham, 1989).

While the basic components of the plan remained consistent, the target number of stars needed for weekly reinforcement activities gradually was increased.

Significant changes in the plan were not necessary because Michael's behavior was improving. However, if this outcome had not occurred, it would have been necessary to make changes in the plan. It may have become necessary to return to the problem analysis phase to further analyze variables such as the setting, intrapersonal child characteristics, or skill deficits. Or we may have had to return to the problem identification stage to determine whether the nature of the problem had changed.

Disengagement

Finally, **treatment evaluation** was undertaken to determine the extent to which the intervention plan was successful. Primary goals during this stage included assessing goal attainment, evaluating treatment effectiveness, and postimplementation planning. Treatment evaluation was essential to the process of behavioral consultation at this point because it facilitated a mutual decision regarding whether consultation should be continued or terminated and whether a postimplementation plan should be initiated to facilitate generalization and maintenance of the desired behavior (Bergan & Kratochwill, 1990; Kratochwill & Bergan, 1990).

The treatment evaluation phase was instituted following five weeks of program implementation. During the Treatment Evaluation Interview (TEI), Ms. Keller and I discussed issues surrounding attainment of the consultation goals, effectiveness of the intervention plan, and acceptability of the treatment to both her and Michael. The process of evaluating goal attainment and treatment effectiveness was accomplished using information from a variety of sources including direct observations, behavioral interviews, rating scales, and social validation.

Single subject design also facilitated determination of whether a functional relationship existed between the specific intervention strategy and the resulting behavior change. It also provided an evaluation of the need for modification, continuation, or termination of treatment.

Results from direct observations of Michael's daily output are presented in Figure 2.1. Data indicate that Michael completed an average of 75 percent of his assignments while the plan was in effect. Likewise, Michael earned enough stars to receive his weekly reinforcement four out of five weeks (all but Week 3). This increase in Michael's assignment production was significant, relative to his completion rate demonstrated during baseline data collection. A decrease in productivity was observed during Week 2 of treatment and may have reflected the presence of a substitute teacher in the classroom at the beginning of the week. It is not unusual to observe variability in client performance during implementation of a new program,

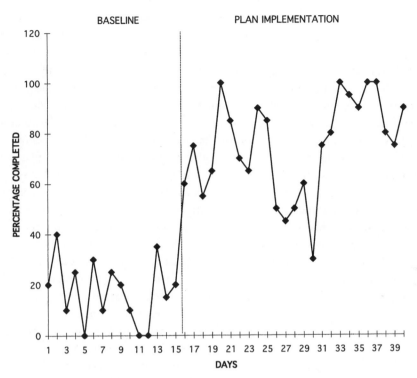

FIGURE 2.1 *Percentage of math assignments completed daily*

and a substitute teacher may have exacerbated this variability.

Results from direct observations of Michael's daily output are presented in Figure 2.1. Data indicate that Michael completed an average of 75 percent of his assignments while the plan was in effect. Likewise, Michael earned enough stars to receive his weekly reinforcement four out of five weeks (all but Week 3). This increase in Michael's assignment production was significant, relative to his completion rate demonstrated during baseline data collection. A decrease in productivity was observed during Week 2 of treatment and may have reflected the presence of a substitute teacher in the classroom at the beginning of the week. It is not unusual to observe variability in client performance during implementation of a new program, and a substitute teacher may have exacerbated this variability.

Social validation criteria also were used to determine whether the intervention program had brought Michael's performance within the range of acceptable behavior as compared to a typical peer of average ability. Ms. Keller collected data on the rate of work production and level of accuracy of the identified comparison peer during the last week of the program. Results indicated that while Michael's level of accuracy was comparable to that of his peer, his rate of production continued to be slightly discrepant. However, Ms. Keller noted that Michael's production rate had improved dramatically and was approaching more acceptable levels of performance.

Information gathered through posttreatment completion of a teacher rating scale and the TEI also revealed consistent findings. Results from the TRF documented improved behavior in the classroom. During the interview, Ms. Keller stated that Michael's rate of work completion in math had improved significantly and that his behavior was less problematic during this period. Informal assessment of the acceptability of treatment following implementation revealed that Ms. Keller viewed the plan as an appropriate and reasonable method of addressing Michael's needs. However, she also expressed concern that Michael had not shown spontaneous improvement in his work production in other subject areas. This information is not surprising in light of the abundant evidence in the treatment literature that specific procedures are needed to facilitate generalization and maintenance of behavior. Although generalization may occur naturally, it typically must be programmed using strategies that may be put into place during the treatment evaluation phase of consultation (Kratochwill, Elliott, & Carrington Rotto, 1995). Since generalization did not occur in non-training settings (i.e., other academic content areas), a decision was made to leave the present plan in effect to continue to modify and maintain Michael's improvements in math while expanding the program to address his difficulties in science. Thus, postimplementation planning focused on modifying the treatment plan, identifying strategies to facilitate generalization and maintenance, and devising a system for follow-up, recording procedures to monitor Michael's progress over time. Given the continuing needs of this case, the consultation relationship was not terminated at this time. Rather, a mutual decision to conclude consultation followed attainment of the consultation goals that included generalization of behaviors and maintenance of treatment gains.

IMPLICATIONS FOR PRACTICE

Traditionally, behavioral consultation has been implemented with classroom teachers in an effort to establish intervention programs in regular education, thereby reducing the number of placements in special education programs.

However, within the past decade, school-based consultation services have been expanded to include work with special education teachers (Kratochwill, Sheridan, Carrington Rotto, & Salmon, 1991) and teachers of early intervention programs for preschool-age children (Kratochwill & Elliott, 1993). While initial efforts primarily targeted behavioral problems in children, behavioral consultation has been used increasingly to remedy academic and socialization difficulties in school settings. This emphasis on retention and direct intervention with teachers is reflected in the present case example, which illustrates the use of behavioral consultation in the school setting to address the academic productivity of an underachieving student.

Behavioral consultation with teachers is an effective method of remedying school-based problems. However, this narrow focus often fails to address the broader ecological context within which the child's problems may occur. Behavioral consultation recently has been expanded to include parents and teachers in a conjoint fashion in an effort to consider the broader behavioral interrelationships across environments and to serve as a link among the significant settings in a child's life (Sheridan, 1997; Sheridan, Kratochwill, & Bergan, 1996).

Conjoint behavioral consultation, when conducted with parents and teachers, has been shown to provide a feasible, effective means of linking assessment to treatment in the provision of indirect services to socially withdrawn children (e.g., Sheridan, Kratochwill, & Elliott, 1990). In this model, parents and teachers jointly and actively serve as consultees, with an emphasis on interactions and collaboration between home and school systems. Strengths of this model include involvement of parents and teachers in a structured, problem-solving framework; the collection of comprehensive and systematic data across extended temporal and contextual bases; and consistent programming across settings to maximize treatment effects, allow for assessment of behavioral contrast or side effects, and enhance generalization and maintenance (Sheridan, 1997).

Use of behavioral consultation also has been extended beyond the schools to address problematic child behaviors that are observed predominantly in home and/or community settings but not in school settings. Parent-only consultation has been used to enhance the effects of competency-based parent training in managing problematic behaviors in school-age children (Carrington Rotto & Kratochwill, 1994). It also has been advanced as a model of early intervention with the goal of decreasing noncompliant and aggressive behaviors in preschool-age children (Carrington Rotto & Kratochwill, 1993). Strengths of this model include parent involvement in a structured, problem-solving framework; use of parent training methodology to teach parents specific skills that enhance plan implementation; and opportunities for early intervention services prior to school entry.

It is likely that the child and teacher outcomes from the present case example would have been enhanced by involving the parents and teacher in a conjoint behavioral consultation approach. Results from a recent study have suggested that conjoint behavioral consultation is an effective model of home-school collaboration in the remediation of academic performance deficits (Galloway & Sheridan, 1992). Although Michael's target behaviors improved in the school setting, his parents did not observe these changes and continued to struggle to get Michael to complete homework assignments. To be truly effective, behaviors taught in any behavioral training program should generalize across time, settings, individuals, and behaviors. Thus, consideration of the use of conjoint behavioral consultation with Michael's teacher and parents would have been appropriate at the inception of this case.

An additional issue arose when Michael's parents later disclosed that they were struggling with significant management difficulties in response to their son's noncompliant and oppositional behaviors at home and in public. Michael's parents did not acknowledge their son's extensive behavioral difficulties until the later stages of plan evaluation, and these problems were not addressed using the teacher-only model of behavioral consultation. In light of their apparent need for parenting support and skills training, later use of parent-only behavioral consultation in combination with parent training services appeared appropriate for Michael's parents.

In sum, behavioral consultation provides a useful problem-solving framework for working within and between family and school systems. This systematic model of indirect service delivery may be conducted with teachers, parents, or teacher-parent pairs to enhance child functioning across home, school, and community settings. Intervention plans may be developed and implemented to address diverse target problems in areas such as academic productivity, socialization, and behavioral difficulties. As research and practice in behavioral consultation continue to expand, consultants must attend closely to the diverse needs of various subject populations and further examine alternative parent and teacher roles and levels of involvement in consultation.

More extensive background about consultation practice and research can be found in seminal works generated to enhance adequate skill acquisition prior to engaging in the practice of behavioral case consultation. Readers are referred to the comprehensive texts by Bergan and Kratochwill (1990), Kratochwill and Bergan (1990), and Sheridan, Kratochwill, and Bergan (1996) for detailed outlines and comprehensive descriptions of the major components of behavioral consultation and conjoint behavioral consultation. Interested readers also may consult Kratochwill, Elliott, and Carrington Rotto (1995) and Kratochwill and Pittman (2002) for more extensive detail regarding the application of behavioral consultation in school-based settings. Finally, Welch and Sheridan (1995) provide a model extending behavioral consultation to educational teams.

TIPS FOR PRACTICE

- Evaluate the plan using multiple measures.
- Consider conjoint behavioral consultation whenever possible.
- Remember to make the goals of consultation as specific as possible.

QUESTIONS FOR DISCUSSION AND REFLECTION

1. What types of outcomes might a consultant expect when using behavioral case consultation in school settings?

2. The consultant and consultee both bring unique skills and understanding to the consultative relationship. What participant characteristics does the consultant bring to the behavioral consultation process? What participant characteristics does the consultee (i.e., teacher, parent) bring to the behavioral consultation process? How might these characteristics influence the outcomes of behavioral consultation?

3. What possible barriers or sources of resistance might be encountered by a consultant who is using the behavioral case consultation model in an applied setting such as a school? What are some signs of teacher resistance and defensiveness? What are some signs of parent resistance and defensiveness? How might a consultant overcome or prevent these challenges while increasing consultee involvement?

4. A current debate in the literature concerns the expert versus collaborative nature of behavioral consultation. Do you perceive behavioral consultation to be directive/controlling or collaborative/collegial? Explain your response.

5. Systematic interventions for school-based problems are believed to be most meaningful and effective when they address environmental variables related to the problems and when they work with significant adults who control those environments (Gutkin & Conoley, 1990). What might the consultant have done differently to better address the environmental variables in this case?

6. What factors might affect a consultant's decision to conduct behavioral consultation with teachers only, parents only, or teachers and parents jointly?

7. What strategies might be employed in this case to facilitate generalization of the target behavior?

8. How might behavioral case consultation services differ in an inner-city school compared to a suburban or rural school?

REFERENCES AND SUGGESTED READINGS

Achenbach, T. M. (1991). *Manual for the Teacher's Report Form and Teacher Version of the Child Behavior Profile.* Burlington: University of Vermont, Department of Psychiatry.

Bergan, J. R., & Kratochwill, T. R. (1990). *Behavioral consultation in applied settings.* New York: Plenum Press.

Carrington Rotto, P., & Kratochwill, T. R. (1994). Behavioral consultation with parents: Using competency-based training to modify child noncompliance. *School Psychology Review, 23,* 669–693.

Carrington Rotto, P., & Kratochwill, T. R. (1993, April). *Competency-based parent consultation and training to modify noncompliance in young children.* Paper presented at the 25th Annual Meeting of the National Association of School Psychologists, Washington, DC.

Conoley, J.C., & Conoley, C.W. (1992). *School consultation: A guide to practice and training* (2nd ed.). New York: Pergamon Press.

Cowan, R. J., & Sheridan, S. M. (2003). Investigating the acceptability of behavioral interventions in applied conjoint behavioral consultation: Moving from analog conditions to naturalistic settings. *School Psychology Quarterly, 18,* 1-21.

Dougherty, A.M. (2005). *Psychological consultation and collaboration in school and community settings* (4th ed.). Belmont, CA: Wadsworth.

Elliott, S.N. (1988).Acceptability of behavioral treatments: Review of variables that influence treatment selection. *Professional Psychology: Research and Practice,19*, 68–80.

Elliott, S.N., & Shapiro, E. S. (1990). Intervention techniques and programs for academic performance problems. In T. B. Gutkin & C. R. Reynolds (Eds.), *The handbook of school psychology* (2nd ed., pp. 637–662). New York: Wiley.

Erchul, W. P., Sheridan, S. M., Ryan, D. A., Grissom, P. F., Killough, C. E., Mettler, D. W. (1999). Patterns of relational communication in conjoint behavioral consultation. *School Psychology Quarterly, 14*, 121-147.

Galloway, J., & Sheridan, S. M. (1992, March). *Parent-teacher consultation: Forging effective home-school partnerships in the treatment of academic underachievement.*

Paper presented at the 24th Annual Meeting of the National Association of School Psychologists, Nashville.

Gresham, F.M. (1989).Assessment of treatment integrity in school consultation and prereferral intervention. *School Psychology Review, 18*, 37–50.

Gutkin, T. B., & Conoley, J.C. (1990). Reconceptualizing school psychology from a service delivery perspective: Implications for practice, training, and research. *Journal of School Psychology, 28*, 203–223.

Kazdin, A. E. (1989). *Behavior modification in applied settings* (rev. ed.). Homewood, IL: Dorsey Press.

Kratochwill, T. R., & Bergan, J.R. (1990). *Behavioral consultation in applied settings: An individual guide.* New York: Plenum Press.

Kratochwill, T. R., & Elliott, S.N. (1993). *An experimental analysis of teacher/parent mediated interventions for preschoolers with behavioral problems.* Unpublished manuscript, Office of Special Education and Rehabilitative Services, U.S. Department of

Education, Wisconsin Center for Education Research, University of Wisconsin-Madison, Madison, WI.

Kratochwill, T. R., Elliott, S.N., & Callan-Stoiber, K. (2002). Best practices in school-based problem-solving consultation. In A. Thomas and J. Grimes (Eds.), *Best practices in school psychology* (4th ed., pp. 583–608). Washington, DC: National Association of School Psychologists.

Kratochwill, T. R., Elliott, S.N., & Carrington Rotto, P. (1995). Best practices in school based behavioral consultation. In A. Thomas & J. Grimes (Eds.), *Best practices in school psychology, III*. Washington, DC: NASP.

Kratochwill, T. R., & Morris, R. J. (Eds.). (1992). *The practice of child therapy*(2nd ed.). Boston: Allyn & Bacon.

Kratochwill, T. R., & Pittman, P. H. (2002). Expanding Problem-solving consultation training: Prospects and frameworks. *Journal of Educational and Psychological Consultation, 13(1&2),* 69-95.

Kratochwill, T. R., Sheridan, S. M., Carrington Rotto, P., & Salmon D. (1991). Preparation of school psychologists to serve as consultants for teachers of emotionally disturbed children. *School Psychology Review, 20,* 530–550.

Kratochwill, T. R., & Stoiber, K.C. (2000). Empirically supported interventions and school psychology: Conceptual and practice issues – Part II. *School Psychology Quarterly, 15,* 233-253.

Martens, B. K., & Ardoin, S. P. (2002). Training school psychologists in behavior support consultation. *Child and Family Behavior Therapy, 24,* 147-163.

Piersel, W.C., & Gutkin, T. B. (1983). Resistance to school-based consultation: A behavioral analysis of the problem. *Psychology in the Schools, 20,* 311–320.

Sheridan, S. M. (1997). Conceptual and empirical bases of conjoint behavioral consultation. *School Psychology Quarterly, 12,* 119–133.

Sheridan, S. M., Eagle, J. W., Cowan, R. J., Mickelson, W. (2001). The effects of conjoint behavioral consultation: Results of a 4-year study. *Journal of School Psychology, 39,* 36-385.

Sheridan, S. M., Kratochwill, T. R., & Bergan, J. (1996). *Conjoint behavioral consultation: A procedural manual.* New York: Plenum Press.

Sheridan, S. M., Kratochwill, T. R., & Elliott, S.N. (1990). Behavioral consultation with parents and teachers: Delivering treatment for socially withdrawn children at home and school. *School Psychology Review, 19,* 33–52.

Sheridan, S. M., Salmon, D., Kratochwill, T. R., & Carrington Rotto, P. (1992). A conceptual model for the expansion of behavioral consultation training. *Journal of Educational and Psychological Consultation, 3,* 193–218.

Stenger, M. K., Tollefson, N., & Fine, M. J. (1992). Variables that distinguish elementary teachers who participate in school-based consultation from those who do not. *School Psychology Quarterly, 7,* 271–284.

Welch, M., & Sheridan, S. M. (1995). *Educational partnerships: Serving students at risk.* San Antonio, TX: Harcourt Brace.

Witt, J.C., & Elliott, S.N. (1983). Assessment in behavioral consultation: The initial interview. *School Psychology Review, 12,* 42–49 Witt, J.C., & Elliott, S.N. (1985). Acceptability of classroom intervention strategies. In T. R. Kratochwill (Ed.), *Advances in school psychology* (Vol. IV, pp. 251–288). Hillsdale, NJ: Lawrence Erlbaum Associates.

3

Mental Health Case Consultation

FRANCES E. TACK AND DEANA F. MORROW

DESCRIPTION OF THE MODEL USED

The following case depicts a mental health consultation that uses the generic model of consultation (Dougherty, 2005). The case involves a consultant interacting with a counselor concerning work the counselor is doing with a particular client. Notably, this case offers the opportunity to analyze the boundaries of consultation, counseling and clinical supervision and it exposes the reader to some of the sensitive issues consultants may encounter.

Specifically, this case demonstrates the use of consultee-centered case consultation (Caplan & Caplan, 1993; 1999), in which a consultant assists a consultee in rectifying a limitation in the consultee's professional functioning. This shortcoming typically revolves around a lack of knowledge, skill, self-confidence, or professional objectivity. The primary goal of consultee-centered case consultation is improvement of the consultee's ability to work effectively with a particular case as well as with similar cases in the future. Improvement in the client is the secondary goal. In this type of consultation, the consultant does not usually have direct access to the client but instead relies on the consultee's subjective views of the case (Caplan & Caplan, 1993; 1999). In the following case, the consultation process revolved around the consultee's lack of knowledge about death and dying and the impasse she was experiencing with her terminally ill client. Lack of professional objectivity was mildly present but was probably ameliorated by gaining knowledge and skill through the consultation.

As the case demonstrates, two of the primary roles of the consultant in this model are that of educator, or trainer, and facilitator. In the education/training role, the consultant typically shares information and teaches skills and interventions.

In the facilitation role, the consultant assists the consultee in discussing the case and outlining problem areas. Through engaging in consultee-centered case consultation, the consultee not only works on immediate concerns, but also cultivates skills and information for application with future clients.

SETTING AND BACKGROUND ISSUES

Setting

This mental health consultation case explores the death and dying issues associated with counseling people with end-stage Acquired Immune Deficiency Syndrome (AIDS) and the behavioral inconsistencies inherent in the transition from living to dying. The consultation resulted from a case at a local AIDS service organization in a medium-sized southeastern city.

This community-based, nonprofit agency employs a total of 12 full- and part-time employees and utilizes over 150 volunteers to provide a range of services to people with HIV/AIDS and their families and caregivers.

This AIDS service organization was founded in the 1980's, beginning as a board of directors without provisions for services, space, or clients. Through community networking and commitment, it has grown into one of the premier nonprofit agencies in the city. It provides comprehensive needs assessment, counseling, financial assistance, resource coordination, and care giving services.

The agency now occupies its own space and, at any given time, has over 200 active clients from as many as 17 counties. Although significant medical advances have been made in helping people with HIV live longer and healthier lives (Barnett & Whiteside, 2003; Gay Men's Health Crisis, 1999), still yet about ten to twenty percent of the agency's clients die each year.

The organization has wrestled with many of the issues common to AIDS service organizations: confidentiality, their duty to warn, employee/volunteer burnout, organizational turnover, and the numerous medical advances in the treatment of HIV/AIDS. Of these issues, employee/volunteer burnout and organizational turnover have been the most impacted due to the high stress of working with chronically ill clients—some of whom will die. For counselors and volunteers it is especially challenging to support dying people who are often rejected by a society that blames them for their illness. For these reasons, the AIDS service organization has become sensitized to the need for, and has developed a policy in support of, employee/volunteer counseling, consultation, extended holidays, and day-to-day grief support.

Background

Some general background on working with people with HIV/AIDS is important to set the stage for the case and to understand some of the underlying issues associated with consultation and counseling related to this population.

In approaching a case such as this, it is critical for the consultant to keep in mind the social stigmatization of people with HIV/AIDS and the dynamics that this can set up for the counselor/client relationship and the consultant/consultee relationship. There are many issues, including heterosexism, substance abuse, and sexism, that have led to the stigmatization of people with HIV/AIDS (Barnett & Whiteside, 2003; Dworkin & Pincu, 1993; Klitzman & Bayer, 2003). Heterosexism is defined here as the belief in the superiority of heterosexuality over other forms of sexual orientation (Morrow, in press; 2003). Prior to beginning a consultation such as this, it is important for the consultant to be certain of his or her personal values on these issues and to be prepared to be open and nonjudgmental. It is also critical to watch for such issues in the consultation as a means of gaining insight into the dynamics between the counselor and the client.

Another concern is the issue of confronting death and dying. The primary goal here is to assist the client in confronting the duality of fearing death and facing life. That is, the client will need help working through unresolved issues that are blocking the emotional progress toward acceptance and, as Powrie (1995) asserts, the client will need assistance gaining "greater insight, which can lead [him/her] to experience more of life, not less" (pp. 113–114). Consultation can be a means of exploring the techniques a counselor can use to facilitate the client in this process. Also, inherent in working with terminal clients (but not always conscious to us) is the fear and contemplation of one's own eventual death. As will be described in this case, the consultee was assisted in becoming aware of some of her own issues about death and was subsequently provided with a referral for counseling.

The particular case that led to this consultation involved a 38-year-old gay male with end-stage AIDS. This client and his life partner of 10 years had been clients of the agency for approximately two years. During this time, the client had received counseling services from one AIDS service organization staff member who had been assigned to the case at the client's first contact with the agency.

The counselor was comfortable with the progress of the counseling until a few months prior to the consultation, when the client's physical health deteriorated rapidly and the progress of the counseling stalled. The counselor was at a loss as to how to emotionally assist this particular client through the next phases of the dying process. She recognized her need for consultation to enhance her effectiveness in working with this particular client as well as other AIDS clients facing issues related to terminal illness.

GOALS OF CONSULTATION

The general goals of the consultation with this consultee (the AIDS service organization counselor) involved facilitating the consultee's knowledge of and comfort with the topic of dying and exploring ways for the consultee to assist her client with the same issues. The consultee expressed a need for more information on the stages of emotional response that a dying client experiences. Further, the consultee wanted to expand her repertoire of techniques and approaches in working with terminal clients.

It quickly became clear that the consultee had some personal issues with death and some boundary issues about how much of herself to give the client in terms of time and energy and how to say "no" when she believed the client was making inordinate demands for time. Therefore, it was also a goal of the consultation to assist the consultee in outlining a self-care and support plan. The consultee was interested in both personal and professional self-care plans. That is, she wanted to develop a better stress management plan for herself and explore her own issues with death and dying, while at the same time clarifying her professional boundaries with clients and defining the level of interaction she could give to this particular client on a routine basis.

CONSULTANT FUNCTION AND ROLE

This consultation required the consultant to take on several roles, including listener, expert, teacher, facilitator, and advisor. Initially, listening and facilitating were primary in assisting the consultee to clearly define her concerns and goals. Once the concerns and goals had been articulated, the consultant's primary role for the remainder of the consultation was that of expert and teacher on the topic of death and dying.

The consultation focused on this topic for the majority of the time since this was the primary reason the consultee had sought consultation. In the role of advisor, the consultant clarified and reflected the consultee's personal issues with death and referred her to personal counseling for further exploration of those issues.

Due to the complexity and sensitivity of the issues in this case, the consultant was required to use strong process skills to facilitate the consultee through clarifying her needs and concerns and defining goals. It was also the consultant's responsibility to structure the sessions and plan processes that would lead to meeting the consultee's goals.

CONSULTEE EXPERIENCE IN CONSULTATION

The consultee's primary roles in the consultation were those of student and collaborator.

The consultee had identified the need to learn more about the death and dying process, and the consultation process resulted in the identification of two routes to accomplish this: training provided by the consultant and continuing education/ professional development.

In her role as student, the consultee took notes and asked questions during the delivery of training, generally interacting with the consultant as she would with a teacher. For example, while discussing the emotional stages that a terminal client goes through, the consultant explained concepts using a flip chart and the consultee participated by asking for clarification, making connections related to her client, and taking notes.

The consultee acted as a collaborator by equally contributing with the consultant in the definition of needs, goals, and plans. The consultee also collaborated in the development of specific interventions and the plan of interaction with the client. Though the consultant acted as an educator, giving information to the consultee (including suggesting various techniques), they worked together to fit the approaches that were developed to the specific needs of the client. It is important to remember that, generally speaking, the consultee knows the client better than the consultant does. In fact, the consultant usually does not know the client at all.

Therefore, the consultee is the prime source of information for the tailoring of various approaches for the client.

APPLICATION: CONSULTANT TECHNIQUES AND PROCEDURES

Entry

During the initial session, the consultant listened actively as the consultee described the case and her concerns. The consultant probed the consultee for additional information concerning the progression of the client's illness and the client's reactions at various stages. The consultee shared the case with the consultant, including her concerns about the client and her interest in gaining additional insight about death and dying. She explained the focus of the counseling with the client over the past two years, emphasizing the last six months in particular.

Though living with full-blown AIDS, the client was generally healthy, and the counselor felt comfortable with the progress of the counseling. However, six months prior to the consultation, the client's health began declining and continued to decline for four months, culminating in the client acquiring a debilitating, opportunistic infection. The onset of the infection caused the client to become bedridden, an event that was quite devastating to him and that pushed him to another level in terms of facing death.

At this point, the counselor's focus shifted to helping the client adjust to the physical changes in his life and to process the frustration, anger, and grief that he was experiencing. It was during this stage of the counseling that the client began to demonstrate the naturally contradictory behavior related to death. He was wishing to die and was concerned about funeral arrangements one minute, saying he didn't want his partner to have to deal with such matters after his death. The next minute, he was concerned about whether his lunch would be delivered on time and was worried about who was going to clean the house.

After pursuing these issues with the client for two months, the counselor felt that the client's progress had stalled, and the counselor was unsure how to proceed. Though having worked with dying clients previously, the counselor felt that this client's history and his strong mixed messages (e.g., not taking medications vs. worrying about nutritional content of meals) created a situation for which the counselor needed consultation relative to the issues of counseling dying clients. It was at this point that the consultee sought consultation from the consultant, due to the consultant's role as a counselor with the local hospice organization.

The consultee discussed her general concerns about assisting the client through the stages of dying and expressed concern over her client's refusal to take his physician-prescribed medications. The consultee saw this refusal as another indication of the client's confusion over accepting versus denying death. Though the client expressed a continuing desire to fight the illness and live, he refused his medications because he feared they would prolong a low-quality existence.

Diagnosis

The second session was focused on specifically defining the areas of concern and establishing goals for the consultation that would meet the needs the consultee had outlined. As the consultee expressed her concerns and needs, the consultant recorded them on poster board. After having discussed all of her concerns, the consultant guided the consultee through combining similar concerns and prioritizing them. Then, through discussion and brainstorming, they established four goals for the consultation:

1. Define interventions to help the consultee facilitate the client's decision making about moving into the death process and reconciling with his death.

2. Explore ways for the consultee to facilitate the client's grief process concerning multiple losses leading up to death and death itself.

3. Provide the consultee with information on death and dying, and identify sources for further training and professional development.

4. Define a plan of action to enable the counselor to take care of herself while assisting the client through the death process.

In delineating these goals, the consultee and consultant recognized that the first and second goal overlapped and were not necessarily separable. Nevertheless, they felt it important to be specific about the objectives of consultation and the concerns the consultee had about the client.

Implementation

The consultee identified that her highest priority was gaining additional information; therefore, in Session 3, the consultant shared information with the consultee in a didactic manner, providing her with resources and teaching her the basics of the death process from spiritual, emotional, cognitive, behavioral, and physical perspectives.

The consultant explained what the consultee could expect in terms of the spiritual issues that might arise for the client, the different feelings the client might experience, the effect dying has on belief systems, the things her client might do and say, and the physical decline of a body that is dying.

Given the consultant's background in working with dying clients, it was fairly easy to compile a resource list for the consultee that consisted of books, professional organizations, and training opportunities (workshops, seminars, conferences, etc.). The consultant reviewed the list with the consultee, and together they generated a plan of specific resources the consultee would pursue and goals for when she would pursue them. The consultee decided that two of the books—one dealing with death and dying and the other with the physiological progression of AIDS—seemed especially appropriate and that she would read those immediately. One seminar on death and dying and one AIDS conference were also singled out, and the consultee planned to check with her supervisor about getting time off from work to attend those.

In Session 4, the consultant shared case examples from her own experience, suggested interventions, and discussed various counseling approaches with the consultee.

Specifically, the consultant suggested the use of the following techniques:

- facilitating the client's guided visualization of the dying experience
- challenging the client to list all unfinished business and fears of death
- encouraging the client to engage in a "dialogue" with his body to understand what, if anything, his body is "telling" him.

With this base, the consultant and consultee developed a plan of action to be implemented with the client over two sessions. This plan recognized the fact that the process of assisting the client through the transition from living to dying and working through grief issues could not be accomplished in only two sessions and actually would continue in some form until the client's death. The intention of the two-session approach was for the consultee to try out some new strategies, discuss the client's responses to those strategies with the consultant, and to adjust the strategies as necessary.

Also, in the fourth session, the consultant and consultee pursued issues related to goal four, in which the consultee takes care of herself while assisting her client through the death process. During this discussion, the consultee spoke of her own grief issues associated with this client and her need for personal support. She also mentioned her own fear of death and her concern that her fear could get in the way of working effectively with her client on death and dying issues.

In response to these concerns, the consultee and consultant brainstormed ways that the consultee could take care of herself while working with the client. The list was narrowed down and prioritized, and a plan was developed. The consultee decided to spend no more than two hours per week with the client, to plan one fun outing for herself per week, to discuss the case regularly with her supervisor, and to seek support as needed from the other agency staff members.

In addition, since the consultee had some personal issues she wanted to deal with surrounding death, the consultant suggested that the consultee seek personal counseling and referred her to a counselor experienced in this area.

In total, the consultant and consultee developed three plans:

• a counseling strategy plan to address goals one and two
• a consultee professional development plan to address goal three
• a consultee self-care plan to address goal four.

In Session 5, the consultee shared with the consultant her progress on the three plans. Specifically, she explained the interventions and approaches she used with her client over the two counseling sessions she had conducted with him since last meeting with the consultant. The consultee shared that the guided visualization had helped her client pinpoint his fears about death and had helped him realize that he wasn't ready to die but, rather, was depressed about his suffering and immobility.

The consultee also indicated that the process of listing unfinished business had been very powerful for her client. Through this exercise he discovered that he had quite a bit of living left to do and decided to start taking the medication that he had previously refused.

The consultee generally felt that the changes in her approach had been helpful, although she questioned her client's readiness for having a dialogue with his body and decided to wait on this approach until he seemed more ready. Overall, she felt that the listing of unfinished business had been the most fruitful in helping the client sort through his mixed feelings of wanting to live and wanting to die.

The consultee also discussed her progress in implementing the professional development plan, which had been established in the third session, and the self-care plan, which had been established in the fourth session. Specifically, the consultee had acquired both of the recommended books and had begun reading the one on death. Her supervisor gave her time off to attend the seminar, but expressed that her taking five days off of work to attend the week-long conference during that particular month would put too much of a strain on the agency. The supervisor had agreed that the consultee could attend a workshop or seminar on end-stage AIDS instead; thus, the consultee and consultant selected one in lieu of the conference.

Lastly, the consultee reported on her self-care plan, indicating that she had done fairly well, but that she would have to put energy into setting clearer boundaries concerning time spent with the client. She had gone on her fun outings, discussed the case with her supervisor, and sought support from her peers at the agency. However, the consultee reported having spent four hours one week with the client, which went beyond the target of two hours she had established. She felt this had drained her substantially and had probably hampered the services she provided to other clients both later that day and the next day. With the consultant's facilitation, the consultee explored this issue further and decided to be more specific with the client when scheduling sessions, indicating to him that, barring unforeseen emergencies, the sessions would need to end as planned. In addition, she decided to openly discuss, in her next session with the client, her need to take care of herself so she could provide the best service possible to him.

Disengagement

At the end of Session 5, it appeared to both the consultee and the consultant that the original goals of the consultation had been accomplished. At this point, the consultant verified with the consultee that there were no additional goals that had arisen throughout the course of the consultation and needed to be addressed. The consultee indicated that, before she tackled any other issues with this case, she needed time to digest the new information and to continue to apply the approaches that had been developed. Therefore, having reached the goals of the consultation, a final session was scheduled to discuss the consultation and reach closure.

In this final session, the consultant solicited feedback from the consultee concerning what had been accomplished during the process of consultation. Although she had worked with dying clients in the past and was somewhat familiar with the death process, the consultee indicated that the consultation had been very helpful and that seeing all the aspects presented holistically had given her a new perspective on death. Because of the consultation she was able to pinpoint specifically where her client was in relation to spirituality, feelings, thoughts, behaviors, and physical decline, and she was able to more appropriately utilize various techniques and interventions. The consultee indicated that this information would allow her to be more aware of what her client was going through and help the client to teach his life partner and other family members about the process.

The consultee also expressed appreciation for now having her own professional development and self-care plans. These were areas on which she had wanted to focus but had not found the time to plan. She particularly felt that seeking her own personal counseling had already had a big impact on her, and she planned to continue with it for several months.

IMPLICATIONS FOR PRACTICE

A mental health consultation case such as this one illustrates many lessons about providing positive consultation and the consultant skills needed to accomplish the goals of consultation. First, it is important to recognize that even an experienced counselor may need consultation. In this case, the consultee had been working with terminally ill clients and had faced the issues of death and dying many times; however, this particular client provided some unique challenges that pushed the counselor into unknown territory, a situation that the counselor healthily recognized and sought to remedy. It was critical for the consultant not to inadvertently shame the consultee into thinking she was an experienced counselor who should already know how to handle this case. Such a misstep could have been very damaging to the counselor's self-esteem and ultimately to the services rendered to her client. Instead, the consultant's openness and validation of the consultee's needs as illustrated in this case encouraged her to be clear about her deficits and fostered a trusting, collaborative relationship.

Second, this case makes clear the issue of self-knowledge for consultants, including their recognition of their own issues, limits, and areas of expertise. In this case, if the consultant had not been an expert on death and dying issues but had tried to "fake it" with the consultee, she would not only have unethically misrepresented herself, but also would not have been able to adequately assist the consultee in accomplishing the goal of gaining more information. If the consultant had found that the consultee's need to learn about the dying process was beyond the consultant's limits of expertise, or if other issues the consultant could not handle had arisen, it would have been imperative for the consultant to have referred the consultee to another consultant.

This case demonstrates some of the sensitive issues a consultant might be exposed to, including chronic disease, death, and consultee personal feelings and values in juxtaposition with services to clients. In addition, the potential influence of forces such as social stigma and heterosexism must be kept in mind as well. Such issues drive home the need for consultants to be clear about their own values and, if necessary, seek personal counseling to work on issues of personal bias. Consultants must also ensure they have the appropriate training for any given consultation, particularly where purchase of expertise is a factor. Hunt (1996) strongly advocates training and values exploration for mental health professionals working with people with AIDS as an essential ingredient to providing effective, ethical treatment.

Issues such as the social stigma surrounding HIV/AIDS, the inevitable death of some clients with HIV/AIDS, and the unpredictable nature of health challenges related to coping with HIV/AIDS can be overwhelming and complex (Dworkin & Pincu, 1993; House & Walker, 1993; Grodeck & Berger, 2003; Irwin, Miller, Fallows, & Farmer, 2003; Keeling, 1993). In terms of process, it is important to recognize that sensitive issues such as these may extend the entry phase. The consultee and consultant may need more time to build their relationship and build trust prior to the consultee feeling comfortable discussing certain topics or sharing certain needs.

This case also highlights the importance of strong consultant process skills. Many cases, including this one, involve complicated scenarios, overlapping issues and needs, and a confusion of possibilities. This was why the consultee requested consultation. Strong consultant process skills help the consultee sort out these issues, make sense of them, and put them into perspective. Once this has been accomplished, goal setting and plans of action become much easier.

The primary process skills used in this case included:

- active listening and clarification
- drawing connections
- brainstorming, combining, and prioritizing.

It is also important here to address the gray area that the consultee and consultant entered when they developed the consultee's self-care plan. Consultation is about working with a consultee on a work-related case involving a third-party (the client); its purpose is not to provide personal counseling for the consultee. As such, the fact that the consultant and consultee developed the consultee's self-care plan during the consultation put them into a sort of gray area; the plan was critical to the consultee's effectiveness with this particular client, but at the same time it was somewhat of a broad personal issue for her. In this case, as they moved into that phase of the consultation, the consultant judged that a high-level, self-care plan, coupled with a counseling referral for the consultee, was an appropriate consultative response to the concerns raised. Though the development of the self-care plan could be construed as counseling, the clear boundaries and open attitude of the consultee led the consultant to believe this positive step could be taken in a reasonable amount of time and could provide immediate strategies for the consultee without crossing the boundary into personal counseling. In another case, with a different consultee, a consultant might not make the same judgment.

Another implication for consideration is the appropriate number of sessions for a mental health consultation. This case involved six sessions over a two month period (somewhat long for a case of this type). Being clear about the boundaries between consultation and counseling helps to guarantee that the consultee's time is truly spent receiving case consultation. In addition, the consultant needs to be aware of the consultee's needs and agenda. In this scenario, the consultee had a clear vision of her needs and was quite motivated to pursue a wide range of goals related to her case. Had this not been the situation, the consultant might have suggested a less aggressive list of goals initially, conducted the consultation in two or three sessions, and invited the consultee to return at some later date to pursue other aspects of the case.

TIPS FOR PRACTICE

- Be aware of your own value system and maintain an observer perspective on how your value system may impact your delivery of consultation services.

- In clinical consultations, resist the temptation to enter into a counseling role with your consultee thus creating a dual role situation with the consultee.

- Make sure you are clear on the consultee's goals for the consultation and don't impose your goals on the consultee.

- Don't be reluctant to refer your consultee for additional services which are beyond the scope of the consultation.

QUESTIONS FOR DISCUSSION AND REFLECTION

1. This consultation case incorporates some very sensitive, value-laden areas, such as heterosexism, HIV/AIDS, and death and dying. What are your values in these areas? How would they impact your handling of this case? How important are the consultant's personal values in determining which consultation cases to accept and how to proceed?

2. The consultant in this case exercised professional judgment in allowing the consultation to push against the boundary from work-related issues to the consultee's personal issues. What ethical concerns does this raise for you? What could have been done differently? What would you have done and why?

3. This case is an example of mental health consultee-centered case consultation. The primary goal is to enhance the consultee's ability to handle a particular case and similar cases in the future. The focus is on the consultee's lack of knowledge, skill, confidence, and/or professional objectivity. The problem is assumed to be with the consultee even though the client's case forms the nexus for discussions. How would you identify and define the consultee's deficits? What are two other strategies you might have used to address these?

4. Given that this model assumes consultee weaknesses, what danger is there to the peer nature of the consultee/consultant relationship? What would you do to minimize the threat to the egalitarian/peer nature of ethical consultation?

REFERENCES AND SUGGESTED READINGS

Barnett, T., & Whiteside, A. (2003). *AIDS in the twenty-first century.* New York, NY: Pulgrave Macmillan.

Cadwell, S.A. (1994).Overidentification with HIV clients. *Journal of Gay and Lesbian Psychotherapy, 2(2),* 77–99.

Caplan, G. (1977).Mental health consultation: Retrospect and prospect. In S. C. Plog & P. I. Ahmed (Eds.), *Principles and techniques of mental health consultation* (pp. 9–21). New York: Plenum Press.

Caplan, G., & Caplan, R. B. (1993). *Mental health consultation and collaboration.* San Francisco: Jossey-Bass.

Caplan, G., & Caplan, R. B. (1999). *Mental health consultation and collaboration.* Prospect Heights, IL: Waveland. (Original work published in 1993).

Corey, G., Corey, M. S., & Callanan, P. (2003). *Issues and ethics in the helping professions* (6th ed.). Pacific Grove, CA: Brooks/Cole.

Dougherty, A.M. (2005). *Psychological consultation and collaboration in school and community settings* (4th ed.). Belmont, CA: Wadsworth.

Dworkin, S. H., & Pincu, L. (1993).Counseling in the era of AIDS. *Journal of Counseling & Development, 71,* 275–281.

Gay Men's Health Crisis (1999). Decline in AIDS death rate slowing. *Treatment Issues: Newsletter of experimental AIDS therapies, 13(5/6).*

Grodeck, G. & Berger, D. S. (2003). *The first year – HIV: An essential guide for the newly diagnosed.* New York, NY: Marlowe & Co.

Hay, L. L. (1988). *The AIDS book: Creating a positive approach.* Santa Monica, CA: Hay House.

Herlihy, B., & Corey, G. (1997). *Boundary issues in counseling.* Alexandria, VA: American Association for Counseling and Development.

House, R.M., & Walker, C.M. (1993). Preventing AIDS via education. *Journal of Counseling & Development, 71,* 282–289.

Hunt, B. (1996).HIV/AIDS training in CACREP-approved counselor education programs. *Journal of Counseling and Development, 74,* 295–299.

Keeling, R. P. (1993).HIV disease: Current concepts. *Journal of Counseling & Development, 71,* 261–274.

Irwin, A., Miller, J., Fallows, D., & Farmer, P. (2003). *Global AIDS: Myths and facts: Tools for fighting the AIDS pandemic.* Cambridge, MA: Southend Press.

Klitzman, R. & Bayer, R. (2003). *Mortal secrets: Truth and lies in the age of AIDS.* Baltimore, MD: Johns Hopkins University Press.

Mancoske, R. J., & Lindhorst, T. (1995).The ecological context of HIV/AIDS counseling: Issues for lesbians and gays and their significant others. *Journal of Gay and Lesbian Social Services, 2(3/4),* 25–40.

Mancoske, R. J., Wadsworth, C.M., Dufas, D. S., & Hasney, J.A. (1995). Suicide risk among people living with AIDS. *Social Work, 40,* 783–787.

Morrow, D. F. (in press). Social work practice with gay, lesbian, bisexual, and transgender adolescents. *Families in Society.*

Morrow, D. F. (2003). Cast into the wilderness: The impact of institutionalized religion on lesbians. *Journal of Lesbian Studies, 7,* 109-123.

Powrie, R. (1995).HIV: Death sentence or opportunity? *Journal of Gay and Lesbian Social Services, 2,* 113–116.

Schein, E. H. (1988). *Process consultation: Its role in organization development.* (Vol.1, 2nd ed.). Reading, MA: Addison-Wesley.

Schein, E. H. (1999). *Process consultation revisited: Building the helping relationship.* Reading, MA: Addison-Wesley.

Stein, T. J. (1998). *The social welfare of women and children with HIV and AIDS.* New York: Oxford University Press.

Werner, J. L., & Tyler, J.M. (1993).Community-based interventions: A return to community mental health centers' origins. *Journal of Counseling & Development, 71,* 689–692.

4

Adlerian Case Consultation
with a Teacher

TERRY KOTTMAN

DESCRIPTION OF THE MODEL USED

In Adlerian consultation with teachers, the consultation process is based on ideas posited by Alfred Adler in his formulation of Individual Psychology during the early decades of the 20th century (Ansbacher & Ansbacher, 1956; Carlson, Dinkmeyer, & Carlson, 2001; Dinkmeyer, Carlson, & Dinkmeyer, 1994; Dinkmeyer & Sperry, 2000; Dougherty, 2005; Sweeney, 1998). The following six concepts are central to the Adlerian consultation process (Dinkmeyer et al., 1994):

1. In order to understand a person's personality, the Adlerian consultant must examine the characteristic pattern of beliefs about self, others, and the world and also examine the choices and behaviors based on those beliefs—the person's lifestyle (Dinkmeyer et al., 1994). A person's beliefs about self, others, and/or the world are frequently "mistaken," or negative and self-defeating.

   Because of "private logic," the person will act as if these mistaken convictions are true, which may result in choices and behaviors that are destructive or harmful to the person in some way (Ansbacher & Ansbacher, 1956).

   One method of looking at lifestyle, or personality priorities, was developed by Kefir (1981) and further refined by several other Adlerians (Dewey, 1991; Kottman, 2003; Kottman & Ashby, 1999; Langenfeld & Main, 1983). Kefir declared that individuals can fall into four distinct categories of coping with life: those who try to please others; those who try to control either themselves or others; those who try to achieve comfort; and those who try to achieve superiority, either over others or over their own past performances.

In consulting with a teacher, the consultant must gain insight into the lifestyles of everyone involved in the consultation process. The Adlerian consultant must understand the beliefs and behaviors of the teacher and any student with whom the teacher needs assistance.

2. The Adlerian consultant must remember that every behavior (positive and negative) is goal-directive and purposive (Dinkmeyer et al., 1994). The goal of children's misbehavior can have one of four distinct purposes: seeking attention, trying to gain power, striving for revenge, or attempting to prove inadequacy (Dreikurs & Soltz, 1964; Lew & Bettner, 1998, 2000). In addition to these four basic goals of misbehavior, Dinkmeyer, McKay, and Dinkmeyer (1980) posited that adolescents may also strive toward three additional goals of behavior: excitement, peer acceptance, and superiority. As teens move toward these goals, they may use positive, socially acceptable, behavior or negative, socially irresponsible, behavior to attain them. If the consultant wants to understand the interaction between a teacher and his or her student, the consultant must strive to determine the purposes of all the parties involved.

3. Adlerian consultants believe that all people are constantly striving for significance (Dinkmeyer et al., 1994). Individuals aim to achieve this sense of success because of perceptions of inferiority that stem from feelings of incompetence they experienced as young children when they compared themselves to older children and adults. They strive for a sense that they "count" (Ansbacher & Ansbacher, 1956; Lew & Bettner, 1998). Each person has a special and unique way of gaining significance; if he or she cannot achieve success in a positive way, he or she will strive in a negative, destructive way. The Adlerian consultant considers how both the teacher and the student gain their significance within the school setting.

4. All individuals involved in the consulting process must be understood from a social context (Dinkmeyer et al., 1994). It is impossible to comprehend behavior in isolation, so the consultant must examine both the teacher's and student's behavior in the context of their interactions with others—other teachers and administrators, other students, school personnel, and so forth.

5. Individuals always have a choice about their attitudes and behaviors. Adlerian consultants believe that people are capable of change because they are constantly making decisions about their own attitudes and perceptions (Dinkmeyer et al., 1994). This belief underscores the idea that teachers and students are responsible for their own choices and behavior. The concept of individual choice

is important to the consultation process because it represents the potentially proactive, constructive nature of the relationship among the consultant, the teacher, and the student.

6. The Adlerian consultant strongly believes that every human being has a need to belong (Dinkmeyer et al., 1994). All human behavior is designed to achieve a sense of belonging, or connection, either in a positive way or a negative way (Ansbacher & Ansbacher, 1956; Lew & Bettner, 1998). Adlerians examine the ways that individuals fit into their families and into other social contexts in order to help them better understand lifestyles and goals of behavior. In consulting with teachers, an Adlerian consultant considers the ways that both the teacher and the student achieve a sense of belonging in the classroom and in the school.

SETTING AND BACKGROUND ISSUES

When I first started work as a school counselor, my idealistic intention was to spend 100 percent of my time working directly with students. However, I quickly found that I could provide help to the children in a more effective and efficient manner if I devoted a considerable portion of my time and energy to consulting with teachers about specific students and about general classroom management and human relationship issues.

Setting

I worked as the school counselor at Starlight, a small private school for special needs adolescents (learning disabled, emotionally disturbed, low IQs). Most of the approximately 100 students who attended this school had been unsuccessful in public schools, usually for a combination of academic, emotional, behavioral, and social reasons. Many of the children had special education labels, such as dysgraphic, dyslexic, dyscalculic, and "slow learner." The school population also included children who had been diagnosed with attention-deficit hyperactivity disorder (ADHD), bipolar disorder, schizophrenia, dysthymia, conduct disorder, and oppositional defiant disorder.

I was the first counselor the school had ever had. Before they hired me to work half time, the director of the school and the school nurse had tried to fill the role of mentor and counselor to the students and teachers. Part of my job during my first year as a counselor was to demonstrate to the staff that I could be helpful to them and that I was not going to try to "tell them how to run their classrooms." Therefore, I was excited and a bit nervous when Mr. Cantrell, the math teacher, came to talk to me about difficulties he was having in his classroom with Jason Jackson, one of his ninth-grade students.

Background

Jason's parents divorced when he was 4 years old, and neither of them had remarried. Jason lived with his mother, who worked nights cleaning office buildings. He visited his father, who was a construction worker, on weekends. Jason was the youngest of four children, and there was an eight-year gap between Jason and the sister closest to him in age, which, in effect, made him an only child. None of the three older children lived with their parents. Both Jason and Ms. Jackson reported that the other three children had not spent very much time with Jason while he was growing up, "except to tell him what to do, which they did a lot, but he just ignored them." Ms. Jackson had worked nights since Jason was 12 years old, and he "watched himself" because he "refused to let me hire a babysitter."

Jason attended public school until the sixth grade. Jason's second-grade and fifth-grade teachers had suggested that he be tested for ADHD, but, based on feedback from the family and several observations conducted by the school psychologist, the Jackson's family pediatrician felt that ADHD was not really the problem. During the fifth grade, Jason had also been tested for special education placement, but he had not met the criteria for learning disabilities (his academic scores were not quite low enough) or behavior disorders (his behavior was not quite difficult enough). Halfway through the sixth grade, Jason was suspended for telling a teacher to take a book and "shove it where the sun don't shine." His parents, concerned that his behavior was deteriorating, decided that he needed a different environment and enrolled him at Starlight. During his tenure at Starlight, Jason's academics improved significantly. He was functioning on grade level in every subject, although sometimes his grades suffered because he refused to do homework or would "lose" his class assignments.

Jason continued to have the same type of behavior problems that he had demonstrated in public school. He was regularly defiant to the faculty and staff, and he refused to participate in many school activities. At other times, when there was no pressure for him to conform to rules or comply with instructions, Jason was a pleasant, fun adolescent. At lunch and before and after school, he frequently engaged teachers and other students in polite and interesting conversations.

In her conferences with school personnel, Ms. Jackson repeatedly told them that Jason "just never did mind anyone." "Don't take it personal or anything," she said. "That is just the way he is. If you let him be, it will be less trouble for everyone." This advice offended Mr. Cantrell, who came to me to talk about "ways to get Jason to do what he is supposed to do in my classroom." Mr. Cantrell reported that, although Jason seemed to like math and spent quite a bit of time around the math room outside of class, during class Jason was consistently rebellious. He either ignored Mr. Cantrell's instructions or actively resisted them. Jason frequently "talked back and sassed" Mr. Cantrell and many times simply refused to do his assignments. Sometimes he would do the assignments, but then he would refuse to hand them in to Mr. Cantrell. The math teacher reported feeling extremely irritated with Jason's defiant behavior during class and feeling mystified with Jason's amiable interactions outside of class.

GOALS OF CONSULTATION

In consulting with Mr. Cantrell about Jason, I had two different sets of goals, several that related to Jason and several that related to Mr. Cantrell. The goals for Jason were:

- Increase Jason's awareness of his own lifestyle and how it might be contributing to the difficulties in his interactions with others, especially with authority figures.
- Decrease Jason's need to prove that others cannot control his behavior by being defiant and refusing to constructively participate in the school curriculum and activities.
- Increase Jason's willingness to cooperate and gain his sense of belonging and significance in school by making a positive contribution to the school atmosphere.

The goals for Mr. Cantrell were:

- Increase Mr. Cantrell's understanding of his own lifestyle (especially his personality priority) and how it might be hampering his attempts to positively interact with Jason.
- Increase Mr. Cantrell's skills in the areas of understanding the goals of behavior, using encouragement, setting up logical consequences, and conducting classroom meetings.

CONSULTANT FUNCTION AND ROLE

In Adlerian consultation, the consultant works collaboratively with the teacher, first forming an egalitarian relationship, then investigating the lifestyle of both the teacher and the student involved in the problem (Dinkmeyer et al., 1994). The consultant may gather information about the problem, the lifestyles of various parties involved, any attempted solutions, and the teacher's feelings related to the student and problem (Dougherty, 2005). Other important data about the student's lifestyle can include information about the family atmosphere (the affective tone of the family) and the family constellation (psychological birth order, family values, and so forth) (Ansbacher & Ansbacher, 1956; Eckstein & Baruth, 1996; Kottman, 2003). The consultant may also observe in the teacher's classroom to further gather information about the teacher's lifestyle and the lifestyles of the student with whom he or she is struggling or to conduct a brief interview with the student to explore lifestyle issues (Dinkmeyer et al., 1994).

Based on the data gathered, the consultant and the teacher collaboratively form hypotheses about the possible goals of behavior, personality priorities, mistaken convictions, and other elements of lifestyle for both the teacher and the student. Although a complete lifestyle investigation would be ideal, in a school setting this may not always be possible. If time is limited, it is still important to gather enough information to give a general idea about the teacher's personality priority, the student's goals of behavior and methods of gaining significance and belonging, and the assets of both the teacher and the student. The consultant and the teacher can then generate alternative ways for the teacher to understand and interact with the student, believing that, if the teacher is willing to change his or her patterns of interaction with the student, the student's behavior and beliefs will also change (Dougherty, 2005).

In each case consultation, I try to tailor my role and function to the specific teacher and the situation. Since I did not know Mr. Cantrell very well before we started working on this case, I spent more time than usual building a relationship and gathering information before I moved toward generating hypotheses and suggestions for alternative methods of dealing with Jason.

CONSULTEE EXPERIENCE IN CONSULTATION

Mr. Cantrell expressed reluctance entering into the consultation process. He told me that he had always solved his classroom problems himself, but that the principal had urged him to try consultation I had observed during the course of the year that Mr. Cantrell seemed to ascribe to several mistaken convictions that can frequently contribute to teacher frustration (Dinkmeyer et al., 1994; Dinkmeyer, McKay, & Dinkmeyer, 1980). These included:

- The teacher must be in control; if the teacher feels out of control, he or she must work harder to make sure that students know who is the boss because being out of control is dangerous.
- Students must cooperate with the teacher; if they don't, there is either something wrong with the student or something wrong with the teacher.
- The teacher must be perfect; he or she must be able to handle every situation and every student in the optimal fashion and if the teacher doesn't, it means that he or she is a bad teacher.

Our initial conversation about Jason lent confirmation to my hypotheses about Mr. Cantrell's beliefs about himself as a teacher and my guess that his personality priority was control. However, it also gave me a great deal of hope because Mr. Cantrell had many assets. He obviously cared about the students, including Jason, and he seemed open to looking at his own motivations and actions and to exploring some new ways of interacting with his students. He was also extremely intelligent and interested in learning about new ideas and new skills.

In my experience with teachers whose personality priority is control, it is necessary to go very slowly in the consultation process, so as to help them feel in control of the interaction. I have also found that it is helpful to be relatively indirect in making suggestions for change. The consultant must also be willing to take a "one down" position in the relationship so that these teachers do not feel as though the consultant is trying to come into their classrooms and tell them what to do.

Therefore, I took the process of consultation with Mr. Cantrell rather slowly, so slowly in fact that after two consultation sessions he urged me to give him more information about Adlerian psychology so that he could learn about these new ideas at his own pace. He got very interested in the concepts underlying Individual Psychology, and, though he did not necessarily become a "convert," he gradually became an active collaborator in the consultation process.

APPLICATION: CONSULTANT TECHNIQUES AND PROCEDURES

Entry

Since I had experienced limited interaction with Mr. Cantrell, I began the consultation process in Session 1 by building a rapport with him, asking general questions about his background and getting him to talk about his philosophical beliefs about children and education. I wanted to convey to Mr. Cantrell that I was interested in him and in his interactions with his students. Without evoking his defenses, it was also important for me to express empathy about Mr. Cantrell's difficulties with Jason and about his fears of being out of control and needing to be perfect. I wanted to acknowledge that Jason was a difficult student without entering into "child bashing." As part of this conversation, I asked about his preconceptions and fears about the consultation process and his feelings about having the principal recommend that he consult me about Jason. As a way of reframing the experience, I suggested that he was in control of whether he consulted me and whether he used anything we discussed in his classroom; in this way, the principal had no power to make him act on any ideas we generated.

In order to reinforce the idea that he was in charge of the process, I asked him to give me an outline of his vision of a successful consultation (Dougherty, 2005). I requested that he think about the following questions: What would my role be? What would his role be? What would Jason's role be? What were his goals? How did he want to be different in his interaction with Jason? How did he want Jason to be different in their interactions?

Diagnosis

In our next meeting (Session 2), we discussed the organization of Mr. Cantrell's classroom and his interaction with past students. He also provided answers to the questions I had posed during the entry phase of the consultation. Mr. Cantrell's comments helped me begin to make some more hypotheses about his lifestyle. He said that he wanted my role as consultant to be very limited: he preferred that I not observe in his classroom or interview Jason. He mainly wanted me to provide him with "some thoughts on how to approach the situation with Jason." Mr. Cantrell stated that his role would be active. That is, he wanted to decide which of my "thoughts" he was going to carry out in his classroom without any "outside interference." In this discussion, he defined Jason's role as relatively limited in terms of having choices. What he really wanted was for Jason to just "do what he was supposed to do," without having a lot of input into the process. In talking about his goals for the consultation, he was a little broader and discussed the fact that he had struggled with students like Jason ever since he started teaching. Noting that he was feeling the need for "learning new tricks" to get the students "to cooperate," he said, "I just feel very defeated and discouraged when things don't go the way I think they should. I have very high standards for my classroom." At the same time, Mr. Cantrell was not sure that he wanted to commit to being different in his relationship with Jason. The thought of his behavior needing to change seemed to frighten him. I reflected this to him, and he acknowledged that, while he thought his current approach had not been working with "this type of kid," he was not sure that he was willing to change his own behavior.

This conversation confirmed my guesses about Mr. Cantrell's personality priority (control) and my guesses about his beliefs about himself as a teacher. He believed that he must maintain control of his classroom and obtain the co-operation (which to him meant obedience) of the students. By admitting that his current methods of discipline were not working with noncompliant students, and by suggesting that he was not living up to his own standards, Mr. Cantrell confirmed that he believed he must do his job perfectly and that he felt discouraged and defeated when he could not.

Mr. Cantrell's remarks also helped me formulate some ideas about his assets as a teacher. He was dedicated to doing a good job and was willing to try to learn and apply new concepts. He was honest about his own reluctance to change, admitting that it would be "more comfortable if Jason would just change." He was also relatively realistic, acknowledging that such a change in Jason was unlikely and that he was not really in control of the behavior of his students.

Since Mr. Cantrell did not want me to observe in his classroom or interview Jason about the problem, I started Session 3 by gathering information related to Jason's lifestyle and by asking Mr. Cantrell about the specific problems with Jason. I asked him to describe several encounters between the two of them. What had provoked each incident? What did Jason do or say during each interaction? What had Mr. Cantrell done to intervene with Jason? How had Mr. Cantrell felt during the interactions? How had Jason reacted to correction? These questions were designed to duplicate the queries usually used in an analysis of children's goals of misbehavior (Dinkmeyer & McKay, 1990; Kottman, 2003; Dreikurs & Soltz, 1964).

There was a definite pattern in Mr.Cantrell's answers that suggested that Jason's primary goal of behavior was power. Jason seemed determined to prove that no one else could control him in any way. Most of the incidents between the two of them started with Mr.Cantrell giving Jason a specific directive, with which Jason consistently refused to comply (usually with openly hostile and defiant behavior). Mr. Cantrell had almost always threatened Jason with punishment (sending him to the principal, calling his mother, giving him extra work).

During these power struggles, Mr. Cantrell had felt angry and frustrated. He had been drawn into verbal arguments with Jason and frequently felt "out of control; as if no matter what I did, I could have no impact on Jason's behavior." When corrected, Jason seemed to escalate his negative behavior, shouting, leaving the classroom without permission, ignoring Mr. Cantrell's demands that he report to the principal's office, and wandering the halls of the school. This was consistent with the usual pattern of children whose goal is power (Kottman, 2003). Their behavior is frequently reported to be out of control. The adults who deal with them usually feel angry and challenged; when the children are corrected, they tend to escalate their negative behavior.

Mr. Cantrell's description fit with what I already knew about Jason's lifestyle from my prior interactions with him. Several other teachers had referred Jason to me for help with anger management and disruptive, defiant classroom behavior. Jason had been unwilling to enter into a counseling relationship with me, telling me that I was "just like the other adults who want to tell me what to do." However, he frequently sought out my company before and after school and at the school functions he attended, engaging me in conversations and telling me stories of his adventures outside of school.

Based on reports from Mr. Cantrell, other teachers, other students, and my own observations of Jason's interactions with teachers and peers, I believed that Jason was also striving toward the adolescent goals of peer approval and superiority (Dinkmeyer & McKay., 1990). Jason received approbation from the other students in the school for not conforming to the rules and for defying authority figures. Many of his peers reported that Jason was "cool" simply because he did not do what he was told. Jason seemed to feel that he was better than his teachers when he succeeded in avoiding doing what they wanted him to do and to feel that he was better than the other students who obeyed the rules.

I shared my hypotheses about Jason's goals of behavior with Mr. Cantrell, asking him to help me make some guesses about other aspects of Jason's lifestyle, specifically his mistaken convictions about himself, others, and the world. I also asked Mr. Cantrell to help me list Jason's assets. We based our hypotheses on what we knew about Jason's interactions with people at the school and what we knew about Jason's family atmosphere and family constellation. In collaboration, we made a tentative list of Jason's mistaken convictions about himself, others, and the world:

• He feels inadequate and insignificant unless he is in control.

• He must show others that they cannot control him.

• He must win every fight he gets into because if he loses, he is nothing.

• Others are always trying to control him.

• Others are weak and unimportant when they don't have any power.

• The world is a place in which he will not be safe unless he is in control.

• The world is a place in which others are either very powerful and controlling or weak and powerless.

We felt that Jason had developed these beliefs partially in response to being both the baby of the family, with several adults (including his much older siblings) telling him what to do, and to being an only child, whose mother tended toward a comfort personality priority, in which she believed the best way to parent her son was to let him do whatever he wanted. We thought that this situation was compounded by Jason's struggles in school and the fact that his learning differences and difficulties, which had not been handicapping enough for him to qualify for special help, left him feeling as if he was incapable and unimportant in school.

Mr. Cantrell and I developed a list of Jason's assets. Jason was charming, interesting, charismatic, intelligent, and resourceful. We believed that a relatively small shift in his beliefs about himself, others, and the world would result in constructive behavior based on a sense of self-reliance, strong leadership skills, and the potential for making many positive contributions to the school and his peers.

Implementation

As suggested earlier in the chapter, the first step in the implementation process in Adlerian consultation is helping the teacher gain insight into how his or her lifestyle is hampering optimum potential for positive interaction with the student. The consultant tries to get a commitment for some type of attitudinal and/or behavioral change in the teacher, with the ultimate goal of a concomitant change in the attitudes and/or behavior of the student.

During Session 4, I began working toward the first goal for Mr. Cantrell, increasing his understanding of his own lifestyle (especially his personality priority and how it might be hampering his attempts to positively interact with Jason). I accomplished this by sharing my hypotheses about Mr. Cantrell's lifestyle. Because of my beliefs about his personality priority, I asked his permission to share my ideas so that he would not feel that I was trying to control our interaction (Kottman, 2003). Because I thought that he was rather hard on himself and that he was worried that I was going to judge him to be inadequate, I first gave him a list of my analysis of his strengths. I then moved toward areas of concern by saying, "I have several guesses about some aspects of a belief system that might get in the way when teachers work with kids like Jason. I was hoping you might think about giving me some feedback on how you think these beliefs might interfere in a teacher's interactions with

Jason." When we had talked about this (with little defensiveness and much insight on his part), I asked him if some of these convictions fit into his own belief system. Although he was initially a bit defensive about this idea, he gradually admitted that he did believe that he needed to be in control of every aspect of his life, especially his classroom, and that this might be interfering in his relationship with Jason.

When there are skills that would be helpful to teachers during the implementation phase of the consultation process, I do some direct teaching of Adlerian management strategies or recommend specific books or book chapters for them to read.

My second goal for Mr. Cantrell was to increase his skills in the areas of understanding the goals of behavior, using encouragement, setting up logical consequences, and conducting classroom meetings. I also believed that increasing Mr. Cantrell's knowledge and application of these Adlerian techniques would facilitate movement toward all three of my goals for Jason. By "spitting in his soup," an Adlerian technique that involves constructively pointing out mistaken goals and faulty convictions to an individual (Kottman, 2003), Mr. Cantrell could increase Jason's awareness of his own lifestyle and how it might be contributing to the difficulties in his interactions with others. By encouraging rather than praising, using logical consequences rather than punishment for inappropriate behavior, and engaging in dialogue with students in classroom meetings, Mr. Cantrell could share some of his power with his students without feeling totally out of control. I believed that this would decrease Jason's need to prove that others could not control his behavior and increase the possibility that Jason would be willing to cooperate and exercise some of his positive leadership skills.

Since Mr. Cantrell had requested that I provide him with a list of materials to read, at the end of Session 4 I gave him several books designed to provide teachers with Adlerian skills to use in their classrooms. Appropriate titles might include *Responsibility in the Classroom:A Teacher's Guide to Understanding and Motivating Students* (Lew & Bettner, 1998) *Cooperative Discipline* (Albert, 1996); *Systematic Training for Effective Teaching* (Dinkmeyer et al., 1980); *Active Teaching* (Popkin, 1994); *Maintaining Sanity in the Classroom* (Dreikurs, Grunwald, & Pepper, 1982); and *Positive Discipline in the Classroom (2nd ed.)* (Nelsen, Lott, & Glenn, 1997).These books cover topics such as understanding the goals of behavior and modifying teacher interaction with students based on individual children's lifestyles, understanding how the teacher's mistaken beliefs can affect the classroom, providing encouragement rather than praise, setting up logical consequences, using effective communication skills, and conducting class meetings.

Rather than telling Mr. Cantrell to read specific books, I gave him a list because of my hypothesis about his personality priority. I have found that teachers whose personality priority is control tend to be more willing to read if they feel that they have the power to choose what they will read.

Mr. Cantrell read several of the books on the list and, after discussing several of the ideas with me during Session 5, he decided to implement logical consequences and class meetings. He liked the idea of giving limited choices to students and involving them in generating alternative behaviors and consequences.

He felt comfortable with this strategy because he would still have the final say in the discipline process, but the students would also feel as though they had some power. Although there was some testing of the limits of this intervention, it worked well with Jason and several other students who had similar lifestyles. Jason responded positively to the idea that Mr. Cantrell was giving him choices, not just telling him what he had to do.

Based on his new understanding of the goals of behavior, Mr. Cantrell also began making guesses about the goals of Jason's behavior. Mr. Cantrell also began "spitting in his soup" when Jason was acting on private logic and behaving as if his self-defeating convictions about himself, others, and the world were true. Sometimes this strategy worked, and sometimes it seemed to backfire. After trying it for several weeks, Mr. Cantrell felt comfortable enough to ask me to observe in his classroom. I noticed that he tended to make his guesses in a rather sarcastic "got you" way to students. Therefore, during Session 6, I gave him some feedback about the way his lifestyle might be influencing the manner in which he presented these ideas to students. He seemed uncomfortable with this direct feedback, so I told him that many teachers like to use a videotape to observe themselves in their classrooms. By videotaping several class sessions and watching the tapes, he was able to learn to recognize when he was doing this and was able to adjust his delivery, which resulted in more positive results from his students, including Jason.

Disengagement

In Session 7 (a brief follow-up visit), Mr. Cantrell reported that Jason was doing "much better" in his class, and we decided to terminate the consultation process. The number of power struggles between the teacher and his student had reduced significantly, and Jason was "more like he is outside class most of the time." Although Mr. Cantrell still seemed uncomfortable discussing his own lifestyle and how it affected his interaction with his students, he had made some rather important shifts in his willingness to share power in positive and appropriate ways with his students. He also gave me credit for suggesting that he videotape his class. Now he could decide "when and where and how it was going to happen and that way," he said, "I can see for myself how things were going." Although he never told me that he was pleased with the consultation process, over the course of the succeeding semesters, he suggested that several other teachers come and talk to me about students who were having problems.

IMPLICATIONS FOR PRACTICE

This case study provided a relatively narrow application of the principles inherent in Adlerian consultation. From a broader perspective, Adlerian concepts are appropriate in a variety of instances. They can serve as a schema for client conceptualization and intervention for use in consulting with school counselors and for mental health counselors working with difficult clients (Dinkmeyer et al., 1994; Dinkmeyer & Sperry, 2000; Eckstein & Baruth, 1996; Kottman, 2003; Manaster & Corsini, 1982; Sweeney, 1998; Watts & Carlson, 1999).They can provide management systems applicable to an entire school or district for use in consulting with school districts (Albert, 1996; Nelsen, Lott, & Glenn, 1993).They can be appropriate in training programs for pre-service and in-service teachers for use in consulting with teacher education faculties or with school district professional development experts (Dinkmeyer et al., 1980; Popkin, 1994). Adlerian concepts can also be applied to parenting programs and can provide information for consulting with parents (Bettner & Lew, 1996; Dinkmeyer & McKay, 1997; Dreikurs & Soltz, 1964; Lew & Bettner, 2000; Lott & Intner, 1994; Nelsen, 1996; Popkin, 1993).

In consulting with mental health counselors and school counselors about difficult clients, the consultant can use several different texts to formulate case conceptualizations and treatment plans. Dinkmeyer et al. (1994) give specific suggestions about the general process of Adlerian consultation. Dinkmeyer and Sperry (2000), Eckstein and Baruth (1996), Sweeney (1998) and Manaster and Corsini (1982) have provided guides to Adlerian theory and to methods that practitioners can use to apply Adlerian concepts and techniques with clients. These authors suggest ideas for conceptualizing clients' lifestyles and for planning intervention strategies to help clients gain insight into their lifestyles, helping them make changes in their attitudes, beliefs, and behaviors. Kottman (2003) integrated the concepts and techniques of Individual Psychology and the strategies of play therapy to develop Adlerian play therapy, a counseling approach for working with young children. All of these models can provide the professional with ideas for consulting with mental health and school counselors on ways to improve their work with clients.

Albert (1996) and Nelsen, Lott, and Glenn (1997) have developed texts outlining methods of using Adlerian principles and strategies for a system of classroom management that can be applied on a school-wide or district-wide basis. These texts would be invaluable to the consultant working with a school district on implementing an Adlerian approach to discipline.

Dinkmeyer et al. (1980) and Popkin (1994) have developed programs for training teachers how to apply Adlerian principles in their classrooms. Consultants can use these resources to work with teacher education faculty members in planning classroom management courses. Also, when consulting with the school district personnel responsible for developing teacher in-service programs, these resources can help suggest specific ways teachers can improve their teaching skills and their ability to comprehend the motivation of students.

Adlerians believe that parent consultation is a key element in working with children of any age, whether their difficulties are home based or school based (Kottman, 2003). Because of the strong impact parents have on the formation of their children's lifestyles, and because parents are invaluable sources of information about their children, any intervention designed to help children should include some component of parent consultation. For successful parent consultation, it is essential to have resources that can help parents both better understand their children and also facilitate them in making changes in their attitudes about, and interactions with, their children (Bettner & Lew, 1996; Dinkmeyer & McKay, 1990, 1997; Dreikurs & Soltz, 1964; Lew & Bettner, 2000; Lott & Intner, 1994; Nelsen, 1996; Popkin, 1993).

QUESTIONS FOR DISCUSSION AND REFLECTION

1. Many Adlerians believe that parents should always be involved in the consultation process, regardless of whether the problem is home based or school based. In this case, do you believe that Ms. Jackson should have been included in the consultation process? Why or why not? If you would have included her in the process, how would you have done this?

2. In this case, both the teacher and the student were clients, but the teacher was reluctant for the consultant to have any direct interaction with the student because he saw the student's role in the consultation process as limited. Would you agree to such an arrangement? Given the premise that consultation is indirect delivery of services, describe your rationale for your decision. If you chose not to agree to this arrangement, how would you have handled the interaction with the teacher to try to get more active involvement with the student?

3. Do you believe you need parental permission to consult with a teacher about a student? Explain your rationale.

4. In this day of accountability, there are many people who would believe that the decision to terminate the consultation process in the disengagement phase of this case study was a bit informal. Discuss ways to make the disengagement more formal and accountable. Remember to take Mr. Cantrell's personality priority (need for control) into account in your discussion.

5. Although most Adlerians have little faith in formal psychiatric diagnosis, many consultants would have considered a psychiatric diagnosis for Jason, such as conduct disorder or oppositional defiant disorder. Explain your stand on this practice and discuss how such a diagnosis would have helped or harmed the interactions in this case study.

6. Jason had trouble with all of his teachers, not just Mr. Cantrell. Describe the kind of difficulties he might have encountered with a teacher whose personality priority was pleasing. What if the teacher's personality priority was superiority? What if it was comfort? Discuss ways you could use your knowledge of a teacher's personality priority to tailor your consultation intervention.

7. How would you handle consulting with a teacher who is adamantly resistant to change if you believed that the teacher needed to change before the student could?

8. Given what you know about the considerations necessary for successful cross-cultural consultation, answer the following questions: How would it have affected the process if the consultant and the student belonged to the same race or culture, which was different from that of the consultee? How would it have affected the process if the consultant and the consultee belonged to the same race or culture, which was different from that of the student? Describe what (if any) adjustments the consultant should make in either of these situations.

REFERENCES AND SUGGESTED READINGS

Albert, L. (1996). *Cooperative discipline.* Circle Pines, MN: American Guidance Service.

Ansbacher, H., & Ansbacher, R. (Eds.) (1956). *The individual psychology of Alfred Adler: A systematic presentation in selections from his writings.* New York: Basic.

Bettner, B. L., & Lew, A. (1996). *Raising kids who can.* Newton Centre, MA: Connexions.

Carlson, J., Dinkmeyer, D., & Carlson, J. (2001). *Counseling: Creating school-based interventions* (2nd ed.). New York: Brunner/Mazel.

Dewey, E. (1991). *Basic applications of Adlerian psychology for self-understanding and human relationships.* Coral Springs, FL: CMTI.

Dinkmeyer, D., Carlson, J., & Dinkmeyer, D. (1994). *Consultation: School mental health professionals as consultants.* Muncie, IN: Accelerated Development.

Dinkmeyer, D., & McKay, G. (1997). *Systematic training for effective parenting: The parent's handbook* (4th ed.). Circle Pines, MN: American Guidance Service.

Dinkmeyer, D., & McKay, G. (1990). *The parent's handbook: Systematic training for effective parenting of teens* (2nd ed.). Circle Pines, MN: American Guidance Service.

Dinkmeyer, D., McKay, G., & Dinkmeyer, D. (1980). *Systematic training for effective teaching.* Circle Pines, MN: American Guidance Service.

Dinkmeyer, D., McKay, G., Dinkmeyer, D., Dinkmeyer, J., & McKay, J. (1987). *The effective parent.* Circle Pines, MN: American Guidance Service.

Dougherty, A.M. (2005). *Psychological consultation and collaboration in school and community settings* (4th ed.). Belmont, CA: Wadsworth.

Dreikurs, R.,Grunwald, B.,& Pepper, F. (1982). *Maintaining sanity in the classroom.* New York: Harper/Row.

Dreikurs, R.,& Soltz, V. (1964). *Children: The challenge.* New York: Hawthorn.

Eckstein, D., & Baruth, L. (1996). *The theory and practice of lifestyle assessment* (4th ed.). Dubuque, IA: Kendall/Hunt.

Kefir, N. (1981). Impasse/priority therapy. In R. Corsini (Ed.), *Handbook of innovative psychotherapies* (pp. 400–415). New York: John Wiley.

Kottman, T. (2003). *Partners in play: An Adlerian approach to play therapy* (2nd ed.). Alexandria, VA: American Counseling Association.

Kottman, T., & Ashby, J. (1999). Using Adlerian personality priorities to custom-design consultation with parents of play therapy clients. *International Journal of Play Therapy, 8(2),* 77-92.

Langenfeld, S., & Main, F. (1983). Personality priorities:A factor analytic study. *Individual Psychology, 39,* 40–51.

Lew,A.,& Bettner, B. L. (1998). *Responsibility in the classroom: A teacher's guide to understanding and motivating students.* Boston, MA: Connexions.

Lew,A.,& Bettner, B. L. (2000). *A parent's guide to understanding and motivating children.* Boston, MA: Connexions.

Lott, L., & Intner, R. (1994). *The family that works together.* Rocklin, CA: Prima.

Manaster, G., & Corsini, R. (1982). *Individual psychology.* Itasca, IL: Peacock.

Nelsen, J. (1996). Positive discipline (rev. ed.). New York: Ballantine.

Nelsen, J., Lott, L., & Glenn, S. (1997). *Positive discipline in the classroom (2nd ed.).* Rocklin,CA: Prima.

Popkin, M. (1993). *Active parenting today.* Atlanta, GA: Active Parenting.

Popkin, M. (1994). *Active teaching.* Atlanta, GA: Active Parenting.

Sweeney, T. (1998). *Adlerian counseling: A practitioner's approach* (4th ed.). Philadelphia, PA:

Taylor and Francis. Watts, R., & Carlson, J. (Eds.). (1999). *Interventions and strategies in counseling and psychotherapy.* Philadelphia: Accelerated Development.

PART III

Organizational and Group Consultation

Organizational consultation has as its main goal the enhancement of the overall effectiveness of the organization. As you will recall from Chapter 1, there are three types of organizational consultation: purchase of expertise, doctor/patient, and process consultation. Although technically a consultant can conduct organizational consultation with an individual consultee, most organizational consultation is conducted with groups of consultees. The client system remains the organization itself.

In Chapter 5, Deck and Isenhour present a case of purchase of expertise consultation using education and training. Noteworthy in this case is the authors' use of the resources of their consultees throughout the consultative process. Also significant in this case is the authors' emphasis on teaching process as well as content.

James, Addy, and Crews, in Chapter 6, present a complex case involving a systems model of program consultation. This case illustrates the importance of communications skills in getting cooperation from various groups that may be in opposition. The authors also raise the issue of parallel processing and how consultants can deal with it.

Tack, Morrow, and I, in Chapter 7, present a case that blends purchase of expertise and process consultation. This case points to some of the issues consultants face when they are part of the system in which consultation is occurring. This case also raises the question, What does the consultant need to know and from whom, before starting the consultation process? In Chapter 8, Becker-Reems presents a case involving process consultation in a health care setting. You will want to note how the consultation starts with one person and then moves to involve others related to the case. This case study also shows the delicate nature of confidentiality in organizational settings. Finally, this case focuses on a variety of goals and illustrates the richness that consultative experiences can possess.

5

Education/Training Consultation with School Personnel

MARY D. DECK AND GLENDA E. ISENHOUR

DESCRIPTION OF THE MODEL USED

This chapter describes a case in which we, as counselor educators, consulted with a school system. We were contacted by a large school system and asked to provide a two-day in-service for teachers, school counselors, and administrators. The in-service was one component of a grant-funded project targeted at designing interventions for students who were potential dropouts. The primary purpose of the in-service was to train school-based teams to work with personnel at their respective schools in developing preventative strategies for use with these at-risk students and their parents. The teams, consisting of a teacher, counselor, and administrator from each school in the system, were invited to participate in the in-service. Upon completion of the two-day in-service training, each school team was to develop and conduct a similar in-service program with their particular faculty and staff. Given this training-to-be-trainers concept, the participants in our in-service were initially consultees and would subsequently become trainers and internal consultants within their own schools.

The model used in our consultation was Schein's (1988, 1990, 1999) purchase of expertise. Purchase of expertise is the most frequently followed model for educational and training purposes and is built upon the expectation that the consultant will share content and information with the consultees. The model is well suited to the limited time constraints that are often part of continuing, professional development and allows for the varying levels of readiness that consultees bring to the training experience (Dougherty, 2005).The consultant's expertise is purchased to design interventions for a problem that has already been defined by the organization or consultee.

The purchase of expertise model has four basic assumptions: the consultee must have made a correct diagnosis of the problem, chosen the right consultant, correctly communicated the problem, and thought through and accepted the consequences of consultation (Schein, 1988, 1999). If the consultee has not made the correct diagnosis, the entire consultation will be invalid: the right consultant might have been chosen, but the wrong problem will have been solved. If it becomes apparent that consultation is solving the wrong problem, the consultant is under no obligation to assist the consultee in making a new diagnosis.

In our case study, our knowledge and skills were "purchased" by the school system to address the previously identified problem of how to train school personnel to be trainers and deliver an in-service within their own schools to help their staffs design interventions for students at risk of dropping out of school.

We were employed as experts to decide what content and information needed to be conveyed in a two-day span to enable the consultees to feel comfortable and confident in their roles as trainers. Our expertise was in planning, designing, and conducting training experiences for a diverse, professional group of adult learners. Other areas of expertise included our skills in understanding and utilizing group processes and in demonstrating inviting consultation behaviors and methods.

SETTING AND BACKGROUND ISSUES

Setting

The school system in which the consultation occurred serves a county with a population of approximately 90,000.The county is the central retail and medical center for an urban metropolitan area of approximately 250,000 people.

Twenty public schools comprise the school system. Thirteen schools are elementary, with either grades kindergarten through five or kindergarten through eight. There are three middle schools serving grades six through eight and four high schools serving grades nine through twelve. The schools' enrollments range from approximately 350 students in the smallest elementary school to about 1,300 students in the largest high school. Sixteen of the schools have at least one full-time school counselor, and the four smaller elementary schools have a counselor on a half-time basis. These same four elementary schools do not have assistant principals. The racial and ethnic descriptions of the student population vary considerably based on the geographical location of the school.

Background

Because we were hired as experts, we were concerned about being stereotyped as "university types." We did not want our consultees to think of us as not having "dirty hands," as "ivory tower experts" who fail to understand the problems of schools in the real world. We were aware that educational professionals required to attend in-service and staff development programs often felt such negative sentiments, whether they expressed them or not. This had, in fact, been our reaction, too, on occasions when we felt forced or coerced to be consultees in staff training. We knew if we ignored such potential perceptions and attitudes resistance could ensue. We were also cognizant of the fact that our consultees were professionals and adult learners with knowledge, experience, and abilities.

We needed to help the consultees feel empowered and confident to return to their schools and share their own expertise. Therefore, we wanted them to be able to access and share their own wealth of information, particularly about the nature of at-risk students and what might work at their individual schools. In addition, we wanted to help them feel a sense of connection and personalization with the training experience itself.

A related concern was how to help the consultees interact, share, and work with one another to problem-solve and develop strategies for helping at-risk students. We were aware that we were bringing together a diverse group of individuals.

Since all schools in the system would likely be involved, there would be persons present with vested interests and questions about at-risk students from kindergarten through high school. With the school teams representing teachers, counselors, and administrators, these professionals would bring differing perspectives and objectives. There was also the potential for some consultees to be intimidated by having administrators who were their immediate supervisors participate, especially when everyone would be asked to identify areas for improvement and offer suggestions for change.

We recognized that, to help our consultees build cohesion and readiness for working together, we needed to structure the in-service using group development principles, group process skills, and the nominal group technique (NGT) (Delbecq, Van de Ven, & Gustafson, 1975).We decided that our entire in-service would be designed to facilitate the consultees' movement thorough the stages of group development and would focus on group problem-solving strategies. By using a group problem-solving approach (Merritt & Walley, 1977), we trusted we would enhance the solicitation of information from consultees and that we then could model for them a format they could employ when they designed their own in-service.

As we considered design and process issues for preparing this in-service, we concurrently considered content issues. We would be working with professionals with different areas of expertise and knowledge bases. We wanted consultees to share their expertise, but we also needed to consider what additional content would be relevant and critical for us to disseminate to all consultees. We focused our content preparation through reading professional literature on students at risk for dropping out of school (e.g., Christenson, Sinclair, Lehr, & Godber, 2001; Downing, LoVett, & Emerson, 1994; Dynarski & Gleason, 2002; Finn & Rock,1997; Jordan, McPartland, & Lara,1999; Pittman, 1995; Rossi,1994; Schwartz, 1995; Van Acker & Wehby, 2000; Walters & Bowers,1997.

GOALS OF CONSULTATION

Consultation through education and training can be exclusively educationally and didactically based, such as when the consultant provides information through a formal presentation or lecture. Or the consultant may be more of a trainer, focusing primarily on experiential learning and assisting the consultees in the acquisition and rehearsal of skills (Dougherty, 2005). Our goal was to combine both education and training. One education goal was to disseminate information and provide resource materials to enhance the knowledge base and confidence levels of our consultees. Another education goal was to expand the purchase of expertise model to include opportunities for the consultees to be the experts, that is, to educate one another about helping at-risk students. We wanted to create an environment in which the information and expertise that the consultees brought to the in-service could be tapped and shared with others.

We also wanted a great deal of the learning to be experiential. This learning-by-doing approach to training would provide consultees firsthand experience with possible interventions they might wish to use or adapt when conducting their own in-service. Experiential learning can assist consultees in giving a sense of self-discovery and accomplishment; therefore our training strategies would transfer more readily into the behavioral repertoire of the consultees (Wallace & Hall, 1996).We also wanted consultees to participate in group activities that would engage them in meaningful interactions with each other. Our overriding goals were for consultees to leave the in-service having been respected for their knowledge and expertise and having had opportunities to experience personalized learning. Meeting these goals would assist consultees in effectively providing information and experiences in their own in-service programs.

CONSULTANT FUNCTION AND ROLE

As educational and training consultants, our primary function was to use our expertise to design and execute an in-service that would meet the expectations and intent of the funding source for the in-service and that would meet the needs of the consultees as participants in the in-service and as future trainers. In fulfilling our consultation contract, we assumed various trainers' roles. We were **planners** of the in-service; **information experts** regarding the content included in the in-service;

facilitators of the experiential components; **process observers** of the small group training experiences; overall **leaders** of the agenda, pacing, and monitoring of the two-day in-service; and **evaluators** of the in-service (Wallace & Hall, 1996).

As information experts, we determined that it was essential for the consultees to understand group development and the dynamics of group process if they were to be trainers themselves. They needed to appreciate and understand experientially how to problem-solve using steps involved in group development and group process. They also needed to design strategies that focused on meeting the needs of at-risk students. We had to plan how to align the sequence and presentation of the needs of at-risk students directly with the steps involved in building a group. Once we solidified this notion of linking content, training, and group development, we structured the total in-service on a group development model created by Merritt and Walley (1977).

Another tool that our consultees needed was familiarity with the nominal group technique (NGT) (Delbecq, Van de Ven, & Gustafson, 1975). The NGT is a group process consultation tool that is useful in helping groups determine possible solutions to identified problems. Employing the NGT would further strengthen our supposition that all consultees possessed useful information and experiences. NGT emphasizes the value of each individual's contribution. Using NGT was also part of our facilitator role, encouraging consultees to experience techniques and tools they might incorporate into their own in-service delivery model. (For additional information about the NGT consult Dougherty [2005].) An additional aspect of our information expert role was compiling a handbook for consultees. We included information on the following topics: steps in group development; nominal group technique procedures; self-concept, self-esteem, and school performance; effective communication; parent-school partnerships; bibliography on at-risk students and dropout prevention; and a step-by-step reference guide detailing the entire two-day in-service (i.e., agenda, timelines, directions for activities, and copies of all handouts). This handbook was to be a primer for the consultees as they prepared for their own in-service. In planning for the in-service, we also moved into our roles of evaluators.

We developed an evaluation instrument designed to assess both content and experiential goals and objectives of the in-service. The instrument included 23 Likert-scale items and five open-ended response items. The school system added one item that asked how the central office staff might be a continuing resource to assist consultees in preparing and conducting other in-service sessions in their schools. As we implemented the in-service, our roles as leaders of the in-service, facilitators, and process observers dominated.

CONSULTEE EXPERIENCE IN CONSULTATION

In working with the grant director in planning the logistics of the in-service, we requested that the in-service be on two consecutive days. We thought that the concentrated time period would increase the momentum and effects of the group development process. We wanted to maintain the energy level and involvement that we felt would be created the first day.

To promote the in-service, the grant director made a brief presentation to the principals during one of their meetings with the superintendent. The superintendent endorsed the in-service and stressed the administrative commitment to this project. With the project director, we helped draft a letter and information packet for prospective participants. The principals were to distribute these materials to those who indicated interest. In this letter, we emphasized the voluntary nature of the in-service. A goal and purpose statement for attending the in-service was included to ensure that those who volunteered were willing to be trainers later in their own schools. We highlighted the experiential nature of the in-service. We hoped to encourage participation of consultees who would be in agreement with, and supportive of, the goals of the in-service. We also requested that volunteers commit to attending both days of the in-service. We explained that, due to the experiential nature of the in-service, it would diminish the impact for everyone if someone had to be absent for part of the experience.

Incentives for consultees included substitute pay for the two days, catered lunch for both days, a videotape with a resource packet on working with parents of at-risk students, continuing education credits, and a certificate of attendance.

APPLICATION: CONSULTANT TECHNIQUES AND PROCEDURES

Entry

During the summer, an administrator from the central office of a large school system asked if we were interested in leading an in-service for teachers, counselors, and administrators. The in-service was one part of an extensive grant being written to focus on dropout prevention. We agreed that we would work with the school system to develop such an in-service if funding became available. Major goals for the in-service, possible numbers of participants and training dates, availability of resources, and payment for consultation services were discussed during this initial contact. No further contact was made until mid-fall, when the administrator informed us that the grant had been funded and the hiring a director to administer it was underway. When a director was employed, we would finalize plans for the in-service.

In early December, the director of the grant contacted us. Our initial meeting was in mid-December at the school system's central office and lasted for about an hour. At this meeting, we clarified expectations and goals for the in-service, explored possible dates, discussed the necessity for committed volunteers who understood fully the expectation to be trainers upon completion of the in-service, reviewed preliminary ideas for using steps in group development as the foundation for the delivery of the in-service, and discussed the kind of training facility that would be needed. During this initial meeting, we were introduced to the school superintendent and other central office administrators. Before leaving, we scheduled a half-day work session for early January with the grant director.

Much of the half-day session was devoted to discussion about the structure of and logistical planning for the in-service. Because as many as 90 persons could be attending the in-service, adequate meeting space was essential. It was decided that the in-service would be conducted in the system's central office in a large multipurpose room with sufficient open space. The room also had movable chairs, so consultees would be able to easily work in dyads, triads, or small groups of 10 or fewer, and they would also be able to assemble in a large circle. We discussed the handbook and evaluation instrument that we, the consultants, would develop and the deadlines for printing these items. Together, we drafted the letter and information that would be distributed to the principals for recruiting consultees.

We established the dates for the in-service in early May. The in-service would occur after the annual systemwide testing and prior to the final crunch of the end-of-school activities. This planning meeting was very productive and, as the consultants, we were now able to plan the details of the in-service.

Diagnosis

In a broad sense, the school system had already defined the problem, (students who were at risk) and an implementation (in-service) prior to our entry. However, there were a significant number of tasks to be accomplished prior to the in-service that required diagnostic procedures. Entering this stage, we had already read the grant, completed our reading of the literature review, and gathered additional information about the system's expectations from the grant director.

We knew the overall goals of the in-service, and we had defined some of our concerns about the in-service (e.g., recruiting volunteers, building the in-service on steps of group development, etc.). Our task now was to design the in-service and to designate specific tasks, strategies, and timelines for its implementation.

We needed to design a systematic approach that linked experiences in group development and group process with relevant content for addressing the needs of at-risk students. To do this, we had three main areas to consider: what model of group development would meet our goals, what content areas needed to be presented, and what activities and strategies would incorporate group development steps as well as focus on at-risk students.

First, we chose to adopt and modify the steps suggested by Merritt and Walley (1977). The steps of interest and involvement, participation, cohesion and harmony, self-disclosure, critical thinking, problem identification, and problem solving met our goals of encouraging the consultees to become acquainted with one another, sharing existing information and expertise with them, and gradually moving them to brainstorming and creative problem solving. The group development model provided us with an outline for developing the specifics of the in-service.

We thought it necessary to include limited amounts of didactic information pertaining to two areas: consultees' roles as trainers and interventions for working with students who were at risk. After brainstorming what content areas to include, we prioritized and selected these four main areas to emphasize: considerations for working with groups, self-concept and self-esteem, invitational learning, and communication skills. We maintained that the majority of the in-service should be experiential learning. Once more we brainstormed about possible experiential activities that we might employ in each of the steps of group development. We then selected those activities that seemed to best fit the group development step *and* foster content learning. We were now ready to construct the in-service format, including timelines, materials, and resources needed.

When we had completed the above procedures, we developed the instrument to evaluate the in-service, and we compiled and organized the materials for the handbook. We also made a materials checklist (e.g., newsprint, markers, overheads, note cards, etc.) that we submitted to the project director.

We met again with the project director to present the outline for the in-service, collaborate on additions and changes to the evaluation instrument, and make final requests for materials and resources for the in-service. At that time, we also heard from the director about possible glitches regarding consultee participation for the in-service. For example, some principals were not recruiting but were requiring certain staff to attend, and a few who really wanted to attend could only be present the second day. We discussed contingencies for handling such concerns within the framework of the in-service. We strongly discouraged the director from including persons who could only attend one day, and particularly only the second day, because of the emphasis on group development as a training model. (As it turned out, four participants were able to attend for the first day only, and on the second day, there were no new participants.)

Implementation

The in-service was scheduled on a Wednesday and Thursday beginning at 8:30 in the morning and ending by 3:30 each afternoon. There were 80 consultees participating on Wednesday and 76 on Thursday. All of the 20 schools in the system had at least one staff person in attendance. Most schools had a three-person team present.

Below, we outline the two-day proceedings by providing a brief description of each of the experiential strategies used (labeled *Strategy*) and explaining how each strategy corresponded to meeting one or more of the steps in the group development process (labeled *Intent*). At the points where we presented content information, we will also provide a brief overview of what occurred.

Day 1

Interest and Involvement: Get-Acquainted, Self-Esteem Strategy Following registration and distribution of materials, we moved immediately into an experiential "get-acquainted" activity. This activity encouraged the participants to describe themselves in terms of four conditions of self-esteem (Clemes & Bean, 1980; Youngs, 1991) and also met the first two steps of group development, interest and involvement. We participated in this activity with the consultees.

Involvement and Participation: Sharing Expertise and Knowledge about At-Risk Students Following the get-acquainted exercise, we spent an hour in a small group activity where consultees identified characteristics, feelings, and needs of at-risk students and their parents and considered current school responses to these needs. We facilitated this activity but did not join in the small groups' generation of information.

Intent: Involvement and participation are enhanced using small groups, assigning structured tasks, and providing clear instructions. The activities are generally focused on identifying content problems as perceived by each member of the small group. By providing a specific task and asking for each person's content-related perception, an atmosphere conducive to sharing, listening, and accepting others' ideas develops.

Strategy: Consultees were randomly divided into small groups, given newsprint with markers, and assigned one or two specific questions from the following set of questions: Who are students at risk? What are characteristics of these students? How do teachers identify at-risk students in classes? What are needs of at-risk students? Which of these needs can be addressed within school? What are feelings and perceptions of at-risk students about school? How can

these students' feelings and perceptions be altered? What are needs of parents of at-risk students? How can schools meet the needs of these parents? After generating responses to their particular questions, each small group reported its main ideas to the large group. For example, some of the reported characteristics of at-risk students were low self-esteem, acting out behaviors, few friends, and unkempt appearance. Some of the identified needs of at-risk students were to be successful, to be accepted by school personnel, to have someone listen and care, and to have academic programs to meet their needs.

After the group reports, we acknowledged and validated the consultees' expertise by linking the literature findings on dropout prevention and at-risk students to their firsthand experience and knowledge.

Cohesion and Harmony: Team Building After the morning break, the consultees met in their school teams for 30 minutes and then met with the larger group for 45 minutes to discuss current strategies they were implementing in their individual schools to meet the needs of at-risk students. Throughout the in-service, whenever consultees met with their school teams, those without teams met in triads to share ideas. The sharing of successful strategies focused everyone on the common goal of the in-service, strengthened the cohesion of the individual school teams, and created a network of resource persons within the larger school system. We facilitated the large group discussion but did not participate during the earlier team discussions.

Intent: In order to experience cohesion and harmony, each consultee needs to feel he or she is an important, contributing member of the group (or team, in this case).At this stage of group development, a sense of belonging and unity of purpose bind group members together. Acceptance of one another, coupled with opportunities for listening and communicating, is essential to the establishment of cohesion and harmony. Activities should encourage openness and foster teamwork through the sharing of ideas.

Strategy: The teacher, counselor, and administrator from each school met as a team to discuss the strategies currently being used to meet the needs of at-risk students and their parents in their school. Each team then reported three of their school's strategies to the larger group. This activity energized the teams by focusing positively on their individual schools and by providing them an opportunity to hear ideas that they might replicate.

Self-Disclosure: Recalling and Sharing Personal School Experiences

The morning activities were relatively safe and non-threatening, centering primarily on content information and revealing few differences of ideas or conflicting opinions. As the afternoon session began, we used an imagery exercise to move the consultees into more personal, self-revealing levels of exploration and sharing. We changed the focus from discussing external issues about students and their parents to examining more personal recollections about what it meant to each consultee to be a student. This experience lasted about a half hour.

Intent: Self-disclosure is a pivotal point in group development as the consultees are asked to take more personal risks. An atmosphere characterized by trust and respect has been established, and consultees now begin sharing more personalized experiences, beliefs, and feelings within the group. Self-sharing helps prepare consultees to engage in more critical, original, and divergent thinking and desensitizes fears about expressing personal ideas and opinions.

Opportunities for self-disclosure help consultees clarify, question, and learn from others in a positive manner while valuing their own awareness and contributions.

Activities designed to solicit self-disclosures need to begin with topics requiring less personal disclosure and gradually move toward topics of a more personal nature. Not everyone will be ready for a deeper level of sharing, and the consultant needs to be sensitive to and respect any hesitancies.

Strategy: Consultees were led through a guided imagery exercise in which they were asked to visualize themselves as children in school and to remember experiences by responding to a series of questions related to invitational education and the development of self-esteem. The questions were: "How were you invited to learn in school?" "In what ways did you feel unique in school?" "How were you allowed to be in control and powerful in school?" "In what ways did you feel a sense of belongingness in school?" "Who were your adult role models in school?" Following the guided imagery exercise, each consultee was invited to share awarenesses from the exercise with a partner (passing was permitted).After five minutes of mutual sharing, volunteers from the larger group were asked to share any thoughts or comments about their experience. This activity helped the consultees connect with their own childhood experiences related to school and personalize the conditions necessary for desiring to learn, feeling a part of the school, and developing self-esteem.

Content Presentation: Guidelines for Working with Groups We blocked out an hour in mid-afternoon to overview the steps in group development and relate them directly to the day's events. We had a worksheet that listed each of the earlier activities and the steps of group development. We also overviewed the following day's agenda and related it to group development. We included a brainstorming session in which we asked participants to share important behaviors and traits for group leaders. We closed this segment by referring consultees to the handbook and the resource materials displayed for additional information on working with groups.

Self-Disclosure: Experiencing Disinvitations We concluded the day with a final self-disclosure activity followed by a homework assignment for the consultees. The self-disclosure activity was designed to foster critical thinking and the homework was to encourage consultees to process what they had experienced during day one of the in-service. Their responses to the homework assignment would be a point of discussion on the following day.

Intent: The purpose of this activity was to place consultees in situations where they felt they did not belong and have them share their feelings and responses to "being on the outside." We wanted consultees to leave mildly distressed in order to prompt their movement toward critical thinking and problem identification. We thought that if they experienced being disinvited and were left to ponder the experience, they would begin to consider ways to change similar "outside" experiences for at-risk students and their parents.

Strategy: The self-disclosure activity required the participants to break into groups of 10. Five persons formed a tight inner circle and five others formed an outer circle (Canfield & Wells, 1976). Persons within the inner circle selected a secret known only to the inner five. This secret was theirs to share or not to share with the outer circle members. Persons in the outer circle questioned, bargained, or pleaded with the inner circle members to learn the secret. After a few minutes, the circles were reversed and the same procedures were followed.

Process questions followed the activity, allowing consultees to express their feelings and perceptions when they were inner circle and outer circle members.

For homework, consultees were asked to consider how we disinvite others from belonging, from learning, from having personal power, and from feeling unique.

Assessment of Day 1 At the close of the in-service, we met for a few minutes with the project director to hear his assessment of the day. He stated that he was pleased with the interaction of the consultees and with the process. The director thought that the strategies were adequately balanced between conveying content and providing for experiential learning. We also processed the day privately with each other. Overall, we were pleased with the way the day had progressed. We were positive and eager to return the next day. Several interactions had come to our attention. We noted that one person in particular seemed to dominate regardless of the group she was with; another consultee had been rambling, long-winded, and somewhat judgmental about at-risk students in his responses; and two persons were particularly reserved when we moved into the self-disclosure activities. We discussed interventions to address these concerns the following day.

Day 2

Most of the morning was devoted to content presentations with the infusion of experiential components. The afternoon session was singularly focused on group work designed to identify innovative interventions to assist at-risk students and their parents. The experiential strategies of the previous day had introduced this day's topical presentations in a personal way to the consultees, and the group development steps had established a foundation of group cohesion and trust to move consultees to the working stage of critical thinking, problem identification, and problem solving.

Interest, Involvement, Participation, and Self-Disclosure: Self-Esteem Graffiti We began the day with an experiential reentry activity to help the consultees regain the spirit and focus of the previous day and to review the four conditions of self-esteem. We participated fully in this activity.

Intent: This warm-up activity incorporated the group development steps of interest, involvement, participation, and self-disclosure. It was meant to re-center the consultees' attention on their personal application of the four conditions of self-esteem in their lives.

Strategy: As consultees arrived, we requested that they rotate to four different stations and draw symbols to represent how each of the four conditions of self-esteem were being met in their lives. Each station had a newsprint graffiti sheet labeled with one of these four conditions of self-esteem: belongingness, personal power, uniqueness, and role model (Canfield & Wells, 1976; Clemes & Bean, 1980). After everyone had arrived and signed all the sheets, the entire group assembled in a circle, and each consultee reintroduced him- or herself by sharing one response from the graffiti sheets. It was gratifying to us to watch how the group of strangers from the previous morning connected this morning as they laughed and talked when signing the graffiti sheets.

Content Presentations: The Self, the Setting, and the Statements We Hear and Tell Ourselves The remainder of the morning session focused on the presentation and discussion of basic information from three theoretical approaches: self-concept/self-consistency (Beane & Lipka, 1986; Hamachek, 1995; Purkey & Schmidt, 1996; Youngs, 1991), invitational learning (Purkey & Novak, 1984; Purkey & Schmidt, 1996), and the facilitative model of communication (Johnson, 1997; Myrick 2003; Witmer, 1992). We also used experiential approaches to supplement the information and personalize the content. For example, to emphasize the interaction of self-concept and school achievement, we gave out self-concept labels to volunteers (e.g., teacher's pet, underachiever, shy child, etc.) and asked them to simulate a classroom setting, behaving as a student with that self-concept might. We then had a short lesson with one of us role-playing the teacher. This improvisation proved to be one of the highlights of the morning.

After the role-play, the group processed how each of the "labeled students" might see themselves as a learner and how they might feel about their place in the classroom and in school. We also asked each consultee who role-played to assess how much the student portrayed was at risk for dropping out of school. This was a very poignant and revealing experience.

After the break, we examined invitational learning and the climate of the school setting. Based on the previous day's homework, we listed ways that schools and school personnel communicate disinvitations to students and parents. We also explored effective communication as a key to invitational learning.

To demonstrate a continuum of facilitative responses, one of us told an everyday story of misadventures (e.g., oversleeping, arriving late for a meeting, being in a traffic jam, etc.) and the consultees formulated statements that were helpful (e.g., understanding and empathic) or harmful (e.g., advice-giving and judgmental).We processed how these same kinds of responses are representative of what different students hear in school.

The experiential aspects of the content sessions allowed the consultees to remain active participants, to take risks (if they chose), and to share in the laughter and spontaneity of learning. Although the morning was very content laden, we felt that the pacing and weaving of experiential activities kept the presentation lively and personal.

Critical Thinking: Brainstorming Ways to Be More Invitational The afternoon session began with consultees using NGT (Delbecq, Van de Ven, & Gustafson, 1975) to generate ideas for being more invitational toward at-risk students and their parents. This experience helped the school teams to consider the broadest possible range of ideas for identifying possible new and innovative interventions that might be implemented in their schools. We facilitated the afternoon sessions, especially keeping track of time and focusing consultees to remain on task during NGT.

Intent: The critical thinking step of group development invites consultees to brainstorm and actively listen as others present their ideas. Consultees are offered opportunities to engage in creative and original thinking. One of the critical rules of brainstorming is that all ideas are accepted without critique or evaluation.

The consultant may need to reemphasize the need to accept and respect the ideas and contributions of others. One way to encourage critical thinking and original ideas is to utilize NGT (Delbecq, Van de Ven, & Gustafson, 1975).

Benefits of NGT are that all group members contribute in the exchange of ideas, all ideas are listed and considered, and, through maximum participation, the pool of possibilities is expanded.

Strategy: Consultees were grouped together according to their school levels and/or school responsibility (e.g., all elementary teachers, all elementary counselors, all middle school teachers, all administrators, etc.). Each group brainstormed how their particular group could be more invitational with students and parents. Five minutes was allotted for each person in the group to brainstorm individually and silently write his or her responses on note cards. Then, in round-robin fashion, each person in the small group offered one suggestion (which was recorded on newsprint) until all ideas were listed. At the conclusion of the activity, each group reported their ideas to the larger group. As the groups reported, they were to omit any ideas that had been previously named by other groups. As a reference for the next and final activity of the in-service, all group suggestions were posted around the room.

Problem Identification and Problem Solving: Prioritizing and Changing

The final in-service activity brought the school teams together to have them experience the last two steps of the group development model. We stressed to the consultees that the teams would experience these steps in an abbreviated fashion.

Intent: The brainstorming activity is linked to problem identification as consultees discuss, clarify, and evaluate the strengths and limitations of the ideas previously generated. Consultees are to discuss ideas in a positive manner, and they should avoid making value judgments and derogatory remarks. It is the role of the consultant to keep the discussion moving, to keep the groups focused on the assigned task, and to help the groups define problems in specific and concrete terms. Problem solving is the final step of this group development model. The preceding steps have systematically built a spirit of teamwork, with the consultees empowered and ready to respond to the question, What *can* we do? The consultees now move to develop a realistic plan to solve problems.

Strategy: As the final activity, the school teams were asked to select three ideas from the brainstorming lists that they felt could realistically be implemented in their school. The teams then listed those conditions that would facilitate and inhibit the implementation of these ideas in their schools. The last charge to the teams was to suggest actions that would sustain the facilitative conditions and would reduce or eliminate the inhibiting conditions.

Closing: Taking It Back Home The last 30 minutes of the in-service was a closing activity. Each consultee was asked to write a personal goal for addressing the needs of at-risk students and to have another consultee witness the goal statement. Consultees were encouraged to take their goal statements back to their schools and use their goals and progress as a model for the in-service they would conduct in their settings. Lastly, each consultee was asked to summarize his or her experience of the past two days with one word and share that word with the group. Afterward, we thanked the consultees for their enthusiasm, willingness, genuineness, and creativity. We wished them well and ended with a poem. The project director made closing remarks, distributed the evaluation instruments, and issued the certificates of attendance and forms for continuing education credit. Our in-service was over; it was now up to our consultees to conduct theirs.

Disengagement

We engaged in formative evaluation as we progressed through the consultation stages. As we moved through the entry and diagnosis stages, we continued to stay in contact with the project director, and we kept one another appraised of progress and developments regarding our mutual responsibilities for the in-service. We continued to engage in formative evaluation during the implementation of the in-service. We periodically checked with one another while the consultees were engaged in group activities to gauge how the process was going. We evaluated the first day's events and pinpointed several small concerns that we tried to modify the following day. We also assessed the second day with the project director immediately after the in-service ended.

We designed the evaluation instrument based on the goals and objectives that constituted the in-service. Based on the outcomes of the evaluations, the majority of the consultees were in agreement that the goals of the in-service were met. While the evaluation results remained with the project director as part of the evaluation materials for the project, we received a brief summary of the results and a list of the items from the comments section. One mistake that we made was in not requesting our own copies of all of the evaluation results. In retrospect, we did not include a copy of this evaluation instrument in the handbook. It would have been beneficial to the consultees to have had a sample evaluation instrument.

We had no planned follow-up contact with the project director. He did not suggest one, and neither did we. This was probably the biggest weakness of this consultation experience. We would suggest scheduling a postconsultation follow-up if only to satisfy one's own sense of incompleteness. Although we saw the director and some of the consultees informally afterwards, we heard only incidentally about the long-range outcomes of our in-service. For us, disengagement and termination in educational and training consultation may be one of the most frustrating elements of this type of consultation. We find it disconcerting to leave and have no continuing responsibility or role once the contract for the consultation has been fulfilled.

IMPLICATIONS FOR PRACTICE

Educational and training consultation is by its nature a contracted, specific, time-limited intervention. Therefore, whatever constitutes the education and training, whether it be an in-service, workshop, or presentation, it is critical to have a framework for approaching consultation. In planning educational and training consultation, Dougherty's (2005) generic model provides a clear and systematic framework for planning, organizing, and designing educational/ training consultation.

If consultees are to benefit from the educational/training experience and feel their time has been well served, consultants need to engage in formative evaluation throughout the consultation process. Formative evaluation allows consultants to stay on track with important elements in the planning and execution of the consultation. As part of formative evaluation, we might have expanded our information gathering to tailor our in-service more directly to the identified needs of the participants. That is, once the teams were identified at the individual schools, we could have surveyed the team members to assess their perceptions of training needs in the content areas and in group process skill areas.

Such data would have provided us with valuable information; in addition, participants would have begun to assume ownership for the in-service prior to the actual training and would have engaged in an assessment process they could later use with their own school staffs.

We also missed an opportunity for formative evaluation by not having a planned postconsultation session. We were left without a feeling of complete closure. Perhaps we would have been able to offer further assistance in helping the school system if we had asked for the postconsultation meeting. Had we focused more on the disengagement phases, we would have avoided this significant omission. An area we could consider more closely is how disengagement is also a process that requires planning.

Another implication for effective practice that our case brings home is the importance of acknowledging the professionalism and expertise that adult learners bring as consultees. When we work in schools, we believe it is presumptuous and demeaning to ignore the background, knowledge, and training of persons who work with students and parents on a daily basis. We appreciate that school personnel resent the ivory-tower-expert approach of some consultants.

We have had the opportunity to consult with a number of school systems on such topics as conferencing with parents, creating positive school environments, establishing school counseling programs, and training in communication skills. We have been well received and attribute that to our regard and respect for the knowledge base of our consultees. When we consult as experts in schools, we focus on being facilitators and collaborators as well. We believe it is important to create an environment in which school personnel, as consultees, feel empowered, encouraged, validated, and supported for what they know. We invite them to share their expertise with one another and with us. We believe that helping school personnel reach out and support one another is perhaps one of the most important contributions we can make as consultants in an educational setting.

Lastly, we believe that as consultants we must model what we are teaching and training others to do. In this way we demonstrate our trust in ourselves and in what we are presenting. When appropriate, we participate in activities with the consultees. We do not ask others to engage in risks that we are not willing to take ourselves. We believe that the best way to encourage others to embrace our ideas, our theories, and our training models is by example.

TIPS FOR PRACTICE

- To the extent possible, encourage that consultees participating in education/ training events be voluntary and have a desire for the knowledge and experiential learning provided through the consultation.

- Review as much organizational data as available in order to design interventions that target the specific skills and content knowledge needed by consultees.

- Schedule formative and postconsultation evaluation across the consultative process.

- Be flexible and open to altering education/training interventions based on formative assessments gathered during the consultation.

QUESTIONS FOR DISCUSSION AND REFLECTION

1. In what ways did these consultants combine Schein's purchase of expertise model with aspects of Schein's process consultation?

2. If you were the consultants in this case, what additional content and experiences might you include to help the consultees become more skilled trainers?

3. What limitations of the purchase of expertise model may have contributed to these consultants' lack of emphasis on the disengagement aspect of this consultation?

4. A weakness in this case study seems to be the limited attention given by the organization (school system) and the consultants to the long-range consequences of the consultation. What might be some of the unforeseen inhibiting consequences for consultees when they attempt to become trainers and conduct a similar in-service?

5. What do you anticipate being some of the frustrations you would encounter as an educational/training consultant?

6. What would be some ethical issues you would consider if asked to be an expert consultant?

7. As you read this case, to what degree did you get the impression that the consultees were adequately informed about the fact that personal material was to be shared? In your opinion is it adequate to provide the opportunity to pass?

REFERENCES AND SUGGESTED READINGS

Beane, J.A., & Lipka, R. P. (1986). *Self-concept, self-esteem, and the curriculum.* New York: Columbia University Teachers College Press.

Canfield, J., & Wells, H.C. (1976). *100 ways to enhance self-concept in the classroom: A handbook for teachers and parents.* Englewood Cliffs, NJ: Prentice Hall.

Christenson, S.L., Sinclair, M.F., Lehr, C.A., & Godber, Y. (2001). Promoting successful school completion: Critical conceptual and methodological guidelines. *School Psychology Quarterly, 16,468-484.*

Clemes, H., & Bean, R. (1980). *How to raise children's self-esteem.* Los Angeles: Enrich/Price Stern Sloan.

Delbecq, A. L., Van de Ven, A.H., & Gustafson, D. H. (1975). *Group techniques for program planning: A guide to nominal group and Delphi techniques.* Glenview, IL: Scott, Foresman.

Dougherty, A.M. (2005). *Psychological consultation and collaboration in school and community settings* (4th ed.). Belmont, CA: Wadsworth.

Downing, H., LoVette, O., & Emerson, P. (1994).An investigation of at-risk students' reasons for staying in school. *Journal of Humanistic Education and Development, 33,* 83–88.

Dynarski, M., & Gleason, P. (2002). How can we help? What we have learned from recent federal dropout prevention evaluations. *Journal of Education for Students Placed at Risk, 7(1),* 43-69.

Finn, J.D., &Rock, D.A. (1997). Academic success among students at risk for school failure. *Journal of Applied Psychology, 82(2),* 221-234.

Hamachek, D. (1995). Self-concept and school achievement: Interaction dynamics and a tool for assessing the self-concept component. *Journal of Counseling and Development, 73,* 419-425.

Johnson, D.W. (1997). *Reaching out: Interpersonal effectiveness and self-actualization.* Boston: Allyn and Bacon.

Jordan, W.J., McPartland, J.M., &Lara, J. (1999). Rethinking the causes of high school dropouts. *The Prevention Researchers, 6(3),* 1-4.

Merritt, R. E., & Walley, D.D. (1977). *The group leader's handbook: Resources, techniques, and survival skills.* Champaign, IL: Research Press.

Myrick, R. (2003). *Development guidance and counseling: A practical approach* (4th ed.). Minneapolis, MN: Educational Media Corporation.

Pittman, R. B. (1995).The potential high school dropout, the 21st century, and what's ahead for rural teachers. *Rural Educator, 16(2),* 23–27.

Purkey, W.W., & Novak, J. (1984). *Inviting school success: A self-concept approach to teaching and learning* (2nd ed.). Belmont, CA: Wadsworth.

Purkey, W.W., & Schmidt, J. J. (1996). *Invitational counseling: A self-concept approach to professional practice.* Pacific Grove, A: Brooks/Cole.

Rossi, R. (Ed). (1994). *Schools and students at risk: Context and framework for positive change.* New York: Teachers College Press.

Schein, E. H. (1988). *Process consultation: Its role in organization development.* (Vol.1, 2nd ed.). Reading, MA: Addison-Wesley.

Schein, E. H. (1990).Models of consultation: What do organizations of the 1990s need? *Consultation, 9,* 261–275.

Schein, E. H. (1999). *Process consultation revisited: Building the helping relationship.* Reading, MA: Addison-Wesley.

Swartz, W. (1995). *New information on youth who drop out: Why they leave and what happens to them.* New York: ERIC Clearinghouse on Urban Education. (ERIC Document Reproduction Service No. ED 396006)

Van Acker, R., & Wehby, J.H. (2000). Exploring the social contexts influencing student success or failure: Introduction. *Preventing School Failure, 44 (3),* 93-96.

Wallace, W.A., & Hall, D. L. (1996). *Psychological consultation: Perspectives and applications.* Pacific Grove, CA: Brooks/Cole.

Walters, K., &Bower, G.L. (1997). Peer group acceptance and academic performance among adolescents participating in a dropout prevention program. *Child and Adolescent Social Work Journal, 14,* 413-426.

Witmer, J. (1992). *Valuing diversity and similarity: Bridging the gap through interpersonal skills.* Minneapolis, MN: Educational Media Corporation.

Youngs, B.B. (1991). *How to develop self-esteem in your child: 6 vital ingredients.* New York: Fawcett Columbine.

6

Systems Consultation: Working with a Metropolitan Police Department

RICHARD K. JAMES, CATHERINE ADDY, AND WALTER CREWS

DESCRIPTION OF THE MODEL USED

This case involved a community-wide consultation with several agencies and groups that were brought together to develop a training program for police officers to deal with the mentally ill. The case is unique in that it describes an initial long-term consultation and followed by a second, on-going consultation. Hence you will read how we proceeded initially and what we are doing now with the same program.

Due to differences in mission, structure, and culture among the groups involved, we chose a systems approach to consultation. A systems approach is often the method of choice when consultants face extremely complex situations like those involved in consulting with a variety of community agencies/groups simultaneously (Fuqua & Kurpius, 1993). Systems theory is based on the concept that the entire target of change (typically a family but in this case a community) should be considered when contemplating change.

According to Fuqua and Kurpius (1993), there are several important concepts related to systems theory. The concept of **interdependence** suggests that forces within a system are always influencing one another. For example, in this case study, the Alliance for the Mentally Ill (AMI) and the Memphis City Police Department were reciprocally influencing one another- mostly in an acrimonious manner. A system has to have some kind of **model** applied to it: Systems are **open**; that is, they are influenced by the interaction of the forces in their internal and external environments and may thus be seen as **an ecosystem** (Bronfenbrenner, 1995). In this case study, the cultural environment of the police department influenced the goals of consultation as did the politics of Memphis City Government. Reciprocally, the local chapter of the Alliance for the Mentally Ill impacted the city government and police department because of their activist role in lobbying for more humane treatment of the mentally ill. While the mentally ill are the identified target population, to service that population the consultation process would have to bring together the police department, the local AMI chapter, and a third group that directly impacted the institution of services to the mentally ill - the mental health service providers in the community.

Systems theory holds that since the elements of a system are interactive, interventions should be targeted at the various subsystems to accomplish change. Hardy (1997) describes systems in terms of relationships, interactions, and context. Because this consultation takes place in a large city with three subsystems that have distinct multiple contexts such as cultural, socioeconomic, racial, and professional roles that influence their interactions and relationships with others, this is a complex approach to a complex problem (Bronfenbrenner, 1995; Dattilio & Jongsma, 2000; Madsen, 1999; Nichols et al., 2000). The major task of the consultants then is first bringing these three sometimes factious parties together.

SETTING AND BACKGROUND ISSUES

Setting

Memphis has a large police department that faces all of the tasks and crimes found in a contemporary metropolitan city of over a million people. The city also has a large population of mentally ill individuals who are in the custodial care of relatives and intermediate care facilities. Additionally, there are scores of mentally ill homeless people, psychotic substance abusers, recently released parolees with mental disturbances, mental hospital patients, and other people with a variety of physical and emotional problems that often lead to irrational behaviors, which are acted out in the homes and streets of Memphis.

Since Memphis police officers do not consider the mentally ill to be "crooks," many of them feel that responding to "mental case" calls is not a true law enforcement responsibility. Because they feel that responding to such calls is not their job, many officers want to get these calls over with as quickly as possible by whatever means necessary (James, 1994). Therefore, any attempt to change their views and operating procedures toward controlling such cases involving the mentally ill was met with a good deal of caution, pessimism, and cynicism by the rank and file of the Memphis City Police Department. It was into this emotionally charged setting, full of intense political pressure and forced compliance to change, that we were called as consultants. This case study describes the systems consultation framework that resulted in the development of a program in which police patrol officers were selected, trained, and deployed as crisis interventionists for the specific purpose of safely and effectively controlling the severe expressive behaviors of the violent mentally ill.

Background

To get a sense of the background issues related to this case, consider the following scenario: A deranged man, standing in the middle of a public housing development in Memphis, stabs himself repeatedly with a butcher knife, screaming incoherently as he makes threatening gestures to neighbors. The police arrive on the scene and attempt to bring the situation under control by taking the man into custody. Over the next 30 minutes, more and more police arrive on the scene. Finally, the man lunges at police officers with the butcher knife, is shot repeatedly, and dies *en route* to the hospital. A huge public outcry ensues, advocacy groups demonstrate against police brutality, the media launches attacks on the police department, lawsuits are filed against the city, and the police department experiences political pressure from the city administration to do something about their apparent ineptness in handling the mentally ill.

Police officers are generally trained to deal with *instrumental* crimes that involve the gain of some material end by a criminal. Catching bank robbers, car thieves, dope pushers, and other fleeing felons is the stereotypical notion of what police work is. However, about 85 percent of all police calls in the United States do not involve "catching crooks" (Luckett & Slaikeu, 1990, p. 228).The great majority of police calls involve *expressive* crimes where smoldering emotions often erupt into violence. Domestic problems, sexual assault, barroom brawls, neighborhood quarrels, and behaviors acted out by the mentally ill all fall into the expressive crime category. Expressive crimes are frustrating, problematic, and very dangerous to police officers because the sole goal of the perpetrator is his or her attempt to reduce emotional tension through any means possible. As a result, the mentally ill perpetrator's behavior is highly unpredictable, and controlling it is complicated by the fact that police officers receive little training in how to deal with it safely (Gillig, Dumaine, Stammer, Hilliard, & Grubb, 1990; Luckett & Slaikeu, 1990).

GOALS OF CONSULTATION

Our primary goal as consultants was to enhance the functioning of the police department in delivering services to one of its constituencies (in this case the violent mentally ill). To attain this goal, we would be working with, not only the police department, but also the entire ecological system of mental health provision in Memphis. As with any system, each part is interdependent upon the other for effective functioning. Family members, community mental health agency staffs, hospital emergency room personnel, advocacy groups, and professional mental health service providers all play important roles in the safe control of the mentally ill. In Memphis, these groups needed to be brought together with the police department in order for all of them to function more effectively.

To highlight the various perceptions these systems can have of one another, consider that mental health workers, the very people the police need most in learning to deal with the mentally ill, are often regarded by the police as softhearted liberals in rose-colored glasses, people who are entirely out of touch with the reality of the mean streets the officers patrol. Likewise, mental health professionals are likely to view the police as uncaring, cynical enforcers of brutal and restrictive laws that do little but exacerbate problems for them and their clientele. As a result, each system typically views the other with distrust and suspicion.

Assessment

Assessment of the ecosystem of the mentally ill in Memphis indicated that there are three clearly defined subsystems interacting within the larger system. First, there is a consumer advocacy group, the Alliance for the Mentally Ill. This group is composed mainly of relatives and friends of long-term, chronic psychotics. Besides functioning as a support group for its members, the Alliance's primary purpose is to lobby for increased social and psychological services for the mentally ill. Their goal is to have police respond quickly to out-of-control relatives, but to do so in a safe and humane manner. At the time of this consultation, the Alliance was extremely irate at the Memphis City police because of a number of mishandled responses to mental disturbance calls.

The second group is comprised of the professional service providers of mental health: the various hospital, community mental health clinics, and other community service providers that deal on a daily basis with the mentally ill. Their goal is to provide service to the mentally ill as best they can, given the limited resources they have, and with as little interference from others as possible. At the time of this consultation, they believed they did not have a stake in the issue, other than to be wary of their interaction with the police.

The third group is the police department itself. Strategically, its immediate goal is to decrease its negative public image of not being able to deal in a safe, effective manner with the violent mentally ill. Tactically, its goal is to learn new procedures for handling mental disturbance calls so that fast, safe, and effective intervention is possible. Logistically, the department needed to obtain the skills and resources necessary to do so.

Initiating Goals

Our first goal was for these often antagonistic and suspicious groups to meet so that a systemic problem-solving process could start to occur. To do so, we attempted to bring all three groups together on a common ground. The critical first step was convincing the groups that each had a vested interest in assisting the Memphis police to deal more effectively with the mentally ill. If we could bring these groups together, then we could use the combined power and creativity of these different subsystems to create a climate for change as well as provide the energy and resources for doing so.

Our second goal was to formulate a training program to teach police officers how to work with the mentally ill so that both parties remained safe and so that their interactions culminated in a positive resolution to the mental disturbance call.

Our third goal had three facets: to determine the best way to use the police department in implementing the program; to develop strategies to monitor and troubleshoot the program as it went into operation; and to determine what additional adjustments, if any, needed to be made.

Our fourth goal was to evaluate the effectiveness of the program by using both quantitative and qualitative outcome measures.

CONSULTANT FUNCTION AND ROLE

Consultants who work with systems, particularly systems that can be antagonistic toward one another, have several roles. First and foremost, we needed to arrange for the systems to meet so that communication links could be established between them. If this could not be accomplished, then any real or lasting success was unlikely. In bringing differing systems together, it is important to keep the geographical and physical setting neutral so that no one has "the home court advantage." To that end, physical settings need to be rotated from group to group, or a neutral setting on no group's "turf" needs to be designated.

Second, it was critical that a chairperson for the group be selected who had the trust, respect, motivation, desire, and ability to work with and understand the needs, fears, and agendas of each of these groups. The selection of a police command officer who had a graduate degree in human services and was also regarded as a credible police officer by the department was an important ingredient in enabling these diverse groups to work with one another. This person will be the major communications link between the lead organization and the other participating groups and needs to be chosen with care. By choosing a person who is a member of the organization that potentially has the most to gain or lose, it is quite likely that he or she will be highly motivated to keep the group moving toward its goal.

Third, both the administrative hierarchy and rank and file of the targeted systems had to have enough belief in the need for such a program and its chances of success that they would be willing to submit themselves to change. It is not enough that administrative fiat is used to dictate that rank and file undergo training. When the police are the targeted system for change, veteran officers may be very cynical about what they are being asked to do, particularly when they may be asked to put their lives on the line. Conversely, if the administration is not vitally involved and is merely committing to the program to "save face" and neutralize political and media pressure, then there is little hope that lasting effects will be achieved. In this case, we needed to convince both commanders and patrol officers that this was a worthwhile endeavor. What we would be calling for was no less than a paradigmatic shift away from a "John Wayne, line up the troops and charge" attitude in dealing with the mentally ill.

We would have to do likewise with the professional staff of the mental health services. There was little money for training. Therefore, training would have to be on a pro bono basis. We would have to convince these professionals that training police officers was worth their time and effort. Besides dealing with some very complex system dynamics, we would be responsible for coordinating assessment efforts to determine what configuration the training and ultimate implementation of the plan would take. We would be in charge of coordinating training. Finally, we were responsible for coordinating follow-up to determine how effective the training was, how effectively the plan was put into operation, and what might need to be done to remedy problem situations as they arose.

CONSULTEE EXPERIENCE IN CONSULTATION

As policing has slowly evolved into a profession in Memphis, and more and more officers have obtained college degrees, a new awareness of the value of outside expertise has developed—particularly when the issues that need to be addressed do not fall within the range of the police department's existing competencies. For this reason, the police administration was astute enough to understand they had a problem and needed the support and validation of mental health professionals to deal with it.

Further, since the Memphis police ran their own police academy, they already had an existing belief in the value of education. They understood that our outside expertise, our combination of experience in law enforcement, education, and mental health, would bring a greater degree of credibility to the program.

Our backgrounds gave us an easier entry into the various systems than other consultants who did not have such experiences would have had. We also brought with us an objective, constraint-free perspective that would not be negatively influenced by the considerable political pressure the department was under to find a rapid and effective solution.

Officers who volunteered for the program reported that they recognized that the old ways of doing things did not work. Although they were unsure whether they could master some of the concepts we were proposing, and though they knew that they would have to radically change their thinking about procedures for handling the mentally ill, they were all volunteers who had committed themselves to come into training with an open mind. Therefore, it was important for us to reinforce the police officers for operating in new and divergent ways and affirm to them that, as learners of new material, it would be okay to make mistakes, ask questions, and voice concerns over what they were being asked to do. Because the police officers had already experienced going through the police academy, had participated in continuing education, and had volunteered to be in the program, they approached training with a healthy skepticism. At the same time, they were also creative in their use of the information and training related to calming and defusing techniques. As the officers carried their learning into the field, they proved to be highly adaptable in turning the lectures and modeling of their instructors into practice.

APPLICATION: CONSULTANT TECHNIQUES AND PROCEDURES

Entry

Doing the Background Work Preparing for consultation is critical. Once we had been contacted, we immediately began polling police departments around the country to determine how they were handling their service calls related to dealing with people with mental illness. We also searched the literature to determine if any new programs or procedures we didn't know about had been initiated.

Exploring Organizational Needs Even though we had many years of experience in the fields of mental health and police work, we realized each system possesses its own unique aspects and consequently needs to be examined thoroughly. Therefore, we wanted to make a comprehensive needs assessment to determine the extent of the local problem, to find out what resources were available, and to ascertain how other programs we'd found out about might be adapted to fit the Memphis Police Department.

To do this, it was necessary for us to bring the different systems together to determine their perceptions of the problem. After deciding who would be representative of, and could make commitments for, all of the systems (the police, the Memphis Alliance for the Mentally Ill, and a broad array of the Memphis mental health provider and social service systems), we called a meeting that invited the systems to become involved in a partnership to help the police deal with the violent mentally ill.

This initial meeting was extremely crucial to getting the project started on a solid footing. We invited middle- and upper-level management of the police department, the paramedics, the veterans hospital, the local state mental hospital, emergency rooms, social service agencies, community mental health clinics, the housing authority, the mayor's office, legal representation for the city, and the Alliance for the Mentally Ill. Everyone was asked to share their concerns with us. The mayor, police chief, and chief executive officer for the city opened the meeting with speeches indicating their support for the project and then gave a charge to the audience to help them. By enlisting the support of these officials, we were hoping to have set the stage and impressed the audience with how important this project was to the city. We invited as many human service organizations to this meeting as possible, including those who might only play a tangential role in the development of the program. In an undertaking of this magnitude, a number of organizations and individuals may have a great deal of initial zeal, but they may later fall by the wayside.

We followed up their comments by indicating that this project was so extensive and so critical that no individual organization could handle it alone. Therefore, we needed the cooperation and input from everyone there. We also indicated that there would be no money and probably little recognition for what they were about to commit to do. We deliberately made these statements to head off any turf wars that might have developed regarding jealousy over which of the agencies might obtain more money or public recognition.

We were still faced with a selling job. Our continuous focus was on two primary issues: safety for the client as well as the officer and overall improvement of the mental health services delivery system (with special attention between filling the gap between lethal and non-lethal force). We had to sell the idea that there was something in this for everyone, and that, in order to get that "something," everyone needed to hang together. (Otherwise, we would all wind up hanging separately!) As we expected, a good number of suspicious questions and some emotional catharsis arose from the audience. To meet the participants' emotional and security needs, we used an extensive amount of the basic exploration techniques of restatement of content, summary of ideas, open-ended questions, reflection of feelings, and nonjudgmental evaluations of the factual information presented. From our standpoint, a good deal of our role at this opening meeting involved our "tuning in" to the different participants. Such an effort enabled us to better understand the dynamics of the different groups, their perceptions of the problem, the roles they might play in its solution, and any hidden agendas that might surface.

A good deal of catharsis occurred about the interaction of mental health and the police. One of the most effective techniques to counter arguments, suspicions, and turf guarding is what we call the "I understand" technique. Essentially, once individuals start to voice their concerns, we incorporate a standard statement that starts with, "I understand that you have a concern about ..." We then complete the statement by giving a summary paraphrase of what the person has just said.

This technique clearly lets participants know we are empathic to their needs and are listening to them. It also allows us to meet complaints in an empathic, affirming way, without getting into divisive squabbles. In this case, after using the "I understand" technique, we used the 'broken record" technique (Canter & Canter, 1982) by repeatedly stating that the police mental health alliance was a critical one and could not be accomplished without their assistance. We intentionally used peer pressure and possible loss-of-face in front of one's peers by asking each organization to commit planning and training time to our proposal. We gained their commitment by passing a sheet around for them to write their names on.

We then prioritized a list of issues to be discussed and activities to be planned. We divided them into task groups to start working on solutions. We then set a two-week turnaround time after which we would come back with working drafts of what the groups were going to do. A strict operational agenda and timeline were adhered to so the planning group would stay highly motivated and on task. We set a tentative future start time of six months to have the program in operation. We pushed hard on both short- and long-range operational goals and planning times because we wanted participants to know they would have to get busy and stay busy in order to get the program off the ground.

Prior to this meeting we sought to arm ourselves with as many facts as possible so that we could mentally compare what was being said with what we knew to be factual. Therefore, we gained access to the police computer and ascertained the number of mental disturbance calls Memphis City officers had made during the last year, the number of times additional assistance was needed, how many people were transported to the local mental hospital for emergency commitment, how many reports of client injuries and officer injuries were made, and other statistics that would give us an objective view of the problem. Armed with these facts we were better able to determine the validity of what was being said and make a more accurate analysis of the problem.

Contracting When working across systems, contracting is essential for a variety of reasons. First and foremost, a contract commits the organization and individual to perform particular, specified tasks. Because the various parties in this setting were involved in a pro bono service, a contract with the force of law behind it was not in effect. However, that does not mean that we did not seek a written commitment from the various parties. This document, called a **memorandum of agreement**, stipulated what each party would commit to the project.

A designated official for each institution was asked to sign it. While there is no legal value in such a document, there is a great deal of psychological value in it. Those institutions that signed the memorandum and then didn't follow through with the terms of the document would lose a great deal of credibility within the local government, other social service systems, and the public. This is especially true in this case because signing the memorandum was given extensive media coverage. The foregoing is particularly true when an advocacy group such as the Alliance for the Mentally Ill serves a watchdog function.

After a series of meetings in which the skeletal form of the program was laid out, the mental health professionals who were present agreed that they would provide teaching staff for training and would also coordinate their institutions in collaborating with the police once the plan was put into action. The Memphis Alliance for the Mentally Ill; the Memphis Police Department; the local state mental hospital the community mental health clinics; the emergency psychiatric unit of the city hospital; the mayor's office; the counseling, psychology, and social work departments of the state university; the psychiatric department of the state medical school; and the Memphis judicial district all signed the memorandum.

Physically Entering the System Because of the numerous stakeholders involved, it was important for the consultants to have more than name recognition or do more than holding formal meetings. As a result, we spent a great deal of time physically going to specific institutions, talking with different professionals, and studying how the individual systems functioned in order to better understand how the various parts could be integrated into the whole.

Psychologically Entering the System Because consultants must earn their way into a system, a critical component of system change is obtaining credibility with those who will be asked to carry out the program. Since the consultants would be involved directly in training the officers, it was extremely important that we establish our *bona fides* with them. While our degrees and titles might get us through the door, they would not guarantee us acceptance or success. We would need to create a psychological bond with these men and women if they were to believe what we said and be willing to literally risk their lives while putting our techniques into practice.

Therefore, we decided that we would cross train with the officers as would the rest of the trainers. That is, we would ride with the officers on the evening shift to learn what they faced every time a mental disturbance call came over the radio. Doing this would provide us with a wealth of practical information to use in training and word would quickly spread among the officers that we were willing to put ourselves at risk with them.

Diagnosis and Gathering Information While local data were being gathered to substantiate the kind and degree of intervention needed, we also surveyed metropolitan police departments across the country with regard to their operational responses to mental disturbance calls. We were particularly interested in programs that could be easily replicated, would be cost effective, and could provide service to thousands of mental disturbance calls a year. Once these surveys were returned, we used the data to brainstorm with the police department.

Although ideas we generated might be well conceived, it would be up to the police to carry them   out. Therefore, it was extremely important that the local department critically appraise any possible intervention plan, focusing on strategic, tactical, and logistical utility.

Defining the Problem Responses to our national survey indicated that some police departments used centrally located specialty units that were specifically trained for crisis intervention with the mentally ill. Other departments had phone linkages to mental health providers that could send crisis response teams of mental health workers to the scene. No programs were found that used what we will call a **specialist-generalist** approach. In other words, none of the other departments used regular patrol officers as crisis interventionists who were given specific training in calming and defusing violent situations with the mentally ill. Even though such a program was not in use, logistically the idea seemed to have merit because it would provide specialists throughout the city who could respond rapidly to calls.

Setting Goals At this point, the goal of the program was to create a crisis intervention team that would be specifically trained in skill areas to understand and deal with the mentally ill. These officers would be initially screened through psychological testing, interviewed from a pool of volunteers, have their performance records reviewed, and be recommended by their commanders.

Generating Possible Interventions Options we considered were the use of the hostage negotiation unit (a specially trained team of crisis intervention officers housed at a central location) and the combining of police with rapid response teams from local mental health clinics. However, these options failed the two critical criteria of meeting the sheer number of calls and responding to those calls quickly. The specialist-generalist approach was still considered to have the most merit, but its major problem was the uncertainty about whether regular patrol officers could be trained to do such a difficult job or whether they would even volunteer to do it.

We believe that, as consultants, the ability to adapt to new and different conditions and to think divergently is highly important to successful consultation. In this case, although the specialist-generalist approach had never been attempted, we felt that its merits justified our taking such risks. Although we are not free from anxiety when we take risks such as these, we believe that well-thought-out risks are warranted. Consultants often have to "get out of the box" and help their consultees to look at radically different options in order bring about successful change.

Implementation: Choosing an Intervention

The first few moments when law enforcement arrives on the scene are the most critical and typically predicate whether or not the call will be resolved peacefully. Therefore, we decided it would be too cumbersome to have centrally located units or specialty response teams when the department averaged over 5,000 mental disturbance calls a year in a heavily populated 200 square mile area. The specialist-generalist approach, which would use regular patrol officers, was discussed at length with the mental health professionals, and consensus was reached that carefully selected patrol officers could be trained to do the job.

Our fears that we would not obtain enough volunteers were groundless. By providing a 50 dollar per month hazardous duty pay to "sweeten" the deal, our initial request obtained over 100 volunteers.

Formulating a Plan Because training patrol officers was a vital component to the program, a great deal of effort and thought went into formulating what the specific training would entail. All of the mental health professionals who had signed the memorandum of agreement cooperated in drawing up a training program. In its final form, that program involved 80 hours of training, which included the following curriculum:

- diagnostic and clinical issues of the dangerous mentally ill
- diagnostic and clinical issues of posttraumatic stress disorder
- basic crisis intervention techniques for controlling aggressive behavior

- suicide intervention techniques

- treatment strategies for crisis intervention

- patient rights and legal aspects of crisis intervention

- types, use, and side effects of psychotropic medications

- alcohol and drug behavior in the mentally ill

- articulation and coordination of police/caseworker roles

- specialized training in non-lethal forms of physical containment such as the Taser electric stun device and pepper gas

- simulation activities that include videotaped role-play and critique of officer performance

- face-to-face discussions between officers and patients at a local mental hospital about their perceptions of one

Implementing the Plan

Two of the more important points about the training program are worthy of discussion. First, we believe that as trainers we should model the behaviors we are asking participants of that training to perform. Simulation activities are one of the most critical components of training because they allow participants to practice in a safe place where they can laugh at one another's miscues, applaud creative responses, and learn from each other.

The other critical component of this training was arranging for officers to have face-to-face dialogues with mentally ill people. While such dialogues were extremely difficult to arrange because of the legal issues associated with confidentiality, they were extremely important both in giving officers a perspective on the mentally ill person's perceptions of the officer and also in helping to allay officers' fears surrounding the mentally ill. We addressed legal issues by having each officer sign an agreement not to disclose any information or reveal the identities of patients they met during training.

Immediately after training was completed, we, along with the police lieutenant and captain who were responsible for the crisis intervention officers' supervision, debriefed all trainers. Besides reviewing written and verbal evaluations of the participants, we also discussed the specific components of training; how they were sequenced; and what we might change, add, or delete.

Once training was completed we had 95 trained specialist-generalist crisis intervention officers available for duty. These officers were placed on duty rosters that would put them in all precincts on all three shifts. This distribution would allow dispatchers to call a crisis intervention officer to respond to a mental disturbance call within minutes in any part of the city.

Evaluating the Plan To monitor the effectiveness of training, we decided to have all trainers ride with crisis intervention officers as soon after start-up as possible. We also committed to having monthly update sessions with the crisis team supervisors, which would include selected mental health professionals who had helped in training. The purpose of these meetings was to troubleshoot the plan and evaluate it for any shortcomings. After four months into the program we concluded the following:

1. Many officers had performed exceedingly well, but there was no vehicle to apprise them of that fact other than word of mouth, which was an exceedingly poor communication method with officers operating on three shifts in five different precincts. Exchange of information between officers as to what worked and did not work was vital. Based upon that finding, the supervisor started a crisis intervention officer newsletter detailing critical incidents.

2. As carefully as we had prepared both top-level administrators and rank-and- file officers, we neglected first-level supervisors, such as lieutenants, who function as field supervisors. As a result, when a crisis intervention officer arrived at the scene of a mental disturbance call, he or she was supposed to be in charge. However, field supervisors sometimes felt their authority was being usurped, and this caused conflicts at the site of the call. It became apparent that we needed to train field supervisors as quickly as possible to alleviate this problem.

3. Crisis intervention officers carried no special identification badges. At times, this lack of identification caused miscommunication. Relatives or friends seeking assistance did not know which officers to talk to, nor at times did other officers, paramedics, or professional staff who might be on the scene of the call. It became apparent that some means of identification was needed. Therefore, a blue-and-silver medallion was designed that would be worn on the officer's uniform blouse and would clearly identify him or her as a crisis intervention officer. However, we were unaware that wearing such a medallion would signify membership in an elite group, and officers started to wear them as badges of honor.

Once we learned of the pride with which these medallions were worn, we suggested that all of the trainers be given them as concrete evidence of their inclusion as equal and contributing partners with the police officers. The mayor and the police chief gave a pinning ceremony and certification of appreciation awards ceremony at the police academy for all the trainers. When the trainers received the medallions, they bonded to the police force and positively identified themselves as an integral part of the program.

Disengagement

The acid test of consultation is whether the plan that has been formulated is meeting its goal. While reports from the general public and personal testimonials from members of the Alliance for the Mentally Ill were highly laudable, hard data was the critical evaluation factor. A series of statistical tests was conducted on pre- and post-intervention measures over a 16-month period. Statistically significant differences were found on increased calls, increased transportation to mental health facilities, decreased injuries to officers and the mentally ill, and decreased barricade/hostage situations. These statistics indicated that the program plan had immediate positive effects. To ascertain if the program had lasting effects, the same statistical analyses were conducted after a three-year period of operation. Again, the same results were found. Perhaps most important of all, no deaths or critical injuries to a mentally ill person have occurred at the hands of the crisis intervention officers during the time the program has been in operation (Carrier-Wright, 1992).

Reducing Involvement and Following Up Disengagement occurred by our systematically removing ourselves from involvement in the program. We do not believe that any consulting assistance should be terminated abruptly or automatically.

As staff members are able to take on more and more responsibilities, many of the consultant's roles can be turned over to them. For example, as supervisory staff became familiarized with the process and procedures and formed bonds with mental health professionals, they took on the responsibility for setting up training and they recruited mental health professionals for it. Fifteen years after start-up of the program, we still do one component of yearly training for new crisis intervention classes, but the day-to-day running of the program is clearly in the capable hands of veteran crisis intervention officers.

Terminating Finally, successful consultation often evolves into requests for assistance with other issues within the system. For example, our original work has led to coordinating school police officers with school counselors in school anti-violence efforts, starting a family trouble center for brokering service for domestic violence incidents that are reported to the police, and debriefing police officers after violent incidents. We are now in the start-up phase of a peer mentoring program for troubled officers.

Our exposure to the initial request by the Memphis City Police Department has been noticed by police departments and departments of mental health from all over the world who come to the training sessions in Memphis. The dramatic material and empirical evidence of the successes of the program has found its way into books and papers that we write and presentations that we make at national conventions. In short, for the consultant, nothing breeds success like success! Because of this success and the Memphis Police Department's desire to formalize the Crisis Intervention Team program for national dissemination, after fifteen years we have been asked to revisit the program.

RE-ENTRY

Statistical analyses indicated that the intervention program was successful – the program's goals were being met three years after implementation (Carrier-Wright,1992). Further, the National Alliance for the Mentally Ill (NAMI) had reported that the effectiveness of the Memphis CIT program was being replicated in outcome studies in numerous municipalities across the United States in the following ways: (1) there was a reduction in the reoccurrence of criminal activity by mental health consumers; (2) more effective relationships between law enforcement and mental health care providers have occurred; (3) less than 1% of the mental health consumers taken to a hospital emergency room did not need emergency medical or psychological care; and (4) officer injury rates decreased (National Alliance for the Mentally Ill, retrieved February 9, 2004). Interestingly, the purpose of this program had been to develop an intervention program for *one* location, Memphis, but now it had grown to be a nationally known and utilized program. It was time for the Memphis Police Department to begin looking at formalizing the program to ensure the integrity of the "Memphis Plan" was maintained both from the standpoint of continuing local integrity and national exportability. Such formalization is typical when innovative programs that were developed to meet a specific need prosper. At some point in time , if they are to survive such informal programs will need to mature and take on institutional trappings (James & Gilliland, 2001, p. 651). In this case to meet national certification standards for police training the program would need to develop a training program that had clear identifiable goals , objectives, methodologies and evaluation components that could be used and implemented nationally.

APPLICATION: CONSULTANT TECHNIQUES AND PROCEDURES

Program Review: Doing the Background Work. To reenter into a consulting relationship with the police department, we would need to complete a review of the training program, specifically to determine the congruency between the current curriculum and the national standards on best practices for training in the field of law enforcement crisis intervention with the mentally ill. The original program had 80 hours of training and included twelve subject areas with two additional components consisting of hands-on-training for the participants and face-to-face dialogues with mentally ill people. Soon after the inception of the program the training was reduced to 40 hours. What training from the original program had been eliminated or reduced and how had the training been affected because of this? Further, what components in the curriculum worked more favorably for disseminating the training information? For example, it appears that the video taped role plays have had more utility for the officers than the lecture format. Has the sequencing of the curriculum had any effect? In other words, would there be a more effective method for ordering the curriculum?

Industry and Literature Review. We would also need to be familiar with the latest research on crisis intervention for law enforcement with the mentally ill. This would include changes in non-lethal forms of physical containment, psychotropic medications, and state, federal laws and guidelines,. Much had changed in 15 years in the field of mental health and we were unaware if any of the new research or practices had been incorporated into the current training program.

To obtain this information, several steps would be implemented. First, an extensive review of literature pertaining to the crisis intervention for law enforcement with the mentally ill will be done. What is now being done on a national level? A good source of information could possibly come from the Criminal Justice / Mental Health Consensus Project, which is a plan authored by the Council of State Governments (CSG). The CSG coordinated a national effort to help local, state, and federal policymakers and criminal justice and mental health professionals improve the response to people with mental illness who have become involved in, or are at risk of involvement in, the criminal justice system (Council of State Governments, 2002).   Second, we would need to conduct interviews with national professionals well-established in the field of mental health crisis intervention and law enforcement would be conducted as well.

Exploring Organizational Needs: the Stakeholders

At the local level we are still interested in the current relationship between the three stakeholders: (1) the consumer advocacy group; (2) the professional service providers, educators, and consultants; and (3) the Memphis Police Department. We would need to determine if the original system is intact and still viable. A dedicated and committed relationship among these three is still critical to the program if it is to continue to be successful and capable of evolving.

Psychologically Entering the System As in the original consultation, we knew it would be critical to have the continued support of the local NAMI chapter. This organization had grown in stature to become one of the most powerful lobbyists for the mentally ill in the nation. NAMI has supported the model currently utilized by the Memphis Police Department crisis intervention for law enforcement officers with the mentally ill through its website (National Alliance for the Mentally Ill, retrieved February 8, 2004). These recommended practices would be important guidelines for addressing any changes to the current program and exporting them nationally.

Our relationship with the officers would also be essential to the success of the program. We knew from the original consultation that credibility was crucial to incorporating the information into practice. To accomplish this we would once again cross-train with the officers to again familiarize ourselves with the officer's experiences during a crisis intervention.

Physically Entering the System Another method of gathering information will be through interviews with the participants so we might have an understanding of their experiences of the program. For example, we would want to know how the participating officers' feel about being in the program. How has the training been effective or ineffective in preparing the officers for intervening with the mentally ill individual and families of the mentally ill? What do the officers see as the advantages and disadvantages of being a CIT officer? How could the program be improved? Do the officers feel adequately supported by the police administration and by the community?

Another important set of interviews would be with those who receive the intervention services, the mentally ill individuals and their families. Has this crisis intervention program made a difference in their experiences of being in crisis, and if so, how? What changes to the crisis intervention program do they believe would improve the service to them? Mental health providers will also provide us with a valuable perspective as to how well the crisis intervention program is helping their clients. This will be a direct reflection on the quality of the training. These questions should facilitate a more complete representation of the environment.

Formal interviews will held with the director and former director of the police department's crisis intervention program and developers of the original training program along with current trainers. These interviews will focus on the original intent of the program's curriculum and manual, program objectives and construction, and, most importantly, opinions on validity of the current program. Another area for review will be with the top administration in the police department and city officials. Is the current top administration still committed to, and involved in, training, continued program development, and evaluation (Patton, 2001)?

We will also consider continuing needs for all the officers. As the fields of mental health crisis intervention and law enforcement crisis intervention are ever-changing with new research as well as advances in best practices guidelines, how is this information provided so that officers are able to incorporate the information into their work environments?

Setting Goals Our current goals have evolved into two different steps: (1) evaluating the effectiveness of the crisis intervention training program for the Memphis Police Department, which targets the current training program; and (2) to determine if this training is exportable, replicable, and financially feasible for police departments no matter what their size or geographical location.

Safety is our second major criterion. One of the major factors in determining the efficacy of the program is to quantify the number of successful interventions where no consumer and officer injuries result. We know that calls requesting crisis intervention have increased from approximately 5000 to 10,000 calls annually (Memphis Police Department, 2003). However, it is unclear as to what this 100% increase has meant in regard to quality of service, response time, injuries to consumers and officers, and the need for additional personnel. These are concrete outcome variables that will need to be examined as part of our comprehensive review of the program.

Evaluating the Training Program We will attend the total 40-hour crisis intervention training class given to the officers to evaluate the training program in action. Review of the training materials and our observation of the instructors' delivery of the training will enable us to determine if there are any inconsistencies between the lectures, manual, and supplemental handouts. This will also provide the opportunity to achieve some sense of the congruency between the training curriculum and the actual services being provided to the mentally ill population.

Analysis and Recommendations

Ultimately, we will need to determine the overall effectiveness of the program based on a two factors: (1) the level of safety to consumers and officers, (2) the efficiency of the delivery system of the intervention. Evaluating current research in the field would enable us to determine what, if any, changes could be made to the program to enhance the delivery system of the intervention. In the case of this particular program consultation, we want to ensure that it is replicable because so many police departments are benchmarking their crisis intervention program from the Memphis Crisis Intervention Team (CIT) program. It must be cost effective so that police departments will choose to provide this service to the mentally ill and their families. Lastly, it must be transportable because police departments will need to be able to implement the program and custom fit it with their own logistical and tactical needs.

Implementation: Choosing an Intervention

Choosing an intervention will be based on the results from the interviews with officers, advocates for the mentally ill, the trainers, and police department administration. We will review the current curriculum and determine the relevance and functionality of each of the sections based on the analysis of the interviews with the officers. Along these same lines we will also determine the utility of the training manual and handouts.

We will also assess the program for cost-effectiveness and simplicity of use by other police departments. This would involve a cost analysis to provide the training curriculum, training materials, and cost-per-officer to train. In the Memphis program, trainers provide services free of cost as a community service in support of the Memphis Police Department and better mental health provision for consumers. However, other jurisdictions may not be able to avail themselves of qualified instructors for free.

Formulating a Plan   After   assessing the efficacy of the current training program and the ability to transport the program to other police departments, we will recommend which of the current sections of training should remain and which should not. We will also make recommendations for follow-up in-service training to provide the department with new and emerging trends in crisis intervention techniques with the mentally ill and provide a platform to troubleshoot issues or problems that occur for officers in the field.

Implementing the Plan

Evaluating the Plan   We will recommend a schedule and a process for reviewing the training program and collecting feedback from the police officers. Information and data gathered from the officers will provide a valuable insight on trends in the community and the needs that develop for the mentally ill as a result. This information will be provided on a timely basis so that it can be addressed and integrated into training.

Disengagement

Disengaging from the consulting relationship would mean that both quantitative and qualitative information indicate a successful program. Post-intervention analysis should indicate that the program is (1) continuing to meet local needs, and (2) is being successfully adapted and adopted by other jurisdictions.

Reducing Involvement and Follow-up It is our expectation that we will turnkey the renovated training program over to the Memphis Police. Our follow-up will involve immediately debriefing with trainers to determine their feelings about working with the new curriculum. We will generate focus groups of crisis intervention team police officers after they have completed six months of field duty. Follow-up with these officers should allow us tot determine what changes should be made in the program. Finally we will do both immediate follow-up with visiting jurisdictions as they undergo instruction to determine how our program may be more adaptable to their needs. We will also plan to do six month follow-ups with these other jurisdictions to determine how effective their adoption of our program has been.

IMPLICATIONS FOR PRACTICE

In the human service business, clear and concrete indications that something works are often few and far between. Probably there is no better test for the consultation process or reinforcement for consultants than to see objective data that their plan or program is working and that their work is being replicated by others. That is certainly true for us. Many other police departments from around the country now send officers to Memphis City for training in crisis intervention with the mentally ill. Further, components of the crisis intervention training we were responsible for are now integrated into all recruit training at the Memphis City Police Academy. At best, working with systems that have different perspectives and may be antagonistic toward the human service worker is difficult for consultants. In working with such clients, consultants will need to vigorously practice empathic listening and responding skills.

At times, the best empathy skills fail with groups whose members have different and opposing agendas. We believe that it is not so much for a lack of knowledge on the consultant's part that this occurs, but rather consultants may fail to accurately gauge their own dynamics as they interact with a group.

Parallel processing is another phenomenon that commonly occurs in counseling and in supervision of counselors when the consultant is engaged with a group that may be fractious (Bernard & Goodyear, 1992; Friedman, 1983; Mueller & Kell, 1972). Parallel process occurs when dynamics in supervision replicate those that occur in the trainee's own attempts at therapy (Bernard & Goodyear, 1992, pp. 29–30).This concept is used particularly in systems therapy (Haley, 1987). It finds its roots in transference and countertransference dynamics. It is applicable to consulting because it is not uncommon for the frustrated consultant to start manifesting the problematic attitudes and responses of the system when recalcitrant and oppositional members stymie him or her.

Consultants need to be very sensitive to this phenomenon. It is easy for the consultant to conclude that a group is stubbornly resistant to change and, consequently, disengage prematurely. Consultants who start to experience negative feelings, such as frustration, or negative behavior changes, such as increased authoritarianism, toward a group should immediately seek consultation themselves to determine if parallel processing is occurring. If this occurs, then the consultant needs to take a long hard look at the baggage he or she brings into the setting. Our axiom is that there are no difficult groups, just difficult problems. When we live by this axiom, it frees us to be proactive and progressive rather than reactive and regressive.

Likewise, it is imperative for consultants to have expertise in understanding the dynamics and techniques for operating within task groups. Possessing and understanding organizational dynamics and knowing how to gain entry and move within the organization are skills critical to effectively coping with political issues, the bureaucracy, and the organization's method of operation. Key to such operations is identifying group members who are open to divergent views, can articulate their own viewpoints, and can coordinate among systems.

Moving these key players into leadership roles is critical when systems are paranoid about one another, when many individual egos are involved, and when organizational "turf" boundaries are being changed.

Illback and Dittmeier (1991) note that seeking entry into such diverse groups calls for understanding that each has a unique and complicated history with one another, which is frequently characterized by stress and strife. The wise consultant who works with a divergent group will take the time to allow individuals to gain a sense that they are part of a task group with its own distinct identity as opposed to the identity they bring with them to the group.

The major initiating task of the consultant to such a diverse group is to develop sufficient trust with each subsystem so that psychological boundaries can be crossed, joining the group together in acting on the problem.

At an initial meeting, it is critical to allocate time for all parties to state desired positive outcomes and benefits. Genuinely reinforcing and accentuating the positive statements each person makes, and tying those statements in with the agendas of other members, goes a long way toward keeping the consultant out of the parallel processing game. We agree with Illback and Dittmeier (1991) that such community-based consultations take longer to get into action than intact groups already in existence. Therefore, patience is a major virtue in this type of consulting relationship.

A consumer advocacy group such as the Memphis City Alliance for the Mentally Ill can be a blessing and a curse. The group can be a blessing from the standpoint that, unlike other organizations and institutions, they can bring a great deal of political pressure to bear on bureaucracies. Thus, they are invaluable in helping the consultant expedite systemic change that otherwise might take years to accomplish. However, they may also be a curse if they are summarily dismissed as agitators who know little of the reality of the situation. If consumer advocacy groups are not carefully involved and given recognition for the critical part they play in making systemic change, they may bring that same political pressure to bear on the consultants! A valuable asset in this consultation was the commitment and involvement of the administration of the Memphis City police force. Consultants should strongly consider avoiding an organization unwilling to have its top administration committed to and involved in training, program development, and evaluation. Unless the policy makers of an organization are personally involved in the training and professional development of rank-and-file personnel, they are implying that the training is not worth their time and effort. That message is implicitly carried to employees, who are then likely to be less than enthusiastic about changes they are asked to make. Further, if policy makers are not involved in training and feedback, they will not be aware of the scope and depth of knowledge and competency that their employees have gained.

The failure to recognize the employees' new skills and the limits of those skills can have serious implications when those skills are carried into practice in the real world.

Perhaps the most potent result of administrative involvement in the system consultation process is the benefit of multidisciplinary thinking when different systems are brought together. A key element in consultation with multiple systems is that people and ideas from different disciplines, perspectives, and cultural and training backgrounds enhance and broaden administrative thinking.

Paradigmatic shifts are not easy for traditionally conservative systems, such as police departments and some mental health agencies, to make. Therefore, it is important to bring such diverse systems together slowly and patiently, reinforcing them and continuously pointing out the benefits of working together.

We would add that one of the most serious mistakes consultants can make is not being willing to model what they are doing. Talking about problems and their theoretical implications is fine, but what most consultees want are clear action plans and models to solve their unsolvable problems. The best way we know how to do this is to show the consultee what we are talking about by demonstrating it.

Examples of such models are our verbal de-escalating, defusing, and calming techniques that we used with trainees in subsequent training sessions after the crisis intervention team went into operation. The consultants and crisis intervention officers collaborated on constructing several written training scenarios directly from crisis situations the officers and consultants had encountered. The consultants and the crisis intervention officers modeled appropriate crisis intervention techniques by reenacting these scenarios and then evaluating with the trainees what they had done and why they had done it. By using these experienced officers and also by subjecting ourselves to critical review, we established program credibility, our own credibility,

and provided an atmosphere that was conducive for trainees to try out their skills
Thus, in this example, consultants were richly involved *with* consultees rather than
doing something *for* them.

Finally, program evaluation and possible change based on that evaluation
is never easy (James & Gilliland, 2001, pp. 649-652). The initial start-up of
the CIT program was a hard birthing. Whether this revision will be as difficult
a rebirth remains to be seen. Consultants should never labor under the fallacious
assumption that re-entry will be any simpler or easier. Once a procedure becomes
institutionalized, it can be very stubborn about changing it ways.

QUESTIONS FOR DISCUSSION AND REFLECTION

1. Entry into the system—physical and psychological—was made more challenging
because there were, in fact, three separate, loosely linked, somewhat antagonistic
subsystems. If you were the consultant, what are two different approaches you
might have used to effect successful entry?

2. This consultation incorporated aspects of education/training, program,
behavioral, doctor/patient, and process consultation. Identify examples of how
each was used. If we had used more narrowly focused interventions or strategies,
would they have been as effective? Support your reasoning.

3. What ethical concerns do you have regarding the face-to-face interactions of
the police crisis team trainees with mentally ill patients? Were there adequate
safeguards? What might you have done differently?

4. A general premise of consultation is that it enables the consultees to better
solve their own problems in the future while fostering independence. This
consultation has spanned several years, and, in fact, after fifteen years the
consultants are still doing annual training and refreshers. Have the consultants
violated this premise? Is their continuing involvement ethical?

5. What are the *key* factors the consultant should consider in helping the client
organization build a coalition or alliance among community agencies and
potential contributors toward attaining the client organization's goals?

6. After examining the consultant techniques and procedures discussed in this
chapter, what additional strategies would you suggest the consultant might use
to enhance the quality and effectiveness of the consultation?

REFERENCES AND SUGGESTED READINGS

Bernard, J.M., & Goodyear, R. K. (1992). *Fundamentals of clinical supervision.*
Boston, MA: Allyn & Bacon.

Bronfenbrenner, U. (1995). Developmental ecology through space and time: A future perspective. In P. Moen, G. H. Elder Jr., and K. Luscher (Eds.), *Examining lives in context: Perspectives on the ecology of human development* (pp. 619-647). Washington, DC: American Psychological Association.

Canter, L., & Canter, E. (1982). *Assertive discipline for parents.* Santa Monica, CA: Canter Associates.

Carrie-Wright, J.T. (1992). *Evaluation of police crisis intervention in mental disturbance calls.* Unpublished doctoral dissertation, Memphis State University, Memphis, TN.

Council of State Governments. (2002). Criminal justice/mental health consensus project. Retrieved July 7, 2003, from Consensus Project Website: http://consensusproject.org/

Dattilio, F. M., & Jongsma, A. E., Jr. (2000). *The family treatment planner.* New York, Wiley

Dougherty, A. M. (2005). *Psychological consultation and collaboration in school and community settings* (4th ed.). Belmont, CA: Wadsworth.

Friedman, R. (1983). Aspects of the parallel process and counter-transference issues in student supervision. *School Social Work Journal, 8,* 3–15.

Fuqua, D. R., & Kurpius, D. J. (1993). Conceptual models of organization consultation.

Journal of Counseling and Development, 71, 607–618.

Gillig, P.M., Dumaine, M., Stammer, J.W., Hilliard, J.R., & Grubb, P. (1990).

What do police officers really want from the mental health system? *Hospital and Community Psychiatry, 41,* 663–665.

Haley, J. (1987). *Problem solving therapy.* San Francisco: Jossey-Bass.

Hansen, J.C., Himes, B. S., & Meier, S. (1990). *Consultation: Concepts and practices.* Englewood Cliffs, NJ: Prentice-Hall, Inc.

Illback, R. J., & Dittmeier, H. L. (1991) Group consultation in community-based programs: Some problems and issues. *Journal of Educational and Psychological Consultation, 2(10),* 91–93.

James, R. K. (1994). Dial 911: Commentary. In P. Backlar (Ed.), *The family face of schizophrenia* (pp. 182–200). New York: G. P. Putnam's Sons.

James, R. K., & Gilliland, B. E. (2001). *Crisis intervention strategies.* Belmont CA: Brooks/Cole-Wadsworth.

Juras, J. L., Mackin, J. R., Curtis, S. E., & Foster-Fishman, P.G. (1997). Key concepts of community psychology: Implications for consulting in educational and human service settings. *Journal of Educational and Psychological Consultation, 8,* 111–133.

Luckett, J. B.,& Slaikeu, K.A. (1990).Crisis intervention by police. In K.A. Slaikeu (Ed.), *Crisis intervention: A handbook for practice and research* (2nd ed.) (pp. 227–242). Boston: Allyn & Bacon.

Madsen, W. C. (1999). Collaborative therapy with multistressed families: From old problems to new futures. New York: Guilford Press

Mueller,W. J.,& Kell, B. L. (1972). *Coping with conflict: Supervising counselors and psychotherapists.* New York: Appleton Century-Crofts.National Alliance of the Mentally Ill (NAMI). (n.d.). *Crisis Intervention Training (CIT) on the Move Across America.* Retrieved November 12, 2003, from http://www. nami.org/Content/NavigationMenu/FindSupport/Education_and_Training/ Education_Training_and_Peer_Support_Center/State_and_Local_ Programs/ Crisis_Intervention_Training_on_the_Move_Across_America.htm.

Nichols, W. C., Pace-Nichols, M. A., Becvar, D. S., Napiers, A. Y. (Eds.). (2000). Handbook of family development and intervention. New York: Wiley.

Patton,M.Q. (2001). *Qualitative research and evaluative methods.* (3rd ed.).Thousand Oaks, MA: Sage Publications, Inc.

Zins, J. E. (1997). Expanding the conceptual foundations of consultation: Contributions of community psychology. *Journal of Educational and Psychological Consultation, 8,* 107–110.

7

Group Consultation with a University Counseling Center Staff

FRANCES E. TACK, A. MICHAEL DOUGHERT Y,
AND DEANA F. MORROW

DESCRIPTION OF THE MODEL USED

Because they are frequently asked to work with groups of consultees, effective consultants need to be skilled in working with a variety of groups. The following case depicts a group approach to organizational consultation, with focus on both process and education/training, utilizing a generic model of consultation (Dougherty, 2005). The case involves a consultant interacting with the staff of a counseling center concerning a particular problem of the center, as well as the staff member's need to learn more about the consultation process through an in-service training setting. This case offers the opportunity to examine the various roles a consultant may be asked to fill, and to examine the evolution of a group consultation and the subsequent flexibility required by a process consultant.

This case also demonstrates the use of Schein's (1988, 1999) purchase of expertise model, in which a consultant is engaged for the purpose of sharing knowledge on a specific topic. In this case, the consultants were selected because of their specific knowledge about acquiring funding and the consultation process, two areas where more information was needed according to the group. As the case demonstrates, one of the primary roles of the consultant in the purchase of expertise model is that of educator or trainer, teaching and coaching the consultee and suggesting interventions from a foundation of knowledge. Through engaging in consultation, the consultee not only works on immediate concerns, but also gains skills and information for application with future consultees.

Another aspect of consultation that this case demonstrates is group consultation, in which the collaborative experience between consultant and consultee group, and also among members of the consultee group, is the heart of the process. As Hansen, Himes, and Meier (1990) point out, in a group consultation the consultant is particularly concerned with facilitating interaction, teaching collaboration, and modeling collaboration. Note in this case how the flexibility of the consultant in response to the group dynamics accomplishes these process goals.

SETTING AND BACKGROUND ISSUES

Setting

The consultation took place at the counseling center of a medium-sized university in a small southeastern college town. The counseling center employs four full-time professional counselors and provides internship opportunities for four students every semester. The center offers individual and group counseling, as well as campus education seminars on a wide range of topics, including multicultural sensitivity, stress management, and conflict resolution. The center is a stand-alone facility with multiple individual counseling rooms and group counseling rooms equipped with monitoring equipment (two-way mirrors and microphones) for supervising interns.

The center serves a total university student population of 8,000, about a six percent of whom seek services from the center annually. The university itself is a private university, dedicated to offering a broad range of bachelor's-, master's-, and doctoral-level curricula, including courses of study in biology, psychology, education, chemistry, and counseling. The students are generally academically focused, and the graduation rate exceeds 70 percent. The school also boasts strong varsity and intramural athletic programs in which about half of all students participate.

Background

The consultation evolved due to staff interest in acquiring funding that would help them pay interns and learn more about the consultation process. For several years prior to the consultation, the director of the counseling center had worked with the staff to acquire funding for clinical graduate assistantships. The director met with little success, primarily due to the tight funding constraints of the university. Having talked with many people through the course of this investigation and having received no commitments, the director decided to approach us to consult with the counseling center concerning the acquisition of funding for interns.

Concurrently, the staff recognized a need for additional training on the consultation process. They agreed that the consultation about internship funding could also be used as training on the consultation process itself. Both of these goals were communicated to us in the request to conduct the consultation.

Though this dual goal presented a great opportunity for us to spread the word about consultation within human services, at the same time it added some complexity to the consultation process. Specifically, we recognized that we would need to plan an approach that would simultaneously produce an action plan related to the funding question and yet that would at the same time leave the participants more aware of and knowledgeable about the consultation process. Furthermore, the director requested that both of these goals be accomplished in a single group meeting with the center's staff.

It was also communicated to us from the beginning that current counseling center interns would participate in the consultation. For this reason, as we planned for the consultation, we had to be aware that the interns would have limited knowledge on the institutional dynamics and the background of the problem. Therefore, we recognized the need to incorporate these elements into the consultation.

It is also worth noting that we had worked with the counseling center director and staff on numerous occasions in the past (though not in the role of consultants) and had a very positive working relationship already established.

This fact helped to shorten the entry process, since trust was established and we already had a wealth of background information on the center and its place within the larger institution.

We were concerned because one of the consultants was an administrator in a department that places interns at the counseling center and therefore had a potential conflict of interest. We discussed this with the director when the initial request for consultation was made. The director did not think the situation would pose any problems, and in fact even suggested that it might be a benefit to the staff, since we would have a "vested interest" in assisting them in acquiring funding. Though the director was not concerned, we kept this potential conflict in mind as we planned the consultation.

GOALS OF CONSULTATION

Going into the group consultation, we understood that the goals of the consultation were to assist the counseling center staff to define the funding problem in greater detail, to generate possible approaches, and to learn more about the consultation process.

The group hoped to leave the consultation with a list of specific avenues to pursue for funding intern positions and an action plan. Though the original goal was to pursue funding for interns, the discussion of goals during the actual group consultation led to an immediate consensus and the establishment of a broader goal—to acquire additional staff. This goal will be discussed in greater detail later in the case.

The consultees also wanted to leave the consultation with a general understanding of the skills and techniques of process consultation. To meet this goal, we planned to review the stages of consultation and to discuss selected techniques.

We knew from the educational backgrounds of the staff that most of them had been exposed to consultation before; therefore, we did not plan to spend a lot of time *formally* teaching consultation. Instead, we planned to conduct the consultation and then to use it as a case example to review the basics of consultation and important issues that emerged.

CONSULTANT FUNCTION AND ROLES

Driven by the dual goals of exploring the funding issue and learning about consultation, this consultation became a hybrid of process consultation and education/ training consultation. This situation generated a subsequent hybrid of roles for us, including fact finders, process specialists, facilitators, collaborators, and educators/trainers.

We acted as fact finders primarily during the initial meeting with the director. During this time we used an interview approach to gain background information about the history of the funding problems and past attempts to solve them. This activity not only helped us to better understand the case, but also provided the director with an encapsulation of the problem at hand. As a result, the director used our fact-finding discussion as the basis for development of a timeline that documented past attempts to acquire funding. This description included a list of which organizations within the university had been approached, names of who had been contacted, a summary of what had been discussed, and the results of the request. (This timeline was later used in the group consultation.)

In the roles of process specialists and facilitators, we served as catalysts for group discussion, summarized input and made connections, and facilitated the brainstorming process. Although the resulting content was important, as process facilitators, our primary focus was on the methodology of the facilitation itself; namely, we engaging all staff members in the dialogue, recording input, and working toward the development of an action plan.

As collaborators, we provided input to the group on our own experiences working to achieve funding for interns and shared our understanding of the system in which their pursuits were taking place. We related a specific attempt we had made three years ago to fund an additional graduate assistant and provided the names of persons we had contacted. We also shared our lack of success in getting what we had requested in our own attempts. This sharing produced mixed results from the group. On one hand, the group seemed validated that they were not the only ones unable to achieve additional funding for interns. However, the group also appeared somewhat frustrated by our experience, which, when added to their own experience, began to make additional funding seem like an impossibility.

As consultants, this presented us with the challenge of keeping the group positive, energized and focused on creative, "possibility thinking" as they had requested. We did this by validating the group's frustration, sharing that we, too, had been frustrated at times in this pursuit; and by reframing the concerns by reminding the group that there were still many options open that we and they had not yet tried.

Subsequent to working with the group directly on the problem of intern funding, we shifted the group into a discussion of the consultative techniques we used and how we had experienced the unfolding of the consultation. We pointed out the markers of where transition from one stage to another had occurred and described the specific elements of each stage that we had accomplished. Further, we reviewed facilitation techniques and the brainstorming process in general, giving examples directly from the funding case we had just completed. We also facilitated the group's discussion of their perceptions of the consultation process they had experienced, debriefing them around roles, stages and techniques. This accomplished the dual objectives of assisting the group to gain clarity on areas that needed further exploration and provided us with useful feedback for our own professional development as consultants.

CONSULTEE EXPERIENCE IN CONSULTATION

During the consultation, the consultees openly discussed their needs and concerns and processed various options with each other. They also explored past unsuccessful attempts to solve their problem and brainstormed possible options for funding, thus acting as problem solvers and collaborators with the consultants. The most significant aspect of the consultees' participation was in generating the action plan, a phase in which the consultants were focused on facilitating the group/creative process and on extracting ideas from the consultees. The consultees provided the actual content as they brainstormed avenues for acquiring additional funding and staffing.

Another significant part of the experience for the consultees was receiving education/training on the consultation process. Since the format for this training was discussion of the case they had just participated in, the consultees played a dynamic part in their own exploration of the consultation process. They heard an analysis of process by the consultants, engaged in dialogue about various elements, and added input from their own past education about consultation and previous experiences as consultees. This added a greater depth and variety to the discussion and allowed the consultees to collaborate in the teaching/learning process.

At the end of the consultation, we facilitated a discussion in which the entire group processed the consultation experience. During this time, the consultees indicated that the process had helped them to "get out of the box" in their thinking to generate options that had not even occurred to them previously. They felt that the group format had allowed them greater stimulation in brainstorming ideas and that having an objective third party to facilitate the process had allowed all of the staff to participate more fully.

APPLICATION: CONSULTANT TECHNIQUES AND PROCEDURES

Entry

The request for us to consult with the counseling center came originally from one of the staff counselors in a memo. In this memo, the counselor explained the staff members' dual needs of exploring intern funding options and learning more about the consultation process. She also explained the staff members' interest in conducting the consultation as a group, including participation of the center's interns.

In our follow-up discussion with the staff member, we expressed our interest in learning more about the center's needs relative to the consultation, and we suggested a preliminary group meeting to help us better understand these needs. The staff member discussed this with the rest of the center's staff, and they decided that they preferred for the center's director to meet with us to clarify their needs.

Diagnosis

The initial meeting with the director took place one week prior to the group consultation. At this meeting, the three of us discussed the history of the concerns and details about the need for funding for interns. The director also shared his frustrations about his past attempts and his interest now in seeking outside guidance to help find a workable approach.

In this initial meeting, the director reminded us about the dynamics of the staff, pointing out that the group was very energetic, intelligent, and interactive with one another. This was important information for us to keep in mind as we planned our approach. Next, we discussed various approaches and agreed that an informal, discussion-based approach was most suitable for this group. This approach included a discussion of the politics of funding, a discussion of our experiences in attempting to get additional funding, and facilitation of the group's generation of ideas using the nominal group technique. Finally, we agreed to plan about an hour and a half at the end of the day to discuss the consultation process in general and have a question and answer time. To further support the staff members' goal of learning more about consultation; we videotaped the initial meeting with the director for use at the group consultation meeting. We included teaching points about the consultation process in the videotape to highlight the various aspects that this meeting demonstrated.

Implementation

The group consultation took place at the counseling center and all staff members were present, including the director, counselors, and interns. We opened the meeting by sharing the agenda that we had developed in the meeting with the director and confirmed with the group that this was indeed the direction in which they wanted to proceed. Next, we showed selected parts of the videotape of the introductory sessions with the director so that the group would have the same background on the case. The videotape also served to begin the education process on consultation, which would be completed during the last hour and a half of the day. A brief discussion processing the video followed.

We then facilitated the group in brainstorming what they wanted, and did not want, from the consultation. Though several "wants" were identified, the primary one was to have a plan of action by the end of the session. They stated strongly that they did not want to hear remarks such as "it can't be done" and "the bureaucracy is too complicated." They wanted to be "possibility thinkers" and did not want us to stifle that process! We expressed to them our understanding of what they were saying and agreed to facilitate them in that vein.

Next, we solicited their input and discussion of their goals in relation to the consultation. The group as a whole was very clear that their goal was to increase the staffing of the center so that they could offer additional programs. This was a somewhat broader goal than was originally stated, but it was a positive revelation in that it permitted broader options when we brainstormed possible approaches. Even though this goal allowed for other options, getting interns funded was still the primary driver and, as we processed options, was seen as one of the most viable. Further, this goal recognized:

- the staff's interest in increasing the services offered by the center
- the center's role on campus as a training ground for psychology and counseling graduate students
- the staff's strong desire to attract quality students to intern positions at the center

At this point, we discussed the background of the center's work to date in searching for funding. The director distributed a timeline narrative of his discussions and results with various administrators over the past several years. This was helpful since not all of the staff members, especially interns, were familiar with the detailed history of this issue. We detected, through the discussion that followed the director's review of the past work, a feeling of frustration and a sense of not knowing what to do next, and it was for these reasons that they sought consultation from us.

Although we had planned to use the nominal group technique to provide a structured framework for brainstorming, the dynamics of the group led easily to an informal brainstorming session that proved very fruitful. The sophistication and knowledge base of the group made the use of a more highly structured process such as nominal group technique unnecessary. So we adjusted our plan.

The brainstorming generated a long list of possible routes they could take to achieve additional staff and funding for interns. Next, we grouped the items according to the campus administrative area that would be involved (e.g., academic affairs, student affairs, development, etc.). Our next step was to turn this list into an action plan. We accomplished this by reviewing the list one item at a time and soliciting the group for consensus on which staff person would be responsible for each particular item, the specific actions that person would take, and when the work would be finished.

The group recognized that implementation of this plan was an ongoing process and that results would probably be slow in coming. This was especially true in light of the university operating their budget on an academic school year basis: even if funding was found, it would probably not get into the budget until the *following* school year. Nevertheless, the group seemed energized to pursue their action plan, and we expressed a willingness to come back at a future date to explore their progress.

Having heard from the group that they felt this topic was adequately covered, we acted as teachers again, reviewing the consultation process and soliciting questions. We used specific elements of the consultation with the group to illustrate the consultation process and techniques.

Disengagement

Since we were not going to actually see the group throughout the entire implementation, we processed the consultation at the end of the group session. To initiate the discussion, we solicited feedback from the group on the consultation and on our performance as consultants.

The group was pleased and felt that they had met the goals of the consultation; they had an action plan for acquiring additional staff/funding, and they had been educated on the consultation process. One staff member did express confusion over our initial plan to use Nominal Group Technique (NGT) and the fact that we did not use it or the flip chart instruction sheet for that technique, which had been posted on the wall prior to the start of the session. We told her that we understood her concern and explained that, because the group had moved so smoothly into brainstorming and had proceeded with it so well, we thought the more structured approach was not necessary. We also recognized to the group that it might have been less confusing if we had explained this at the time we made the adjustment. The group agreed that an explanation would have been helpful.

IMPLICATIONS FOR PRACTICE

This process consultation leads to several general implications regarding consultation with groups and organizations. First, consultants need to be able to walk the thin line between being a group collaborator and a group member.

There can be a strong urge to pick a side and become a player, but it is important for the consultant to resist the temptation to jump into the dynamics and politics of a situation. On the other hand, the group needs to view the consultant on some level as part of the team, as a collaborator, as someone who truly understands their issues. In this way, the consultant needs to relate to the group and find some common ground of interest or experience that can unite the consultant and the group. This situation was somewhat eased for us in this consultation because we were already acquainted with the staff and had developed a positive working relationship. We did have to put energy into maintaining a balanced, objective stance as we processed options, particularly in light of the staff's wish that we not stifle their process with "it can't be done" type remarks.

Another message that we can learn about consultation from this case is the importance of strong process skills and flexibility. As with so many organizational consultations, at the counseling center there were many players with many ideas and with different levels of influence within the group. Our use of strong process skills kept the group on track yet permitted exploration, allowing everyone to contribute and be heard. This was especially true considering that there were four levels of employees in the group: manager (the center's director), supervisor (one of the counselors who acts as a lead person), direct workers (counselors), and apprentices (interns). For example, during the brainstorming, we noticed that one of the interns was being very quiet and was not active in generating ideas. When this was observed, we made a special effort to draw her into the process and solicit her input. Consequently, the intern began sharing and generated a couple of very creative ideas that were added to the action plan.

In terms of flexibility, we changed our plan during the consultation in response to our observations about the group. Had we not been flexible in letting go of the original plan to use the NGT, the group might have felt stifled. This could have resulted in resistance to further techniques and discussion through such behaviors as shutting down (passive resistance) or disagreeing with our facilitation (active resistance). As indicated in the disengagement discussion, we did not communicate to the group that we were changing direction and this caused some confusion. In the future, when we have shared an agenda with a group and then decide to change it, we will share this with the group and solicit their support.

In this particular consultation, knowledge of the system in which the organization was operating was very helpful. It permitted us to assist in assessing options and in prompting the generation of options. It also provided us the basis to share our own experiences and do so in a manner to which the group could relate. Regardless of whether a consultant is part of the system in which he or she consults, it is important for the consultant to have some background and understanding of the dynamics of the larger organization. Further, the consultant needs to be aware of the norms and vocabulary of the organization and use that in communicating with the consultees. Clearly, consultants should avoid using their own jargon, as it may distance them from the consultees or cause confusion.

Consultants need to be open to feedback during and after the consultation. It is easy to hear the positive feedback, but it is not so easy to hear the things one could have done better. However, this is how we improve as consultants and how the consultees become *our* teachers. Being receptive and non-defensive is especially important when working with groups because the group may sometimes appear to "gang up" on the consultant, uniting around a point of feedback. In this case, we solicited feedback from the group and made a point to be open and receptive to it. This was particularly important when the staff member shared with us that she was confused by the fact that we did not use nominal group technique. Instead of becoming defensive, we heard her message, agreed with her, and suggested that it might have been helpful if we had let the group know we were changing plans and why. She agreed, felt that she had been heard, and we learned a valuable lesson.

In addition to soliciting feedback, consultants can themselves point out areas in which they feel the consultation could have been improved. We did this by expressing that we probably should have given the director more time to discuss and explain the timeline narrative that he distributed. Had we done this, everyone would have had a clearer idea of the types of things that had been tried. As it was, we ended up spending some time during brainstorming removing ideas that had been generated but that had already been tried. This approach of discussing our own areas for improvement showed our genuineness as consultants and the true investment we had in facilitating the most useful outcomes. The consultees commented that our sharing had enhanced our trustworthiness in their eyes.

This case illustrates how important it is for consultants to be aware of group dynamics and group development during their work with multiple consultees. This particular case was easy, in that the group was one in which strong collegial relationships had long been in place and the group had functioned as a work team in many capacities. Further, the consultees were all trained mental health professionals who had expertise in group skills. With a different group, dealing with the various group dynamics and controlling the pacing of the group as it approached its task with the consultant could be critical elements related to a successful outcome.

Finally, it is worth considering which parties should be included in preliminary sessions. In this case, at the request of the counseling center staff, we conducted the preliminary exploration with the director only. Though staff members were comfortable with the director representing them, it might have been more helpful if all parties had been present initially. If that had been the case, we all would have had a solid understanding of the background and issues involved from a variety of perspectives. As it was, we processed the issues with the director in our initial meeting and then again with the staff at the group consultation. Therefore, the staff did not have the opportunity to hear the details of the director's perspectives, and we did not have time to recreate these or to play the entire videotape during the group consultation. Though this point was not particularly problematic in this consultation, it could pose a very large problem in organizations where hidden agendas and power games are prevalent. This was not the case at the counseling center.

TIPS FOR PRACTICE

- Be willing to be flexible with your plans/agenda and adapt as group dynamics and needs dictate.
- Make sure to include all interested parties in as many phases of the consultation as possible; don't be afraid to repeat a step of the process if you discover that input from an interested party was overlooked.
- Communicate with the group about the process regularly throughout the consultation, particularly if a change in plans/agenda seems warranted.
- Ask for feedback…your next consultee will thank you!

QUESTIONS FOR DISCUSSION AND REFLECTION

1. Schein's model of process consultation assumes consultees must acquire and maintain ownership of their problems, that they do not fully understand these problems, and that they can learn to design and manage change on their own. Cite three examples from this case study that illustrate these assumptions.

2. The focus of process consultation is, as its name states, on the process of problem solving rather than on solving the problem. In what ways was this consultation structured to focus on the process? From your viewpoint, is this an effective way to enter into consultation? Give rationale to support your view.

3. In the education/training model the consultant is the expert, sharing knowledge and/or skills through some kind of training, workshop, or lecture. How does this model complement the process model? How does it conflict? Was it an effective "marriage" in this case? Why or why not? 4. Assess your personal strengths and weaknesses with regard to receiving and asking for feedback. When do you "hear" what's being said? When do you discount or defend?

5. Soliciting feedback entails some risk and can sometimes be uncomfortable or downright unpleasant. Is it ethical, in consultation, to avoid the evaluation/feedback stage? Support your answer.

6. Try this exercise. (To the instructor: Please make sure that the class is well familiarized with the generic model of consultation.) Divide the class into dyads, with one person taking on the role of consultant and the other person portraying the consultee. Assume that you are the consultant in this case study.

Conduct an interview in which the consultant does a preliminary exploration of the needs leading to the request for consultation. Then engage in the same process again only having the participants switch roles.

As a follow-up exercise, have one student, acting as the consultant in this case study; conduct a group interview of the members of the counseling center. Then have the class compare the differences between conducting group and individual interviews in consultative situations similar to this.

REFERENCES AND SUGGESTED READINGS

Association for Specialists in Group Work. (2000). *Professional standards for the training of group workers.* (rev.) Alexandria, VA: Author.

Dougherty, A.M. (2005). *Psychological consultation and collaboration in school and community settings.* (4th ed.). Belmont, CA: Wadsworth.

Hansen, J.C., Himes, B. S., & Meier, S. (1990). *Consultation: Concepts and practice.* Englewood Cliffs, NJ: Prentice-Hall.

Kuh, G.D. (1993). Appraising the character of a college. *Journal of Counseling & Development, 71,* 661–668.

Randolph, D. L., & Graun, K. (1988). Resistance to consultation: A synthesis for counselor-consultants. *Journal of Counseling and Development, 67,* 182–184.

Rockwood, G. F. (1993). Edgar Schein's process versus content consultation models. *Journal of Counseling and Development, 71,* 636–638.

Ross, G. J. (1993). Peter Block's flawless consulting and the homunculus theory: Within each person is a perfect consultant. *Journal of Counseling and Development, 71,* 639–641

Schein, E. H. (1978). The role of the consultant: Content expert or process facilitator? *Personnel and Guidance Journal, 56(6),* 339–343.

Schein, E. H. (1987). *Process consultation: Lessons for managers and consultants.* (Vol. II). Reading, MA: Addison-Wesley.

Schein, E. H. (1988). *Process consultation: Its role in organization development.* (Vol. I). Reading, MA: Addison-Wesley.

Schein, E. H. (1999). *Process consultation revisited: Building the helping relationship.* Reading, MA: Addison-Wesley.

Westbrook, F.D., Kandell, J. J., Kirkland, S. E., Phillips, P. E., Regan, A. M., Medvene, A., & Oslin, Y.D. (1993). University campus consultation: Opportunities and limitations. *Journal of Counseling and Development, 76,* 684–688.

8

Process Consultation in a Health Care Setting

ELIZABETH D. BECKER-REEMS

DESCRIPTION OF THE MODEL USED

"Process consultation is a set of activities on the part of the consultant that help the client to perceive, understand, and act upon the process events that occur in the client's environment" (Schein, 1987, p. 34).

When we talk about process events in this context, we are talking about methods that people use to communicate, to problem-solve, to lead and share leadership responsibility. We also look at other internal systems or methods that people use for getting things done, such as meetings, planning, goal setting, performance evaluations, and so on.

The key to process consultation is the involvement of the consultant and the consultee in a problem-solving partnership. The consultant develops a relationship with the consultee that engenders trust and depends on mutual respect. Through this relationship, the consultee is able to identify and admit the problems that exist, as well as work with the consultant to resolve the problems (Dougherty, 2005).

Process consultation depends on the willing participation of the consultee. At the end of the process, it is the consultee who has the authority to perpetuate the changes, and the ability to stop the changes before they are truly integrated into the culture.

Actions that need to be taken to solve the problems will only have a lasting impact if the consultee is involved in the diagnosis, problem solving, and implementation of change. The consultee possesses knowledge of the organization that the consultant does not have. It is the application of this knowledge, along with the skill of the consultant in problem solving, that helps assure that the interventions are successful and of a long duration (Dougherty, 2005). Consequently, it is essential for the consultation process to be characterized by a collaborative approach, in which the consultant and consultee pool their resources.

SETTING AND BACKGROUND ISSUES

Setting

This case study is a composite of several consultation experiences that I had while working in a large acute care regional medical center located in the southeastern United States. This successful and progressive medical center possesses values and a culture that include respect for the individual and an emphasis on excellence.

With more than 3,000 employees organized into 100 different departments, the organization is complex and diverse. The medical center is recognized nationally for its clinical excellence, sound financial position, and state-of-the-art technology. As a fast-moving organization with a strong power and achievement focus, it is unusual for the medical center to allow performance problems to exist for long, without taking strong and decisive action to resolve them.

Background

The Human Resource Division of the medical center provides organizational development and consultation services to individuals, teams, departments, and to the entire organization. Although the services are readily available, there is reluctance among middle management to seek consultation for existing personnel problems. Instead, consultation services are sought for building something new, rather than repairing existing problems or systems. Management commonly seeks consultation and organization development services when a new program or service is being implemented, a new organization structure is contemplated, and when planning or collaboration with others needs to occur.

Directors perceive seeking consultation help as admitting a performance deficiency or personal lack of knowledge or skill and are therefore unlikely to use internal consultants. They want to project a strong "in-control" image in this power-oriented organization. It is more common for a vice president to recommend consultation services for a subordinate director who is experiencing a problem, than for directors to seek the services themselves.

The grapevine within the organization usually reveals problems to the Human Resource Division staff before they are approached to offer their help and support. I had learned that there were problems in the Respiratory Therapy Department from several sources, but not from the director himself. I was only slightly surprised when I received a call from the vice president of the Respiratory Therapy Department asking me to attend a meeting with him and the director of the department. They wanted to talk about a possible consultation.

GOALS OF CONSULTATION

The primary goal of this consultation was to help the consultee gain insight into the methods he was using in managing his department, and to recognize how those methods were detrimental to his performance and the overall performance of the Respiratory Therapy Department. As the case unfolds, it will become apparent that the goals of consultation were to help the consultee change his own behavior. If the consultation proved successful, the director, the department, and the entire organization would benefit (Dougherty, 2005).

CONSULTANT FUNCTION AND ROLE

In process consultation, the consultant's role is to help the consultee help himself. Process consultation builds knowledge and skills in the consultee that help him address future problems successfully (Rockwood, 1993). It does not require that the consultant be an expert in any specific area. Rather, the consultant is an expert observer, facilitator, questioner, and confronter, who helps the consultee through a self-diagnosis process and ultimately helps the consultee achieve specific goals (Schein, 1987, 1999). To be successful in process consultation, it helps to establish a collaborative mode for guiding the activities of the consultant and consultee (Kurpius, 1991).

Establishing a collaborative relationship is not an easy task. There may be barriers in the relationship between the consultant and consultee. They may have no prior knowledge of each other and must spend time, and be successful in, developing a relationship of trust and mutual respect. Or, they may have prior knowledge that leads them to question whether they can comfortably collaborate together.

As an internal consultant, one of my goals is to ensure that the relationship that is built during consultation is a positive one—one that will last so I can work effectively with the consultee in the future in additional consultations.

When the consultation is ordered, as it was in this case, developing a lasting relationship becomes even more difficult. When the consultee has not entered the consultation willingly, she or he can be defensive and suspicious. The consultee wonders whether the consultation will help personally, or merely benefit the organization. The consultee may see the consultant as the "tool of administration," rather than as a person committed to the consultee and the consultee's needs.

CONSULTEE EXPERIENCE IN CONSULTATION

In this case, the consultee had no prior experience with process consultation. He had sought expert consultation in the past from Human Resources to address disciplinary problems with staff and to resolve compensation issues.

During this consultation experience, the consultee was an active collaborator throughout the process. He defined the diagnosis steps, set goals, and developed action plans to accomplish the goals. He possessed knowledge of his department and the people and systems within it. The success of the consultation was directly related to his knowledge of his staff, his willingness to work hard to make personal changes, and his commitment to creative problem solving. It was assumed that the entire organization would benefit from the changes the consultee made (Dougherty, 2005).

APPLICATION: CONSULTANT TECHNIQUES AND PROCEDURES

Entry: A Meeting to Explore Possibilities

We scheduled the initial meeting for an hour, to be held in the vice president's office. It would not be a meeting of strangers: I had worked with the vice president on several previous projects and had come to know the director of Respiratory Therapy in the three years he had worked for the medical center. The director and I had served on task forces together and mutually attended meetings and work-related social functions throughout his tenure with the organization. I was wondering how serious the problem was and how he would view consultation.

After several minutes of congenial social talk, the vice president stated the purpose of the meeting. "Liz," he said, "I have asked you here to meet with Larry and me to start a discussion on how we can improve the situation in Respiratory Therapy. Larry and I have some ideas of what might be going wrong, but we would like some outside help. I've talked to your boss, and he is willing for you to work with us, if you have time. I believe you can be of assistance." I asked the vice president to explain the problem. Apparently, two long-term supervisors in the department had "backdoored" the director (Larry) and gone directly to the vice president for help in improving the work environment in Respiratory Therapy. Backdooring is a way of undermining the legitimate position authority of someone. It is the process of skipping your immediate manager and communicating to the next organizational level, without your manager's knowledge, consent, or approval.

The vice president and Larry met weekly as part of their routine communication process. During those meetings, Larry had shared his concerns over the high rate of turnover in the department, his frustrations with trying to make improvements with a resistant staff, and his apprehension over the department's severe morale problems. The information the two supervisors brought to the vice president was not a surprise. However, their perspective was very different from the viewpoint that Larry had expressed.

From Larry's view, the two supervisors were part of the problem. They, along with several other "old-timers," frequently expressed dissatisfaction with Larry's management style. In addition, these supervisors had a history of not communicating with him about the department's problems. These two concerns, along with the recent incident of backdooring, had created an intolerable situation. Larry was ready to take disciplinary action against the supervisors, at the very least, and fire them if there was sufficient justification.

The vice president was opposed to any disciplinary action and thought Larry needed to take a rational look at what was happening in his department.

Larry did not appear too happy with the vice president's position. I was concerned about Larry's reaction. I wondered what his relationship with his vice president was. I had hoped that the request for consultation was a mutual decision by Larry and his vice president, resulting from their desire to attempt to improve the situation in Larry's department. At this point, I was becoming concerned that Larry was not a willing participant.

Trying to put the consultation process in a positive light for Larry, I suggested that consultation might be of some help in exploring and addressing the turnover, morale, and supervisor problems. We reviewed the main elements of the consultation process and discussed how Larry and I would work together.

As we talked, I outlined the basic steps on my note pad, a copy of which I later gave to Larry for his reference. I then spent some time discussing confidentiality.

I did this deliberately to make sure the vice president would not pressure me to share information about the consultation, and to fulfill my ethical objective to acquire Larry's informed consent.

Larry had said little after his vice president told him he would not support disciplinary action with the supervisors. He asked no questions about the consultation process. His lack of responsiveness made me feel uncomfortable and caused me to wonder whether Larry really wanted to be involved in a consultation relationship with me. If Larry didn't want to be involved in this consultation, then ethically I would need to terminate the consultation relationship.

So I asked, "Larry, do you think there will be any benefit in our working together?" He stated that he really did need some help and wanted to engage in consultation. Although I still sensed some hesitation from him, I decided not to pursue it at this time. I sensed that Larry felt pressure from the vice president to participate in consultation. On the one hand, I saw Larry's ambivalence as a normal reaction to the anticipation of having to change, but, on the other, I was concerned about the effects of the pressure to participate from the vice president.

We would explore this ethical issue later, in a setting that did not include the pressure a superior can place on a subordinate.

I felt that it was important to clarify with whom I would be working during the consultation, as I was concerned about how the vice president would fit into all of this. If the vice president was bent on managing my consultation, the fact that he was Larry's immediate supervisor could have disastrous results. So I asked the vice president, "After our meeting today, I will be working directly with Larry. Is that correct? And how will you be involved?" The vice president stated that it was an assignment for Larry and me, and that he would rely on Larry, not me, to give him progress updates. I made a note of this agreement. From past experience, I knew that communicating with the vice president would be an important part of Larry's role and was something that would continue to build their relationship. Our meeting adjourned with the understanding that additional data gathering on the problem was necessary. Larry and I decided to meet again the next day to further discuss the consultation and to develop a plan for our work together.

Follow-Up to the Exploratory Meeting

When I got back to my office after the meeting, I went to my computer and documented the meeting. I summarized the content of the meeting, agreements we had reached, and observations I had made about Larry. As I completed my notes, I realized that I did not know whether the vice president had any expectations about the length of the consultation and that we had not established the specific results that he expected. I thought about sending him an e-mail message, so that I would have the information when Larry and I met the following day. Then I realized that I had almost broken one of our first agreements: Larry was supposed to communicate with the vice president, not me.

I asked the personnel staff to provide me with a list of all the employees in the Respiratory Therapy Department that included individuals' job titles and employment dates. I created a paper file and put this information into it, along with a copy of my notes. I would not gather any other data until Larry and I met and decided what information was necessary.

I believed my first meeting alone with Larry would be critical to determining how well we would relate during the consultation. I wanted to help Larry feel comfortable with the consultation process, and me. Based on my observations at the meeting with the vice president, I felt that Larry wasn't sure about the process. I also believed that he did not have full confidence in my ability to help him. I felt the need to build my credibility in Larry's eyes. I drew up a brief agenda for the first meeting I would have with Larry. I would go over the agenda with him at the beginning of our meeting and seek his approval to follow it. The agenda looked like this:

1. Share some of my educational and consultation experiences with Larry to build up my credibility.

2. Ask Larry to redefine the problem from his perspective.

3. Ask Larry his expectations for the length of the consultation relationship.

4. Come to an agreement on the roles each of us will take during the consultation.

5. Assess the degree to which we believe the culture of the medical center supports collaborative consultation.

6. Determine what Larry expects to get out of the consultation.

7. Develop a preliminary plan.

8. Ask Larry what he thinks his vice president's expectations are for results and the length of time that we have to produce such results.

9. Ask Larry how he plans to keep his vice president informed of our progress.

As I reviewed the proposed agenda, I anticipated that the meeting would take approximately two hours.

Our First Session

My office, along with all the other human resource offices, was located in a separate building from the main hospital. Larry and I agreed to meet in my office.

He wasn't ready for me to come to his office, since this would make public that he and I were engaging in problem-solving activities. Larry was not ready for that degree of commitment to this process. As Larry talked, I sensed that he felt inadequate as a director because he could not solve the problems facing his department by himself. So I initiated a discussion of how major organizations such as AT&T, GE, and Xerox have their top level of management rely on the services of internal and external consultants to deal with problems and change issues.

I tried to clarify with Larry how he might benefit from the consultation. I wanted him to know that experiencing consultation was a learning process, and, after being a consultee this one time, he would acquire the foundation of a system that he could use independently for future problem solving. He might use his newly acquired process consultation skills to help his supervisors resolve problems in the future. I wanted him to know that we would be collaborating partners, working together on solving the department's problems, and that all important decisions would be his. I also explained that my involvement would save time, provide a sounding board, and allow him to gather more information than he might obtain on his own. Finally, we discussed that either of us could terminate the consulting relationship without any fallout.

In planning our work together, I walked Larry through the steps of the consultation process. I provided him with copies of some of Edgar Schein's works (1987, 1988, 1999). We determined that this project might take four to six months if we devoted several hours each week to it. We did not set a firm termination date because we felt we needed more information to determine the scope of the problems to be solved and we still needed feedback from the vice president on his expectations.

At the end of our meeting, Larry and I spent some time talking about the culture of the medical center. Since the culture of the organization is increasingly identified as a potential barrier to a collaborative problem-solving process, I thought we should compare our perceptions and discover if the culture of the medical center would be a potential barrier. If the culture of an organization does not accept change, or if it is not open to collaboration and teamwork, then process consultation can fail. Schein strongly advocates an exploration of the underlying assumptions that exist within the culture prior to finalizing the interventions (Rockwood, 1993). Through our discussion, we identified that the culture of the organization encouraged change and that both independent and team efforts to make improvements in the organization were supported. The culture would not be a barrier to our process consultation.

The Problem Statement

During our discussion, Larry and I arrived at these statements of the problems we needed to deal with during our consultation:

- The turnover rate in the Respiratory Therapy Department was higher than desirable.

- Department morale appeared to be at an all time low.

- Backdooring was being engaged in by some of the supervisors as well as by Larry himself.

- The night shift was unhappy and felt ignored.

- Two long-term supervisors had generally negative attitudes toward the department.

These problems were multifaceted. We didn't know if these were symptoms of a larger problem or problems in their own right. We wouldn't have the answer until we completed gathering data.

Diagnosis

We decided to gather some preliminary data. I would get data about the departmental employees from the personnel files. Larry would put some subjective data together based on his knowledge of the department, its people, and its problems. Larry was to generate a list of employees and identify those he believed were positive about the department and the work environment, those who were unclear, and those who were slightly or very negative. It was during this stage that I finally got the feeling that Larry and I were connecting as a team. Really working together on the problem, combined with the nonjudgmental attitude I was projecting, helped free Larry from the worries he held about how this consultation might harm him, or worries that he had about us venturing into areas he didn't want to enter. By demonstrating the importance of his own personal view of the situation and his department, I was able to develop an atmosphere of mutual respect and validation.

For my part, I obtained turnover data for the past five years by job type, shift, and for the department as a whole. In addition, I retrieved exit interview information over the past two years. Once I had gathered the data, I analyzed it to see if there were trends or surprises. I noticed that there was no turnover in the clerical staff and little among the technicians. However, turnover was unusually high with the registered respiratory therapists who had been with the organization fewer than three years, the supervisors, and the therapists who worked the night shift. The exit interview data identified the following as the contributing reasons for leaving the medical center: lack of trust, lack of commitment of the director to his staff, and the undesirability of working the night shift.

Our Second Session

Larry and I met to review the data we had gathered. Larry's review of the subjective data indicated problems with five out of seven supervisors, four out of five night shift employees, and more than half of the registered respiratory therapists.

As we discussed the implications of the data, Larry stated that he felt the basic issue was that the supervisors were working against him. If he could get rid of several long-term supervisors, who he believed were undermining him, then the work environment of the department would improve. The more Larry and I talked, the more I realized that he was accepting little or no responsibility for contributing to the problems in the department. He did recognize, however, that getting rid of several long-term supervisors would be extremely difficult to achieve.

I shared the data I had gathered from the personnel files. I suggested that Larry and I focus on the exit interview information. The issues of lack of trust and commitment of the director to the staff seemed to hit Larry like a sledgehammer.

He suggested the possibility of gathering more data from current members of the staff because he was certain that it was "just those two supervisors who were stirring up all the trouble." We talked about the concept of 360- degree feedback, which includes input from parties at every level of the organization involved with a director. We agreed to gather one more set of data by interviewing all the supervisors, several registered therapists, and all the night shift workers. Together we designed the interview questions for the current employees.

At Larry's request, I agreed to conduct the interviews. We agreed the results of the interviews would be shared with Larry and all the people who were interviewed.

Entry Again!

Larry introduced me to the department's employees at a regularly scheduled staff meeting. Larry said that I was there to help improve the work environment through data gathering, analysis, and problem solving. He expressed his commitment to improving the environment in the department and reducing turnover. There was no discussion by the employees. I could sense the level of distrust within the department. I hoped I would be accepted as someone who wanted to help, not as one who would create more problems for the staff.

The Interviews

I scheduled meetings with the supervisors and began interviewing them. I planned an hour for each interview. After interviewing the supervisors, I interviewed the registered therapists and then the night shift employees. As it turned out, Larry was mistrusted by all but two of the supervisors. However, even those supervisors accurately corroborated the problems the other supervisors described. Apparently Larry himself was guilty of backdooring in his relationships with his supervisors. If Larry wanted to involve an employee in a project, he would go directly to the employee. The supervisor might not learn of the employee's involvement until the project was underway. If the supervisor attempted discipline and the disciplined employee went to Larry, Larry might reinterpret the problem and dismiss the disciplinary action that was taken by the supervisor. Consequently, the supervisors felt justified in their own backdooring behavior.

In addition, Larry was viewed as spending very little time in the department. He was not present for staff meetings, and in fact rarely held routine monthly staff meetings which were an organization-wide expectation for directors.

Many employees alleged that he spent most of his time enhancing his relationship with his peers, the doctors and nurses in the medical center; building a statewide reputation for himself; and making himself look good to senior management. Their message seemed to be, "A good department director stays home and Larry doesn't stay home!" Several of the people I interviewed noted that Larry had a bad habit of using the word *I* frequently during his conversations with others. This gave the impression that Larry was very self-centered and that he cared more about himself than his department and the people in it. The supervisors and all the other staff members I interviewed agreed that Larry was very intelligent, charming, and forward thinking. However, they did not trust him and did not like working with him. They claimed he was cold, insensitive, and manipulative in his communications. The supervisors were even losing respect for senior management because the communication problems had been there a long time and senior management had done nothing to alleviate them.

Based on the interviews, it appeared that the supervisors were willing to work on the problems as a group as long as they had some assurance that Larry would be willing to change his behavior. The issues with the night shift employees seemed to be tangential to the emerging problem. Larry decided to postpone addressing the night shift issues.

From the information I had gathered in my interviews, I determined that Larry was going to have to face a reality different from the one he perceived. I planned my next meeting with Larry carefully. I could envision Larry rejecting the information, rejecting me as a supporter, and rejecting the entire consultation process. During the course of my interviews, I had obtained specific examples of the problems as seen by the supervisors and other employees. I hoped the specifics would help Larry understand the problems and prevent him from dismissing them as glib generalities. If I could provide Larry with concrete examples, he might not only own them, but he might have more specific ideas about how he could change.

Our Third Session

When Larry and I met, we reviewed the information from the interviews, along with the data from the personnel files and Larry's own assessment of the morale in his department. I had already drawn some conclusions from the data but I wanted to see what Larry thought about this new information.

Larry was dismayed by the results of the interviews. After reviewing the information, he sat silently for a few moments. I suggested that we look at each item and test the validity of the supervisors' perceptions. He agreed. We started talking about what he had been able to accomplish while spending time with the doctors and nurses within the medical center. He said he didn't see his role as spending all his time in the department, and that progress would stop if he wasn't out talking and negotiating with directors and physicians every day. We talked about the excellent reputation the department had in the state and the nation. The department was highly regarded as professional and forward thinking.

Then we got to the bad news. I asked about his role within the department and the necessity for his support of his supervisors. He said that he hadn't realized that he had been backdooring the supervisors, but as he listened to the examples they shared, he knew that what the supervisors were saying was accurate.

He asked me if I had noticed that he was overusing the word *I* in his conversations, and I said yes. I suggested that he try counting the number of times that he uses *I* in conversations and simply try to use the word *we* more. At that point, Larry sighed deeply and said, "Maybe I need to make some changes first if we are going to get anywhere."

Based on this discussion, we agreed on goals and implementation plans (see Table 8.1). We did this by discussing what Larry meant when he said he would have to change. We then tried to frame these proposed changes into goals. We evaluated the goals and determined that they were very ambitious. Larry and I knew we needed supervisor involvement and agreed to share the goals with the supervisors and get their input. We also took this opportunity to discuss the nature of feedback as an intervention itself and how the feedback session would start to bridge the communication gap between Larry and the supervisors.

TABLE 8.1 *Goals and Implementation Plans*

Goal	Intervention	Action Steps
1. Clarify the organizational structure of the department by assessing the roles and responsibilities of staff, particularly Larry and the supervisors.	Implement role clarification.	a. Conduct role clarification exercises. b. Develop revised job descriptions. c. Communicate the revisions to all parties.
2. Improve the internal department communication process.	Restructure department communication process. (Munter, 2000)	a. Select a staff task force. b. Evaluate the type of meetings needed. c. Decide how to use e-mail, mailboxes, and bulletin board. d. Revise the new employee orientation program.
3. Spread ownership for the effectiveness of the department to the supervisors.	Conduct a survey feedback session with supervisors.	a. Feedback the data and interview results gathered. b. Involve supervisors in a review of the consultation goals. c. Revise goals as necessary.
4. Improve Larry's interpersonal communication skills so that he will be perceived as a more sensitive and less self-centered administrator.	Obtain communication and sensitivity training for the director.	a. Identify alternative training opportunities. b. Select an opportunity. c. Schedule and attend the training. d. Modify behavior. e. Get feedback on behavior.
5. Improve the professional relationships that Larry has with the supervisors.	Conduct team building among the management team.	a. Decide on team-building activities. b. Schedule and communicate the team-building sessions. c. Conduct the activities.
6. Discontinue any backdooring by anyone in the department.	Conduct a force field analysis.	a. Brainstorm barriers to faceto- face communication. b. Identify measures that can be taken to overcome those barriers. c. Implement those measures.

The Feedback Session

Larry decided to lead the session even though it was somewhat threatening to him to do so. He shared the information that he and I had gathered. It was a very uncomfortable meeting for everyone involved, but at the same time there was a sense of hope and an atmosphere of honesty that had been missing in recent department interactions. Many of the employees were pleasantly surprised that Larry owned some of the responsibility for the problems the department was experiencing. Several employees offered ideas about the goals that should be pursued to enhance the department's effectiveness. No one suggested that Larry should be replaced. The goals that we came away with after the meeting with the staff were much the same as the goals Larry and I had agreed upon earlier.

Our Fourth Session

After the feedback meeting, Larry and I spent two hours in my office unwinding and rehashing the meeting. It had been a long and difficult day. Larry and I had achieved a new level of trust and understanding. It was as if he understood that his staff did not want a different director, just a changed Larry. They would be willing to change if he would.

Implementation: Our Fifth Session

Larry and I met the following week. We took the goals, interventions, and action steps, added time frames and assigned responsibility for taking the action. We included regular "How's it going?" meetings between Larry and me and progress update meetings between Larry and his vice president.

Disengagement: Subsequent Sessions

At our "How's it going?" meetings, we adjusted the timeline and talked about the reception the various interventions were receiving in his department. By now, Larry had the supervisors involved in conducting some of the sessions, and I was becoming less involved.

As the consultation was drawing to a close, I wanted to get some feedback from Larry. Instead of a formal evaluation, we agreed to meet to discuss how things had gone from both of our perspectives. I wanted answers to the following questions:

- Was I clear in communicating with him?
- Did he feel like he could trust me?
- Did I respond to him and his department in a timely manner?
- Was I sensitive to his needs and concerns?
- Did he believe the interventions were helpful?
- Did I stay within my role as collaborator, or did I step out of it and give advice?
- Did he learn process consultation skills during the consultation?
- Did he feel like we had truly collaborated?

Larry was glad to see the consultation come to an end. He said that he felt like his behavior was under a microscope and that he was under tremendous pressure. He had not slept well in the period encompassing the consultation and had been concerned about his job security. He said that one thing he liked about me as a consultant was how, when he asked for advice, I had suggested that we brainstorm together, rather than give him easy solutions. He liked the give and take of collaboration and noted that he would miss that. In addition, he discussed the benefits of being able to come to my office to talk about what was happening. We agreed to update each other every two weeks for the next two months to see how things were progressing. He asked me to let him know if I heard him use the word *I* frequently in his conversation. It had become something of a joke between us.

I had also established a fairly close relationship with several of the supervisors. I told them that I would stop by their offices occasionally to see how things were going. I let them know that I could come to a staff meeting or management team meeting to observe progress if they wanted to invite me. I knew I would miss my meetings and appointments with Respiratory Therapy, but that is part of what consultation is about. Near the end of our consultation experience, Larry and I wrote a brief report of the consultation process. He gave a copy to his vice president, and I gave one to mine.

IMPLICATIONS FOR PRACTICE

The consultation experience outlined in this chapter has several implications for practice. First and foremost, each time I am involved in a consultation, I learn something new that I can apply to subsequent consultations. For example, from this consultation I realized that working with Larry as the primary consultee did not negate involvement with other consultees. The purpose of the consultation was to help the department director solve problems with his supervisors and staff. However, as the consultation progressed, the supervisors became direct as well as indirect recipients of consultation services. Since the consultation lasted almost six months, relationships were formed with supervisors as well as the director. Those relationships enhanced the quality of the consultation experience for me, provided learning opportunities for the supervisors, and assured a more lasting impact from the consultation.

Second, consultants need to be careful not to assume that the problem has been correctly identified until data has been gathered and analyzed (Cooper & O'Connor, 1993; Beer & Spector, 1993). Initially, it appeared that two long-term supervisors were the problem. However, the data gathering eventually identified a variety of causes for the problems, including that one cause was the consultee himself. Larry's involvement in the problems only became apparent after interviewing the supervisors and several employees. Individual interviews are a rich source of data and, though they are time consuming, frequently provide pertinent information that cannot be gathered elsewhere. My experience with interviews suggests that their quality is enhanced by opportunities to focus on specific ideas that emerge from the process. Quality interviews often allow room for the interviewee to elaborate in detail when appropriate.

From the outset consultants need to stress the benefits and learning opportunities gained by participating in consultation. In order to maintain the self-esteem of the consultee and to ensure the success of the remedies or solutions that are eventually implemented, consultees themselves need to be in charge of the change process from the outset of the consultation relationship. (Kotter, 1996)

Collaboration in process consultation is an essential tool in assuring the lasting effectiveness of interventions. It would seem likely that the success of collaboration as a tool for the consultant could be measured by the ability of the consultant to establish a relationship with the consultee. However, that is just part of the equation. There are a number of other variables that influence how well the collaborative process will work. According to Kurpius (1991), the consultant needs to consider relationship issues, faulty expectations of roles, or the lack of a clear definition of the problem. Beyond these issues, the work culture will also have a significant bearing on one's ability to establish a collaborative relationship. If the environment is unsettled, it is more receptive to changes that may arise due to the consultation. If the organization and the consultee are open to new ways of working, then collaboration is more likely to be a workable methodology for problem solving. If either element of the work environment is not present, then collaborative consultation will likely not work (Kurpius, 1991).

Formative evaluation is very important in process consultation. At the beginning of the consultation, I told Larry that one of the benefits of consultation would be learning. During the consultation relationship, we need to remember to take the time to process with consultees what has transpired. By reflecting on actions taken, and the results that such actions produce, we can facilitate the learning of the consultee.

Consultation needs to be viewed as a desirable and legitimate enterprise within the organization (Schein, 1990, 1999). Larry initially resisted the idea of involving an internal consultant to help solve the problems in his department. He saw needing help as a personal weakness and did not recognize that the use of internal resources could be a productive management technique.

He believed that consultation is used in organizations when all else fails. But consultation should be like other problem-solving strategies; it should be part of our daily work lives. Then, it would become a more acceptable endeavor in which directors and other prospective consultees might engage.

TIPS FOR PRACTICE

• Building a strong positive relationship with the consultee will smooth the entire consulting process.

• Look at the consultee's environment as an organic system, with interconnecting parts that are all affected by changes in any segment.

• Be realistic about your limits; involve others when you don't possess the necessary knowledge or skills.

• Work diligently at maintaining the self-esteem of all who are involved. People are more willing to change when they sense that they are respected and valued.

QUESTIONS FOR DISCUSSION AND REFLECTION

1. A goal of process consultation is for the consultee to take away new skills that she or he can apply to similar situations in the future. How was this goal met? How was Larry empowered by this process?

2. The voluntary nature of consultation, the boundary between counseling and consulting, and confidentiality were all potential ethical landmines in this case. Were there ethical compromises? If so, define and indicate what you might have done differently. If not, what specifically was done to avoid the ethical breaches?

3. Was the consultant able to maintain confidentiality with the consultee? How was confidentiality maintained? Could the consultant have done anything differently?

4. Process consultation is supposed to address the human processes in an organization. It is becoming an increasingly relevant activity in today's work environment. What are characteristics of work environments today that make this consultation model more applicable now than in the past? What were the human processes that this consultation experience addressed?

5. A key premise of all models of consultation is that consultation is a totally voluntary activity for all concerned. Given the "top down" nature of the referral in this case, was this premise in place at the outset? What concerns would this raise if you were the consultant?

6. The line between counseling and consulting can become very thin. In this instance, the consultee's personal issues were clearly involved in the work-related problem. How would you evaluate the consultant's handling of this sensitive area? What are two ways you might have approached it differently?

7. Internal consultants face challenges to a different degree than external consultants do. What are some of the challenges of internal consulting that were identified in this case study?

REFERENCES AND SUGGESTED READINGS

Beer, M., & Spector, B. (1993).Organizational diagnosis: Its role in organizational learning. *Journal of Counseling and Development, 71,* 642–650.

Behring, S.T., & Ingraham, C. L. (1998). Culture as a central component of consultation: A call to the field. *Journal of Educational and Psychological Education, 9,* 57–72.

Block, P. (2000). *Flawless consulting: A guide to getting your expertise used* (2nd ed.). San Francisco: Jossey-Bass.

Bramlett, R. K., & Murphy, J. J. (1998). School psychology perspectives on consultation: Key contributions to the field. *Journal of Educational and Psychological Consultation, 9,* 29–55.

Carson, A. D., & Lowman, R. L. (2002). Individual-level variables in organizational consultation. In R. L. Lowman (Ed.), *Handbook of organizational consulting psychology: A comprehensive guide to theory, skills, and techniques* (pp. 5-26). San Francisco: Jossey-Bass.

Cooper, S. E., & O'Connor, Jr., R.M. (1993). Standards for organizational consultation assessment and evaluation instruments. *Journal of Counseling and Development, 71,* 651–660.

Dougherty, A.M. (2005). *Psychological consultation and collaboration in school and community settings* (4th ed.) Belmont, CA: Wadsworth.

French, W. L., & Bell, C. H., Jr. (1999). *Organization development: Behavioral science interventions for organization improvement* (6th ed.). Englewood Cliffs, NJ: Prentice- Hall.

Fuqua, D. R., & Kurpius, D. J. (1993) .Conceptual models in organizational consultation. *Journal of Counseling and Development, 71,* 607–618.

Hicks, M.D., & Peterson, D. B. (1997). Just enough to be dangerous: The rest of what you need to know about development. *Consulting Psychology Journal, 49,* 171–193.

Kilburg, R. R. (1998).Coaching and executive character: Core problems and basic approaches. *Consulting Psychology Journal, 49,* 281–299.

Kotter, J.P. (1996) *Leading change.* Boston, MA: Harvard Business School Press, 20-23, 95-100 and 101-115.

Kurpius, D. J. (1991).Why collaborative consultation fails: A matrix for consideration. *Journal of Educational and Psychological Consultation, 2,* 193–195.

Levinson, H. (1996). Executive coaching. *Consulting Psychology Journal, 48,* 115–123.

Levinson, H. (2002). Psychological consultation to organizations: linking assessment and intervention. In R. L. Lowman (Ed.), *Handbook of organizational consulting psychology: A comprehensive guide to theory, skills, and techniques* (pp. 415-449). San Francisco: Jossey-Bass.

Munter, M. (2000) *Guide to managerial communication.* Upper Saddle River, NJ: Prentice Hall, 95-103.

Rockwood, G. F. (1993). Edgar Schein's process versus content consultation models. *Journal of Counseling and Development, 71,* 636–638.

Schein, E. H. (1987). *Process consultation: Lessons for managers and consultants.* (Vol. II). Reading, MA: Addison-Wesley.

Schein, E. H. (1987). *Process consultation: Its role in organization development.* (Vol. I). Reading, MA: Addison-Wesley.

Schein, E. H. (1990).Organization culture. *American Psychologist, 45,* 109–119.

Schein, E. H. (1999). *Process consultation revisited: Building the helping relationship.* Reading, MA: Addison-Wesley.

Tobias, L. (1996).Coaching executives. *Consulting Psychology Journal, 48,* 87–95.

PART IV

Collaboration

Over the past decade, collaboration has become an increasingly important service function for counselors, psychologists, social workers, and other human service professionals. In collaboration, human service professionals serve as team members and take on some responsibility for the outcome of the case or program being dealt with.

In Chapter 9, DeEsch and Murphy present a case involving collaboration in a university reading and writing center. One interesting aspect of this case is its illustration of the necessity of a team leader. Boat and Boat, in Chapter 10, present a case of school-based mental health collaboration.

You may want to note that in this case the team members did not always function smoothly together. Pay particular attention to the relationship between the school counselor and the school psychologist in this case.

9

Collaboration in a University Reading and Writing Center

JESSE B. DEESCH AND JAMES MURPHY

DESCRIPTION OF THE MODEL USED

The case described in this chapter details the experiences of a collaboration team comprised of graduate student interns from a school counselor, school psychologist, school administrator, and a reading/language arts programs. The primary purpose of the collaboration was to develop a pre-service model for collaboration training and to provide collaborative educational and psychological services for the students, parents, and staff of a Center for Reading and Writing.

Caplan and Caplan (1993) define collaboration as "an interprofessional method in which a mental health specialist establishes a partnership with another professional worker, network, group, or team of professionals in a community field or a human services institution" (p. 295). According to West (1990) it is a process of shared decision making; it is an interactive-planning, decision-making, or problem-solving process involving two or more team members. The outcome of an educational collaboration focuses on changes in knowledge, skills, attitudes, or behaviors at one or more of three levels: student, staff or parent, or the system. The purpose of collaboration is to improve assessments, delivery of interventions, and intervention results with all team members equally responsible for the well-being of the student or the presenting concern (Caplan & Caplan, 1993). Phillips and McCullough (1990, p. 295) summarize the central tenets of collaboration as the members of the team having a:

- joint responsibility for problems
- joint accountability and recognition of problem resolution
- belief that pooling talents and resources is mutually advantageous
- belief that teacher and/or student problem resolution merits expenditure of time
- belief that correlates of collaboration are important and desirable

In the case of Brad, as presented in this chapter, the members involved in the collaboration team all shared in the responsibility of assessing the student needs and determining educational and psychosocial interventions. In collaboration, all professionals can be involved in interventions, whereas in traditional consultation, the consultant is not involved.

In recent years there is an increase in the function of educators' uses of collaboration and consultation, especially for the school counselor. More school professionals value collaboration with colleagues and view it as an accepted and expected aspect of professional behavior. The school counselor ideally serves as a catalyst for promoting systemic school wide and district wide collaborative services to meet the developmental needs of students (Rowley, Sink, and MacDonald, 2002). School counselors, in the evolving comprehensive developmental school counseling curriculum initiative, are expected to work cooperatively with other school professionals to better serve the students (Shoffner & Briggs, 2001; Sink & Yillik-Downer, 2001). Counselor education programs have increased the focus on preparing school counselors to initiate effective collaborative partnerships with other school professionals (Bemak, 2000; Sabella & Booker, 2003). This increased emphasis is especially true for the school counselor and the school psychologist working more collaboratively in the delivery of their respective functions (Staton & Gilligan, 2003). As is emphasized in this article, preservice level collaborative experiences in which counselor educators and school counseling intern students having an actual collaborative experience together can serve as a valuable learning experience (Clark & Horton-Parker, 2002). Also, the emphasis in school counselor education programs is increasing in promoting the school counselor and the school administrator working more cooperatively and with increased appreciation of the functions and responsibilities of the respective professions (Shoffner & Williamson, 2000).

However, the evolution of formal education in Western cultures continues to lead to an isolation of teachers in closed classrooms. Teachers are charged with the ultimate responsibility for their students' outcomes. "There is a shift away from the Newtonian ideas of simplicity, hierarchy, mechanics, assembly, and objectivity that have nourished our current view of the world. The new view is more integrative, holistic, collective, cooperative, and organizational" (Dettmer, Thurston, & Dyck, 1993, p. 386). With this continued changing view and with the continued relatively limited prospect for increased material or human resources, it is imperative that existing human resources be used more effectively. This effectiveness can be accomplished through collaboration among members of the school community.

In the wake of school violence and national trauma, children have needs that require school professionals who are versed in mental health knowledge as well as traditional pedagogy (Marlow, Bloss, & Bloss, 2000). The entire school community is now an integral part of the education program and collaboration among professionals must be present. Collaboration is intrinsic to school reform and to responding to the changing needs of students (Dettmer et al., 1993; Friend & Cook, 2003).

In collaborative schools professionals are resources for one another in attaining the common goals of delivering high quality services (Rowley, 2000; Smith, 1987). Collaborating school professionals reduce overlapping roles and functions, fill gaps in existing services, and increase their self-efficacy by identifying with colleagues who share a common mission while possessing unique and complementary knowledge and skills. School counselors and teachers working together produce a more nurturing environment (Marlow et al., 2000). Collaboration yields many benefits, including reduced competing for diminishing resources, elimination of service duplication, and diversified problem solving (Dougherty, 2005). Facilitating communication and cooperation among the relevant collaborative members is essential (Friend & Cook, 2003).

SETTING AND BACKGROUND ISSUES

Setting

The setting for the case study is the Rider University Center for Reading and Writing. The Center, located on the Rider campus, has an international reputation for serving children in the local geographic area. Offerings include programs for gifted and average students, and for those with special needs. Center staff offer students specific strategies for dealing with varied types of reading materials and strategies that help children become effective writers.

Educational and psychoeducational evaluations are offered throughout the year; psychological assessment is also available. All offerings are designed to improve students' self-esteem as learners. In addition to the services for students and their parents, the Center has a long-standing history of providing research and training opportunities for undergraduate and graduate students in education. The Center serves approximately 250 students and parents annually.

Background

Collaboration at the Center had been occurring sporadically and unsystematically between the Rider University Graduate Reading and Language Arts Program and the School Psychology Program. In recent years, a close, ongoing collaboration had developed between the Rider University School Counseling Program and the School Psychology Program. It reached the point where the two programs were combined for educational and administrative purposes with a commitment to include collaborative training experiences in counseling, consultation, and intervention development (Rowley, 2000). More recently, faculty of other graduate education programs agreed to commit to systematically promote the value of teamwork in public school settings. The faculty shared the belief of others who stated that collaboration and teamwork must be experienced directly by future professionals during their pre-service education period to maximize the possibilities they would enter their fields with a strong commitment to, and skills for, effective collaboration (Clark & Horton-Parker, 2002; Shofner, 2000).

The faculty believed that modeling collaboration directly with each other, in the presence of student interns who were functioning as a separate collaboration team, would facilitate a mind-set in the interns for using collaboration in their professional lives. It was determined that the Center for Reading and Writing was an ideal setting to establish these collaborative teams. Three teams were established for the project described in this chapter. The *Intern Collaboration Team* consisted of graduate students who were completing some portion of their required field experience. This included students from graduate programs in school counseling, school psychology, educational administration, and reading/language arts. The *Faculty Collaboration Team* consisted of the program advisors from School Counseling, School Psychology, Educational Administration, and Reading and Language Arts. The *Intern/Faculty Collaboration Team* consisted of all members of the Intern Collaboration Team and the Faculty Collaboration Team.

GOALS OF COLLABORATION

Within a collaborative format, the goals are for participants to learn about boundaries, alliances, coalitions, family and school structures, triadic relationships, and other systemic and ecosystemic concepts and to work on their own professional problems individually or in groups.

Successful schools are identified by the frequency and extent to which staff discuss academic practices, collaboratively design materials, and share and critique one another (Little, 1982). When assimilated throughout the school, the collaborative ethic empowers professionals to assist each other in solving problems.

Attaining and maintaining a collaborative ethic in the schools is not a simple task. It has an underlying theme of shifting from an individual locus of control to a systems-thinking process. Although school systems are not totally opposed to systems thinking, most educators have not been trained in it. There are, in addition, many political, economic, and personal obstacles to be overcome when attempting to function as a team versus working individually or when working as an interdisciplinary team (O'Callaghan, 1993). Collaboration recognizes the complexity of the goals in the school that require a joint effort. The process respects the creativity generated by professionals working together, appreciates the sharing of joint problem solving, and recognizes the power of group process. Professionals committed to collaboration create a climate of a community of learners. The process goes beyond the sharing of ideas; it requires a desire to search through creative efforts to reach mutually agreed-upon strategies. Collaboration among professionals is based on the philosophy that all professionals have something important to contribute to the process. Collaboration formally recognizes the expertise and competence of those who work in schools to make decisions to improve learning, focuses accountability for decisions, nurtures and stimulates new leaders at all levels, and increases both the quantity and quality of communication (Keys, 2000).

The two primary goals of the collaboration presented in this case were to develop a pre-service model for training professionals to have a direct experience as collaborative team members and to provide professional educational and psychological collaborative services for the students attending the Center for Reading and Writing. The training component was designed to investigate the possibility of:

- establishing a formal component in the university professional training programs
- gathering data on how effective collaboration develops among experienced professionals and graduate students in the disciplines of school counseling, school psychology, and school administration
- gathering data on the value of effective collaboration on the delivery of services to students

The service component involved collaboration for the Center and was to provide:

- support for the staff
- direct service to the students
- direct service to the parents
- academic and psychological support services for the Center

COLLABORATORS' FUNCTIONS AND ROLES

For collaboration to develop, participants must share a common vision and agree on a common mission. In the case described in this chapter, all collaboration team members, on all three teams, had the common vision of a holistic approach.

Emphasis was placed on creating a climate of trust, respect, openness, active listening, clear communication, and willingness to risk in sharing ideas.

All of these traits have been identified as fundamental requirements for effective collaboration. The motivation for a common mission for each team was to identify and resolve problems, focus on the issues presented by the Center's staff, and achieve quality results through consensus of the collaboration team members.

A critical issue related to successful collaboration is the need for one team member to be recognized as the leader. Caplan and Caplan (1993; 1999) strongly endorse this concept that one person be responsible for initiating and maintaining the collaborative endeavor. Likewise, O'Callaghan (1993) states that, for school-based collaboration to work, someone has to direct it. Someone has to identify the relevant collaborators, assess their level of functioning, conduct collaborative team meetings when necessary, and monitor follow-up efforts.

Initiating and maintaining collaborative efforts is an appropriate role of the school counselor. Counselors, with their unique training in communication skills, problem solving, team and group facilitation, consultation, and coordination, play key roles in the current reformation taking place in the schools. The evolving functions of the school counselor as a human relations specialist, a facilitator of team building, a resource broker of services, an information processor, and a promoter of positive student outcomes are all traits of one whom ideally initiates collaboration (Allen, 1994).

Concurrent with the shift of the school counselor's role and function, the American Psychological Association (APA) Task Force on Comprehensive and Coordinated Psychological Services for Children adopted a recommendation for professional psychology to take a leadership role in collaborative services.

There is a growing support for school psychologists to facilitate a service integration approach that emphasizes interdisciplinary coordination and collaboration (Bemak, 2000; Paavola, Carey, Cobb, & Illback, 1996).With these noted evolving trends, school counselors and school psychologists share a holistic orientation to human development, along with a common knowledge and skills base in many areas.

Training standards for both professions include skill development in the areas of assessment, consultation, and counseling, and in facilitating the delivery of comprehensive services within a team concept (Council for Accreditation and Related Educational Programs, 1994; National Association of School Psychologists, 1994). Thus, the basis for effective collaboration exists between school counselors and school psychologists.

For the training project described in this chapter, all members (faculty and interns) agreed to maintain a journal chronicling their experiences during the collaboration. The Intern Collaboration Team met with their respective faculty supervisors for individual supervision. The Intern/Faculty Collaboration Team met weekly to process concerns of the Intern Collaboration Team. At these meetings Faculty Collaboration Team members shared their conceptions of the roles and functions of professional issues of collaboration and the respective professional disciplines. Special effort was made by faculty to model effective collaborative behaviors throughout the experience. Each Intern/Faculty Team meeting was videotaped for use in individual and group supervision.

Collaborators' Experiences during the Process

As the Intern/Faculty Team met on a weekly basis, trust, honesty, and openness became the accepted norms, the identified traits of effective collaborative teams. As each collaborative team developed, the traits were expressed in the following behaviors of all team members:

- willingness to self-disclose and ask questions of other members
- understanding of and respect for the contributions of other members
- understanding of and appreciation for the potential value of each discipline in helping children
- awareness of the best practices in each profession
- understanding of the need to continually attend to the group process as well as the individual reactions of team members
- awareness of the fragile nature of communication and collaboration
- awareness of the factors that dilute group cohesiveness and the inevitability of these factors in field settings

As noted earlier, the need for a designated leader of the collaboration team is clearly expressed by Caplan and Caplan (1993;1999). They note that for mental health professionals to succeed as collaborators, there must be an accepted hierarchical quality to the collaboration team. From the onset of this project, no one person was designated as the leader. In the absence of a designated leader, confusion arose on several occasions. For example, the primary confusion was about which element of the project was more important: the observation of how collaboration works or the actual delivery of collaboration services for the students at the Center. As the semester progressed, serving students evolved into the primary goal of the Intern Collaboration Team. Although still important, the investigation of the development of the collaboration process was minimized by the Intern Team during the early and middle stages of the project. We believe this was a result of a lack of a designated collaboration team leader.

Early in the experience, each team became very sensitive to the need for active leadership. Members of each team requested clear direction and purpose for the teams' existence. As the teams matured, their focus became more group process directed and less content directed to a point where both elements became balanced (in this sense, the term *group process* refers to interactions and relationships among members in the group). The identification of a team leader for each of the teams might have hastened the team maturation process. Viewing the process and content as two threads of one string is a means of conceptualizing group facilitation and group membership. Each collaboration team increasingly experienced the importance of the process of the groups' functioning and how this was significant to the quality of the respective groups' performances.

The awareness of the impact of group process is consistent with the findings of Blackman, Hayes, Reeves, & Paisley (2002), Gladding (1995), Kormanski (1995), Kottler (1994), and Yalom (1995).

APPLICATION: COLLABORATION TEAM TECHNIQUES AND PROCEDURES

Entry

The collaboration took place in the University Center for Reading and Writing, as described earlier. One of the first functions of the Intern Team was to observe the class during instructional periods with a reading specialist. During the early phases of team development, all interns observed the interaction between the teacher and the children and then discussed their observations during their team meeting after the students left the Center. As a result, the interns developed a common understanding of the type of observations that the Faculty Team recommended and developed a trust in each others' observations. This increased the reliability of specific behavioral observations. The Faculty Team also observed the children in the class and the Intern Team meetings and shared their observations at appropriate times during the Intern/Faculty Team meetings.

During the early Intern/Faculty Team meetings, each intern team member shared her observations about each child in the class. As the meetings progressed, the team meetings began to take a collaborative, problem-solving tone.

Diagnosis and Problem Analysis

During the routine sharing of observation data, Brad was identified as a student about whom each Intern/Faculty Team member had some concern. By the third week, the team began to focus on Brad and one other student as needing team intervention. The collaborative process was already evident at this point: Brad was referred to the Intern Collaboration Team, by the Intern/Faculty Team. While this is not an unusual practice in clinical and hospital settings, it is not a typical mode of operation in public schools. Faculty wanted to closely observe this aspect of the collaborative team model for future applications in inclusive school settings, that is, in schools where more than one professional, working on a team, might routinely interact with the same class or group of students. Although all Intern Team members described specific concerns about Brad, the counselor, psychologist, and administrator deferred to the intern teacher team member. The teacher identified some concerns of her own, which were similar to those of other team members, and accepted the concerns described by other team members as valid and in need of intervention. Specifi- cally, Brad tended to rush through his weekly contract. At the beginning of each session, the teacher shared with each student a preliminary contract that she had developed in advance. The student provided input and, within a few minutes, a final contract was agreed upon concerning the workload of the student for that two-hour session.

Brad always agreed to his contract but without the enthusiasm displayed by most of the other students. When the teacher mentioned this to Brad, he would shrug his shoulders and tell her it was "okay." He would then work rapidly and somewhat impulsively and complete his work about 15 minutes before the end of the allocated contracted time. When the teacher suggested to Brad that he engage in other activities after completing his contract, he would state that he had completed his contract and really did not have to become involved in additional work because it was not in his contract. All Intern/Faculty Collaboration Team members observed these behaviors.

The counselor and psychologist also observed that Brad seemed to hang back and avoid socializing with the other students in the class, and that he frequently moved his chair away from the other students. They also noticed that Brad looked at them and the other observers in the room much more frequently than did the other students in the class. The counselor, psychologist, and teacher also noted that Brad frequently was off task during the segment of the class during which students worked on composing text on the computer.

Teacher attempts to redirect Brad's attention to the task frequently resulted in his engaging the teacher in conversation, resulting in even more time off task. The counselor and psychologist observed an increase in off-task behavior following individual attention by the teacher aimed at assisting Brad in completing the assigned task. Brad would continue to use the computer but would shift screens to access options other than the task at hand. His immediate response to attempts to set limits was to try to prove to the teacher that he was complying with the "letter of the law." Within the framework of the collaborative model taught by the counseling and school psychology programs, the counselor and psychologist used a problem identification protocol similar to the process employed in behavioral consultation (Bergan & Kratochwill, 1990). Since Brad was new to the Center, the teacher did not have much of the information necessary to engage in problem analysis. Brad's Center records contained no information provided directly from the sending school. When Brad was identified as a student in need of assistance, the administrator on the Intern Collaboration Team reviewed his records again and gathered background information concerning his parents' perceptions of his functioning at home and at his sending school.

The administrator also contacted Brad's parents, outlined some of the initial concerns identified by the Intern/Faculty Team, and obtained permission to exchange information with the sending school. The counselor and psychologist continued to conduct systematic observations of Brad's time on task, conversations with the teacher and other students, and his degree of compliance with teacher directives.

The counselor scheduled an Intern Team meeting, involving herself, the school psychologist, and the teacher, with Brad's parents to engage their participation in the intervention process.

The Intern Collaboration Team made decisions regarding specific functions of team members, with occasional consultation with the faculty supervisor team. The ongoing communication among team members had resulted in increased understanding of both the contemporary roles and functions of each profession represented on the team and also of the individual strengths of each team member. This familiarity compensated to some degree for the fact that none of the collaboration teams identified a leader, nor had one person emerged as the team leader.

The Intern Team appeared comfortable making decisions by consensus. The counselor and psychologist, having the most familiarity with problem-solving skills, tended to facilitate the team meetings aimed at problem identification and problem analysis. During the problem analysis phase of this collaboration, goals were clarified and information that had been gathered by team members was shared and analyzed by the group. It was the group's consensus that Brad's behaviors appeared to be compliance based as opposed to skill based and that similar behavior patterns had been observed in his sending school.

The Intern/Faculty Team reviewed the strategies implemented by Brad's sending school classroom teacher to help Brad increase his time on task and to reduce his avoidance behaviors when redirected to the task by the teacher. The parents had acknowledged that the sending classroom teacher had noted these concerns to them. The counselor and psychologist felt that the parents did not fully understand the potential negative effects of Brad's behaviors. The team added another goal for the collaboration: the parents would more clearly understand the nature and consequences of Brad's apparent low level of commitment to his educational program.

Following the data collection process, which took one week, the Intern/ Faculty Team identified the goals for this collaboration:

- explore and possibly revise the contracting system to address the issue of a student rushing through his contract and refusing to engage in other activities

- increase Brad's time on task during his sessions at the Center

- increase the reading teacher's awareness of when Brad might be using avoidance behavior

- increase the reading teacher's repertoire of strategies to redirect students' attention to the task with a minimum of avoidance behavior

- increase Brad's active participation in his program at the Center, as evidenced by his increased participation in developing his contract and his increased on-task behavior during the computer segment of his session

The Intern/Faculty Collaboration Team developed a plan to address each of the preceding goals. It was decided that the Intern Collaboration Team would meet with the director of the Center and the Faculty Collaboration Team to explore the system of developing and revising student contracts. The Intern/Faculty Team decided that the teacher, in turn, would conference with Brad and state her observations and concerns to him. Brad would be informed of the rationale for contracts and that each contract specified a minimal expectation for completed work. Brad and the teacher would then generate a menu of acceptable activities in which he could engage to meet the requirements of the contracts. The Intern/Faculty Collaboration Team then discussed ways to increase Brad's on-task behaviors. This discussion took into account the values and skills of each team member involved in the direct implementation of the intervention. It was decided that the counselor would continue to chart Brad's time on task and the teacher would, when appropriate, provide smiles and positive verbal statements to Brad relating to his on-task behavior. In addition, the psychologist would meet with Brad for 15 minutes at the end of each week.

The goals of these meetings would be to identify Brad's interests, validate his strengths as a learner and as a person, and identify potential school-related issues that might be contributing to his low level of compliance to school-related demands. The counselor, psychologist, and administrator interns planned two additional meetings with Brad's parents, aimed at increasing their awareness of the ramifications of his current behavior patterns. The agenda for the meetings included the communication of Brad's strengths, his reactions to the team's interventions, and the solicitation of additional strengths, reward preferences, and other ideas from the parents as to what strategies might be effective with him.

With regard to Brad's tendency to engage in arguments and discussions when prompted by the teacher to refocus on the task, the Intern/Faculty Team decided that the teacher would conference with Brad and review her expectations for behavior during his time at the Center. The Director of the Center made herself available to assist the teacher, should the need arise. The teacher wanted to meet with Brad alone. In addition to the conference, the team decided that the teacher would clearly state each directive to Brad, after ensuring that she had captured his attention, and that she would reinforce him with a smile and a light pat on the back when he complied. When he did not comply with the initial verbal prompt by the teacher, she would stay with him and initiate the next step of the task herself, engaging him nonverbally. The teacher would remain with him and model the appropriate response while providing no other attention to him during this time.

When Brad attempted to change the subject or engage in argumentative behavior, the teacher would ignore these statements and continue to engage in the appropriate task. If Brad continued to avoid the task, the teacher would accompany him to the office and call his mother, who had previously agreed to assist the team in this intervention. His mother would direct Brad to comply with the teacher's directive. These procedures were clearly communicated to Brad by the teacher during their conference and agreed to by his mother.

Implementation

The interventions were implemented during the fourth week of the nine-week cycle. During the implementation phase, which lasted for four weeks, the Intern Team set aside a period of time during which they shared information, provided the teacher with feedback and encouragement for her efforts, monitored the plan, and made necessary revisions. Brad quickly developed a positive relationship with the psychologist and looked forward to their weekly meetings. Brad also continued to connect positively with the counselor, who was in the classroom each week monitoring his on-task behaviors.

The teacher expressed confidence in her ability to clearly state her expectations to Brad and to review the purpose and implementation of the contract with him. The teacher did share doubts about her ability to remain focused on the redirection of Brad's attention to, and participation in, the appropriate tasks during the computer portion of the sessions. The Intern/Faculty Collaboration Team helped the teacher rehearse her strategies and used role-playing to assist her in preparing herself for various responses by Brad. The team also demonstrated possible parent meeting scenarios by using role-playing techniques. All team members expressed an awareness that they were not working alone; all team members were "present" with each other in spirit. This increased the confidence and willingness of the Intern Team members to take reasonable risks.

Evaluation/Disengagement

The effectiveness of the interventions was monitored on a weekly basis during the implementation phase. Following the initial conference Brad had with the teacher, there was a noticeable difference in his attitude toward being in the Center and in his willingness to actively participate in his educational program.

He assisted in developing a menu of additional activities to be pursued if he completed his initial contract before it was time to move to the computer room. Beginning with the fifth week, and continuing through the end of the eighth week, his time on task improved significantly and was consistent with that of the other students in his class. This level of time on task was quite satisfactory to the teacher and other Center personnel.

With the facilitation of the psychologist, Brad identified several strengths of which he was proud. He enjoyed this activity and remarked to the psychologist that at his sending school he never had an opportunity to talk about what he liked about himself. He also expressed surprise that the staff at the Center seemed to enjoy spending individual time with him. Brad identified several reward preferences to the psychologist during these sessions, which were later communicated to the reading teacher, his parents, and his sending school teacher.

During computer time, Brad continued to experience difficulty remaining on task during the fifth and sixth week. The teacher implemented the intervention plan, and Brad did return to the appropriate task following one verbal prompt and several minutes of teacher modeling, during which his off-task verbalizations were ignored. It was not necessary to call Brad's mother on any occasion. During the seventh and eighth week, he returned to the appropriate task following the one verbal prompt by the teacher.

The meetings with Brad's parents were held with limited success. They reported that they appreciated being treated as full partners in the process and not blamed for causing Brad's difficulties. They continued to be critical of the efforts of the sending school and believed that the same positive results that were obtained at the Center could have occurred in the sending school, had sufficient attention been given to solutions as opposed to identifying problems. The Intern/Faculty Collaborative Team offered to communicate with the sending school and work with the school personnel. The parents were reminded that the Center had resources that might not be available in the public school and that the interventions developed by the sending school might vary from the Center's due to differences in their environments. The parents were encouraged to develop a partnership with the sending school.

During the final week of the Center's cycle, the collaborative effort was evaluated. Each team member concluded that the desired changes in Brad's behavior had occurred and that each of the goals was met. They further determined that the interventions were the most probable reason for the observed positive changes.

IMPLICATIONS FOR PRACTICE

Based on the collaboration project, the case reported in this chapter, and the review of the related literature, we recommend consideration of the following factors when implementing a collaborative effort in a school setting: It is important for all persons participating in a collaborative endeavor to be part of the initial phase of identifying the purpose of why the collaboration team is being established. A team's overall functioning is significantly more effective when each member has a strong sense of affiliation and ownership in the team. Affiliation is more likely to occur when all collaborators are included in the development of the team mission, goals, and norms. Ownership is enhanced when the team has the freedom to develop the methods to achieve its ends.

Someone should be identified as the collaboration team leader. The ideal leader is knowledgeable about group process and is skilled at facilitating a group with a distributed functions style. *Distributed functions* means the ability to identify and utilize the unique skills of each member of the team. Knowledge of group process and group leadership skills is a common required program standard for school counselors and school psychologists. Therefore, it is recommended these professionals serve as the collaborative team leaders.

Goals, roles, and functions of the collaborators need to be constantly monitored and refined during the period of collaboration. An effective group is not stagnant. For example, in this case, the Intern/Faculty Team members were constantly sensitive to evaluating the team's effectiveness and were responsive to the changing goals and respective members' roles. Team members also evaluated the effectiveness of the team's functioning and the clarity of the final results of the team's purpose.

Team meetings must have clearly stated goals, effective facilitation, and clear follow-up procedures. Without clear goals, teams can flounder and never "get on with it." Meetings often become complaint or gripe sessions with little or no attempt to take constructive action. Without effective facilitation, teams can easily become stuck at various points in the problem-solving process. For example, a team may move from problem definition to the first course of action that comes to mind and by-pass important processes such as brainstorming possible interventions. If follow-up is not conducted, teams not only miss critical information about their functioning, but they also miss potentially rich feedback that can be used in subsequent team projects.

Clear and relevant meeting agendas are critical to a team's effectiveness. It is important to adhere to timelines set for items on the agenda. Further, regularly scheduled team meetings are essential to the team's success. In spite of the heavy workload of team members, common planning time is necessary.

- Administrators should be encouraged to allow teams the time necessary to work effectively.

- A primary purpose of the team is to use the synergistic energy of all members.

- An effective team ensures that what might be important to one member is of value to all members. Creative brainstorming is a value in collaboration.

- Group process evaluation is essential. There are two critical elements to a team's work. One is the content of the team's purpose: is the team accomplishing its identified tasks? The second is the process by which the team is attending to the identified tasks: is the team attending to the means by which it is working toward accomplishing its tasks? Time must be made available to address team maintenance and team development issues.

- No elements or experiences should be taken for granted. An effective team is sensitive to the broad spectrum of overt and covert patterns of behavior.

- When in doubt, talk it out. Mind reading is dangerous and usually counterproductive to clear communication.

- Conflict and controversy are valued as positive traits in an effective team.

Conflict is viewed as a valuable aspect of the team/group process; it needs to be invited, harnessed, respected, and worked through. During the initial phases of the team-building process, it is important that conflict be framed as creative tension resulting from a confluence of diverse yet valuable perspectives. Conflict within the framework of a common mission and mutual respect allows for a synthesis of useful ideas. Ground rules for addressing conflict should be stated clearly and must be issue focused in order to facilitate team goals.

An effective collaborative team respects the unique professional functions and contributions of the respective disciplines on the team. Protecting one's professional "turf" is an inhibitor to an effective collaborative team. It is critical that respect be clearly communicated to team members. Appreciation for the knowledge base of each discipline and for the contributions of each team member must be overt. Passive appreciation does not guarantee that each team member will experience being respected.

We further recommend that a collaborative process become a clearly delineated approach to delivery of student and staff services. The quality and respect for collaboration is enhanced by providing these services at the developmental, preventive, and crisis levels for students, staff, and school system. In Brad's case, he received attention, the teacher was supported, the parents were involved, and the Center benefited from the recommended changes in the manner in which contracting was used. In essence, professionals committed to collaboration create a climate of a community of learners.

TIPS FOR PRACTICE

1. When involved in a collaborative relationship the defining characteristics are:
   - Voluntary involvement
   - Mutual goals
   - Sharing resources
   - Sharing responsibilities

2. As in any helping relationship the use of effective feedback is important. Critical skills in giving feedback in collaboration include:
   - Focus on the patterns of behavior that can be changed
   - Sensitivity to the process of the team discussion
   - Focus on the specifics rather than the general
   - Use perception checks to ensure clarity of the communication

3. Traits of more effective types of questions to use in the collaboration process are:
   - Open rather than closed questions
   - "How" or "what" rather than "why" questions
   - Avoiding multiple choice questions
   - Avoiding rhetorical questions

4. Basic rules for effective collaboration team brainstorming include:
   - Do not reject ideas that are shared
   - Facilitate the discussion of the ideas to generate other ideas

- Avoid evaluating the ideas as they are shared
- Encourage openness of divergent thinking in the sharing process

5. The effective traits of a collaborative team are:

- The purpose of the team's goals are clear
- The unique skills of the team's members are utilized

10

School-Based Collaborative Teaming in Special Education Services

MARY BARBARA BOAT AND BARBARA WALLING BOAT

DESCRIPTION OF THE MODEL USED

The purpose of this case study is to illustrate a collaborative effort between school-based mental health, education, and education-related service professionals. There is increasing consensus within school communities that mental health issues are significant risk factors leading to poor academic and social outcomes for children (Anderson-Butcher & Ashton, 2004). Simultaneously, schools have recognized the importance of consistent communication among school-based personnel (Tourse & Surlick, 1999) in creating successful school environments. Identifying ways to confront mental health issues through shared resources and responsibilities is critical to the effectiveness of school personnel. The scenario provided demonstrates processes by which collaborating professionals work as a team to create an effective education program and supportive learning environment for a 9-year-old child receiving special education services. The primary focus of this case study is on the diagnosis stage of Dougherty's (2005) generic consultation model. The case is written from the perspective of one of the collaborating professionals, the school psychologist. It is important to note that the child's family played a critical role in the overall team process, as is both legally mandated and ethically required by the special education service delivery process. However, the focus of this case study is on professional collaboration and, therefore, the importance of family involvement may be underscored.

The model employed in this case study was a collaborative model, the cornerstone of which is team effort. Terms such as "collaboration", "teamwork", and "collaborative teaming" imply an environment of shared work and shared results (Gardner, 1999). Collaborative teamwork in education settings is an interactive process (Hohmann & Weikart, 1995; Thomas, Correa, & Morsink, 1995) founded in the notion that promoting child well-being requires addressing the "whole child." Achieving this goal most certainly requires the expertise of individuals (professional and nonprofessional) from a variety of disciplines who represent a cross section of relationships with the child. Such varying perspectives allow for better-informed decision making (McWilliam, 2000). Developing comprehensive and compassionate programming for a child with special needs also necessitates a shared commitment to child well-being (Bailey & Wolery, 1992) and the group decision-making processes that result in such an outcome (Bruder & Bologna, 1993). Using this approach, the expertise I brought to the team as the school psychologist (primarily in the areas of testing and mental health) was considered vital to the team processes, but it was no more and no less important than the expertise of any other member of the team.

Thus, the relationships between our team members were coordinated in terms of team functioning.

In addition to the critical component of perceived equity of importance among the team members, collaborative teamwork involves the recognition that the knowledge and skill one brings to the situation are best used in context of the knowledge and skill possessed by the other team members. This is even the case when one of the team members has responsibility only for a specific aspect of the case. In other words, the best decisions are likely to be made through systematic efforts to share information, competencies, and skills and problem-solve according to all the information and expertise provided (McWilliam, 2000; Rosin et al., 1996).Thus, collaborative team efforts involve reciprocity (Thomas, Correa, & Morsink, 1995). As stated by Hohmann and Weikart (1995), "At its best, teamwork is a process of active learning that calls for a supportive climate and mutual respect" (p. 89).

Support for Using Collaborative Models

Support for using a collaborative model in this case may be drawn from both the legal and logical domains. First and foremost, collaborative team efforts in meeting the needs of children receiving special education services are both legally mandated and encouraged by the federal legislation and state and district policy governing services to children with exceptionality. More specifically, the Individuals with Disabilities Education Act (IDEA) provides a federal mandate for collaborative efforts in developing individualized programming for children receiving special education services. IDEA provides for free appropriate public education in the least restrictive environment for children qualifying for special education services. Critical aspects of free appropriate public education include the requirement of multidisciplinary evaluation of students' strengths and areas of need across all domains relevant to effective functioning in the school environment and the need to include in the evaluation process persons qualified to gather information from each of these domains. Qualified persons may include teachers, parents, psychologists, counselors, speech-language pathologists, physical therapists, occupational therapists, vocational specialists, and social workers (Turnbull & Turnbull, 1997). This mandate provides the framework by which professionals and families may develop a comprehensive understanding of a child by incorporating the observations, information, and viewpoints of others into their knowledge base as they *work together* to meet the needs of the child and the requirements of the law.

In addition to the legal mandates for collaboration between professionals and families, collaborative approaches to providing services to children with special needs are logically more appropriate than service delivery efforts by individual disciplines. The collaboration process recognizes that, while professionals may function in a discipline-specific capacity, children do not. Collaboration provides the framework for viewing a child in a more holistic and integrated manner and, thus, creates a foundation for more comprehensive service provision. Additionally, collaborative teamwork decreases duplication of services (Lawson, Anderson-Butcher & Barkdull, 2000; Rosin et al., 1996).

While the focus of this case study is on a child with identified special education needs, collaborative models in education settings need not be limited to children receiving special education services. Clearly, the notion of providing comprehensive services to and meaningful learning environments for all children should be goals of the entire education system. Collaborative models provide means through which such goals become feasible.

The legal and ethical arguments for collaborative teams are supported by research on the effectiveness of multidisciplinary teams. For example, Gashelis and McConnell (1993) found in their evaluation of the effectiveness of multidisciplinary teams that these teams were more accurate in their identification of family priorities and needs than any single practitioner, even those practitioners considered to be highly perceptive. Others have noted improved academic performance and behavior among school children (Smith, Armijo, & Stowitschek, 1997) and enhanced inter-professional communication (Lawson et al., 2000) as a result of professional collaboration. The value of collaborative teaming through increased competence among students and professionals affects environments well beyond the school doors.

Types of Collaborative Teams

Multidisciplinary, interdisciplinary, and transdisciplinary teams are the three types of team models most commonly associated with educational settings. All three models involve some level of collaboration between individuals representing separate disciplines or important persons in a child's life. These team structures differ in how they approach team goals and, subsequently, in the level of outcomes achieved (Rosin et al., 1996).

In multidisciplinary models, team members have common goals but usually work independent of one another to complete the tasks necessary to meet the goals. Communication between team members may be part of the team process, but formal lines of communication are not built into the structure (Rosin et al., 1996; Bruder & Bologna, 1993; Council for Exceptional Children, 1988).

Interdisciplinary team models are similar to multidisciplinary models in that the team members from the different disciplines often work on tasks separately, however, communication between the members of the team on team activities is facilitated by formal lines of communication (Bruder & Bologna, 1993; Council for Exceptional Children 1988).These formal lines of communication provide team members with the opportunity to learn from one another (Rosin et al., 1996).

Transdisciplinary team models utilize a systematic method of working across disciplines (Rosin et al., 1996; Bruder & Bologna, 1993; Council for Exceptional Children, 1988). Participants in transdisciplinary teams must be committed to working collaboratively across discipline boundaries. This process requires role release; the team members play roles within their discipline as well as take on the roles of other disciplines (Rosin et al., 1996).

Dimensions of Collaborative Teams

At the heart of any collaborative effort is the concept of teamwork, the realization that many complex issues are best addressed through the mutual exchange of information and development of ideas. Beyond including at least two individuals, teams may take on a variety of sizes, compositions, and affiliations, and serve a variety of functions (Spencer & Coye, 1988).The success of any one team is dependent upon a number of factors individual to the composition and purpose of that team. However, there are some generic elements necessary to effective collaborative efforts (Spencer & Coye, 1988).

First, any team must have a super ordinate goal, purpose, or philosophy. Second, there must be positive interdependence between the team members, meaning that each team member must acknowledge the importance and necessity of each team member's contributions if the goals of the collaborative effort are to be successfully accomplished. The third element involves commitment to the concept of teamwork. That is, each team member must embrace the belief that this collaborative approach is the best way to accomplish the goals of the team. The fourth element is accountability. Accountability refers to the idea that any team is responsible for answering to a larger organization or group of organizations. Furthermore, the entire team must be credited for successes and be held responsible for any shortcomings. Finally, any effective team must have qualified leadership. It is shortsighted to believe that even a group of mature, committed professionals can collaborate successfully without leadership. How leadership is determined is likely to vary from team to team, but developing a method of maintaining direction and movement is necessary (Spencer & Coye, 1988).

SETTING AND BACKGROUND ISSUES

Setting

The setting for this case study was a large suburban intermediate school. The school housed all 1,200 fifth- and sixth-grade students in the district and represented the consolidation of students from five elementary schools. The school faculty numbered 230. Additionally, the school maintained a full-time school psychologist and a school counselor whose responsibilities included testing, evaluation, and providing mental health support activities and programs.

Background

This case study involved a 9-year-old girl, named Katy. Katy received special education services under the category of developmental disabilities. She transferred to our school district midyear from a k–4 urban elementary school. Although Katy was only 9 years of age and technically a fourth grader, she was placed in the intermediate school setting to avoid an additional transition at the end of the school year. The administration, in conjunction with Katy's parents, determined that this placement was acceptable, given that Katy would spend a significant amount of her time in special classrooms.

As the school psychologist, I was approached by the special education teacher regarding some issues related to the development of Katy's education program. According to the teacher, Katy was demonstrating significant emotional and behavioral concerns, and these issues were preventing her from effectively accessing the education environment. The special education teacher expressed her belief that any effective educational program developed for Katy would require substantial supports to address her emotional and behavioral needs.

GOALS OF COLLABORATION

The goals of our collaborative efforts can be examined on two levels: child- and family-related goals and team-related goals. The fundamental purpose of our team efforts was to develop and implement an appropriate individualized education program (IEP) for Katy. This process included identifying student strengths and areas of need, developing goals and objectives for student growth based on these identified areas, and designing and providing an instructional environment that supported student attainment of the goals and objectives. Thus, the overriding goals of our collaboration were child and family related, in that we sought to improve child functioning with the participation and consent of the family.

However, achieving this end required effective team functioning. In short, the team was charged with the responsibility of engaging in effective decision making activities based on the mutual sharing of information and expertise and team-based problem solving. Achieving this level of functioning was a critical goal as well.

One crucial aspect of team-based decision making is the development of systematic procedures for making decisions (Spencer & Coye, 1988). Given that no best systematic approach to team decision making has been identified, the team was required to establish a set of guidelines for this process. Our team chose a modified version of the decision-making process proposed by Project Bridge (American Academy of Pediatrics, 1986).

The Project Bridge is a program designed to support interdisciplinary teams associated with early intervention services. The decision-making model put forth by this project is a five-step approach. The five steps, in sequential order, are: defining the problems and gathering information, generating alternatives, selecting alternatives, implementing the alternatives, and monitoring outcomes. This decision-making model is later discussed under the section entitled "Application: Collaboration Team Techniques and Procedures."

COLLABORATORS' FUNCTIONS AND ROLES

My function as a member of this collaborative team was to work cooperatively with the other team members to develop an integrated and meaningful education program for Katy. My purpose on the team was similar to that of every other team member in that I was there to give information, receive information, and problem-solve in the context of these shared exchanges. Therefore, my role as a professional member of this team was to support the team (and ultimately Katy) by providing information and options related to Katy's social-emotional and behavioral functioning. My role also involved listening to and supporting the views of the other team members and participating in all aspects of the decision-making process.

COLLABORATORS' EXPERIENCE DURING THE PROCESS

Having worked both in early childhood and elementary school settings, I have been exposed to a variety of team experiences including multidisciplinary, interdisciplinary, and transdisciplinary models. Most of these activities have centered on the assessment phase of individualized programming for children with special needs and their families. However, it has been my experience that most interdisciplinary school-based teams employ a multidisciplinary model. A brief survey of the team models experienced by the other team members revealed a pattern of experiences similar to mine. Given the extensive and to some degree urgent nature of Katy's needs, we agreed that this team needed to function at least on an interdisciplinary level, with systematic efforts to share information and problem-solve.

To facilitate the interdisciplinary team process, we first designated the team leadership. In this case, the leadership was identified by consensus. All the team members believed that, as the case manager, Katy's special education teacher should facilitate the team process. Additionally, the team decided to meet on a weekly basis until the individual education plan (IEP) goals and objectives were fully developed. This development met with some resistance from the team members, particularly from those individuals who were itinerant (the physical therapist and the occupational therapist). However, the commitment was made to go ahead with weekly meetings but to maintain flexibility and understanding in the meeting arrangements if the scheduling created difficulties for team members. Furthermore, the team unanimously agreed that significant effort needed to be made to encourage parent participation in whatever ways and at whatever levels possible. Thus, the team decided that beyond simply asking Katy's parents to join the team meetings, one team member would be designated to communicate consistently with the family.

While all of the team members knew one another, not all the members had served on teams together prior to this experience. Therefore, our initial interactions were quite formal, and the team members tended to provide and request information specific to their respective disciplines. Additionally, team members were very guarded in their comments and went out of their way to avoid "stepping on toes." During this phase of team development, it was clear that we were seeking clarification and definition of our roles on *this* team. This process created some tensions as team members became more comfortable sharing the traditional requirements of their roles with one another (role release). A specific example of such tensions occurred between the school counselor and myself. Within the day-to-day school context, we have overlapping job responsibilities.

Therefore, we were, at first, a little uneasy about who would be responsible for collecting additional information regarding Katy's social/emotional functioning and problem behaviors, since each of us felt that we had specific expertise in the areas of social/emotional development. The team facilitator suggested that we work together on this process. The school counselor and I agreed to do so and set up a time to get together and come up with an approach.

I suggested that we each come to the meeting with a list of tasks to be accomplished (based on our observations and the information we had gathered from the team) and any methods or tools we know of that would be helpful in collecting the information. At our meeting, we immediately discovered that the list of tasks was so extensive that one person would have difficulty accomplishing everything. Additionally, we found that, in general, we were interested in focusing on different aspects of data collection. Thus, we determined that I would be primarily responsible for gathering information about Katy's social/emotional functioning as it related to the context of school, and the school counselor would gather information about Katy's functioning in the home and other community contexts. We would then share the information to develop our report jointly. The only major disagreement we encountered pertained to the use of the established standardized measure. The school counselor suggested that we share with the team the issue of standardized testing for discussion as a group. I thought this was an excellent suggestion.

By the third meeting, team members were beginning to express themselves, although primarily through reactions to suggestions made by team members that appeared to be outside the traditional boundaries of their disciplines. For example, the classroom teacher brought up an observation she had made in the classroom regarding some of Katy's outbursts. She suggested that Katy was more likely to become upset during activities that required handwriting skills, and that it might be worth assessing these contexts to see if we could identify alternatives for some of these activities. The classroom teacher added that she did not think that handwriting would ever be a truly functional skill for Katy. The occupational therapist immediately responded that, as she had pointed out in her initial assessment, Katy's fine motor skills were very poor, and neglecting handwriting at this point would disadvantage Katy significantly as she got older.

The occupational therapist added that the team needed to remember the emphasis Katy's parents had placed on handwriting as a goal, and the importance of respecting parent priorities as contributing members of the team. Realizing that she unintentionally offended the occupational therapist by suggesting that Katy's handwriting requirements be reconsidered, the classroom teacher attempted to clarify her position: she indicated that she, too, considered handwriting an important goal for Katy but wondered whether they could, at this point, look at incorporating handwriting into Katy's daily activities in ways that did not frustrate her as much. Other team members agreed with the classroom teacher's assessment of the situation, stating that any strategy that increased the likelihood of Katy's behavioral outbursts was interfering with Katy's opportunity to work on goals anyway. Sensing that the occupational therapist was feeling somewhat "ganged up on," I asked her what types of fine motor activities might allow Katy to continue working on fine motor skills but not pressure her as much. The occupational therapist reluctantly said that she would develop a list of options, but she asserted her belief that these activities be considered temporary and that the classroom staff reintroduce the more difficult activities. All the team members agreed.

Over the next two months, the team evolved significantly as a decision-making body. We discovered that there was plenty of work for each team member within and across disciplines. In fact, we became grateful for the opportunity to share the responsibilities and our resources with one another. The team's increasing level of comfort with one another was evident in member willingness to ask questions and make suggestions related to other areas of expertise.

Additional evidence of our growth as a team could be seen in member willingness to raise sensitive issues and to ask difficult questions. This process was enhanced by the team facilitator's ability to remind us of our team goal at this point in time. Specifically, the facilitator was able to refocus our attention on assessing and addressing Katy's behavior issues. This leadership was tremendously important to our success as a team.

APPLICATION: COLLABORATION TEAM TECHNIQUES AND PROCEDURES

School-based professional collaboration and the Project Bridge's five-step approach to collaborative decision making (American Academy of Pediatrics, 1986) can be viewed in the context of the generic problem-solving model provided by Dougherty (2005). Using this model as a framework, we viewed the entry stage as the point at which the child's *current* educational team came together.

Although the team had some sense of purpose at this point, the issues to be addressed and goals of the team required further development. The entry stage activities were a prerequisite of team-based decision making. During the diagnosis stage, the point at which we gathered relevant information, we identified the major issues to be tackled and proposed options. The diagnosis stage included steps one and two of Project Bridge's five-step decision-making model (identifying the issues and gathering information and generating alternatives).

Stage three of the generic model, implementation, involved developing, implementing, and evaluating the plans of action. This stage of the generic model encompassed steps three, four, and five of the five-step decision-making model (selecting alternatives, implementing alternatives, and monitoring outcomes).

Stage four of the generic consultation model, disengagement, was the only stage to which the collaborative efforts in this case study did not have a direct counterpart. According to Dougherty (2000), the disengagement phase refers to the time period during which consultant involvement is decreased. Ways in which this school-based collaborative effort may be conceptualized in terms of this phase will be discussed later in this section.

Entry

After Katy had been in our school for about one month, as the school psychologist, I was asked to join Katy's educational team to help develop appropriate supports in the school environment and educational programming to meet Katy's special needs. Other members of Katy's new educational team included the special education teacher (and Katy's case manager), a regular education teacher, a physical therapist, an occupational therapist, the school counselor, and Katy's parents. The first team meeting was held as an opportunity for the team to get together and generally discuss assessment and programming options for Katy. All of the educational team members were invited to participate and were asked to suggest convenient times to meet. Additionally, each team member received copies of Katy's existing IEP, and I received copies of her most recent three-year comprehensive assessment outcomes.

In attendance at the initial meeting were myself, Katy's primary special education teacher, the school counselor, the physical therapist, and the occupational therapist. Having just moved, and feeling somewhat overwhelmed by all that required their attention, Katy's mother and father expressed that they would prefer not to attend the preponderance meetings. However, Katy's mother indicated that she would be attending the annual IEP meeting and would be happy to provide any information needed prior to that event over the phone or through written correspondence. Katy's annual IEP meeting was scheduled to take place the following month.

Diagnosis—Step One: Defining the Issues and Gathering Information

Step one involved defining the problem areas and gathering important information. In this case, the sharing of basic information enabled the team members to develop a basic framework for what issues needed to be addressed and, subsequently, to identify areas where additional information was needed. At the first meeting, we proceeded directly to better familiarizing ourselves with Katy's case. Katy's special education teacher (and case manager) assumed leadership in facilitating and guiding the team meeting. She began by describing what the classroom staff members were observing about Katy since her arrival. She went on to share the information she had gathered from Katy's education file, former teachers, and mother. As Katy's teacher spoke, I was able to ask questions about issues that had arisen during my review of Katy's education file and her classroom and home activities.

From the conversation with Katy's special education teacher, I received the following information about Katy: Katy was born very premature and spent the first 18 months of her life in and out of the hospital. She is very small for her age (about three-and-a-half feet tall and 45 pounds). In addition to her small physical stature, Katy has slight spastic cerebral palsy primarily affecting her lower legs (she walks and runs pigeon-toed) and her fine motor skills (handwriting is a very labor intensive process for Katy). She also has a slight visual impairment necessitating corrective glasses and health concerns including asthma, allergies, and frequent bouts of pneumonia. Katy has received special education services since the age of 3 and currently has been identified (labeled) as having moderate developmental disabilities.

At the new school, Katy spent most of her day in segregated special education programming. Katy's primary placement was a separate special education classroom focused on meeting the needs of the children with more pervasive special education needs. Katy spent approximately half of her day with this group. In addition to the special classroom, Katy spent about one-and-a-half hours each morning in a resource setting for students with mild to moderate disabilities working on academics. Katy spent the remaining portion of her day with her chronological age-mates in the regular education setting for activities such as homeroom, music, physical education, recess, and special school activities (assemblies and field trips).

According to information from Katy's previous school and from recent assessment results (within the past year), Katy was working at a first- to second-grade level academically. The special education teacher indicated that Katy had a substantial sight word vocabulary and was able to do some phonetic reading.

Additionally, she had memorized single digit addition up to the number five and could add and subtract larger numbers using either her fingers to count or various math manipulative. The special education teacher added that, while maximally Katy performed well academically (higher than the levels at which she tested), her performance was very inconsistent and appeared to be compromised significantly by her limited attention span and reactivity. In fact, the special education teacher felt that Katy's most significant area of need at that point was behavioral.

In discussing Katy's specific behavioral issues in the classroom (observed by the classroom staff), the special education teacher stated that Katy's behavior ranged from being off task to being aggressive toward others. Examples of inappropriate behavior in Katy's repertoire included: getting up and walking away from an activity; running out of the room and wandering the halls or going outside; standing on tables and chairs; destroying property (knocking items off counters, throwing classroom materials and furniture); and hitting, kicking, and spitting at peers and school staff. She also exhibited such inappropriate verbalizations as perseveration on nonsense words, name-calling ("You baby," "You butthead"), profanity, and statements such as "I'm going to kill you" and "I'm going to kill your mother." Historically, Katy's problem behaviors related to off-task inattentiveness, wandering, and name-calling. However, the teacher reported that Katy's behavior problems were escalating in frequency and severity.

Specifically, Katy was becoming increasingly aggressive, more verbally abusive, and often was being "sent back" from her other classrooms because she was not attending to the activities and was being disruptive to the other children. The teacher stated that when staff tried to redirect Katy, she would drop on the floor and "tantrum." Additionally, Katy was doing substantially more running from the room and was beginning to hide in places such as the boys' bathroom. She was also removing articles of clothing, such as her pants and her shirt, in public places (e.g., the hallway). The special education teacher expressed particular concern about these increases given the fragility of one of Katy's classmates (a child with brittle bones). Specifically, the teacher was worried that during one of Katy's outburst she might either intentionally or unintentionally injure this child.

Further discussion with the special education teacher revealed that, while Katy possesses strong verbal skills (she had previously scored well on measures of social skill) and interacts well with adults (particularly one-on-one), she has a great deal of difficulty interacting with peers. I asked the teacher to expand on any specific interaction issues the staff had observed, and she indicated that Katy is able to initiate interactions; however she has trouble maintaining and appropriately terminating these exchanges. Additionally, the teacher indicated that Katy talks continuously, often repeating herself with statements such as, "We're having fun, aren't we?" After discussing the observed behavior issues, the special education teacher noted that Katy had many strong areas. She pointed out that Katy often is an affectionate child, who loves to help others. She often approaches the staff, hugs them, and makes statements such as "I love you" and "You're my friend." Katy also seems to enjoy having special responsibilities such as taking the lunch cart back to the cafeteria and collecting cans for recycling. Furthermore, Katy's teacher revealed that Katy seems to take a great deal of pride in her accomplishments and "beams" when she is praised for her efforts and successes.

In addition to providing details about Katy's school-based activities, the special education teacher provided information she had gathered from correspondence with Katy's mother. From these communications, Katy's teacher had learned that Katy is the oldest of three siblings, each approximately one year apart in age. Katy's father works odd hours (evenings, nights, and weekends) and, therefore, often cannot attend school meetings. Katy's mother works caring for an elderly neighbor. Katy's mother indicated that they moved from the city to the suburbs because of the location. They chose Katy's current educational setting (not her home school) because they wanted Katy to have more functional skill training.

Katy's mother described Katy's previous educational setting as "okay," but she felt that Katy was not learning much there and had a great deal of freedom in choosing what she did during the day. A conversation between Katy's previous and current teachers seemed to corroborate this information.

In discussing Katy's behavior issues, Katy's mother indicated that there were difficulties at home as well. She was particularly frustrated by Katy's interactions with her siblings. The mother noted that Katy often got angry with her siblings and resorted to name-calling and hitting. She felt that, although Katy was the oldest child chronologically, she often was treated as the youngest because she acted like the youngest. Furthermore, the mother was concerned both by the addition of derogatory and profane words and phrases to Katy's vocabulary over the past month and also to Katy's increasing fascination with human anatomy.

When asked about Katy's activities at home, Katy's mother indicated that Katy liked to play outside in the yard and in her room, moving quickly from one activity to another and frequently wandering aimlessly around the house.

Katy's mother also related that Katy helped out around the house and could act very sweet and caring, but that she was becoming increasingly difficult to control. The mother felt that Katy's age (approaching pubescence) was making normal life adjustments at home and school difficult for Katy.

Step Two: Generating Alternatives

Step two of the five-step decision-making approach consisted of generating solutions, options, and alternatives. To meet this objective, each team member provided a general overview of their impressions of Katy's needs-based information they had received to that point. Through the sharing process, we determined that there were inconsistencies between Katy's demonstrated abilities and her psychological profile. The special education teacher indicated that the classroom staff would continue to collect data on Katy's academic and social activities in the classroom so that we could determine if there was a need to reassess Katy's intellectual and social functioning. We also decided that the occupational therapist and the physical therapist would make several independent observations of Katy throughout the school day to explore Katy's motor functioning in her new school setting. To develop a comprehensive profile of Katy's social/emotional functioning (strengths and areas of need), we decided that I would compile a comprehensive overview of the existing information and additional formal and informal assessment data. We agreed that the school counselor would be in contact with Katy's parents to gather additional information about Katy by assessing family needs (e.g., coping with stress).

During the course of our initial discussions, each team member indicated that they were concerned by Katy's inability to focus on school-related tasks for an appropriate period of time and her strategies for dealing with situations that frustrated her. The possibility of whether Katy should be evaluated for attention-deficit hyperactive disorder (ADHD) was addressed in the meeting.

The team decided that, before this issue was raised with the family, extensive environmental analyses were needed to explore Katy's patterns of behavior (to look for consistencies/inconsistencies in behavior strengths as well as difficulties and contingencies that may be encouraging and/or maintaining Katy's problem behaviors). I offered to provide the tools and general structure for the analyses.

The format for the meetings leading up to the IEP meeting was an elaboration on the theme of the first meeting. Each week, team members provided a general overview of their findings and progressed to more in-depth discussions centered around specific areas of development and/or specific issues identified (substeps taken from Bailey & Wolery, 1992). Due to the limited amount of time we were able to meet each week (one-and-a-half hours), we took turns sharing the information we had gathered. Specifically, the special education teacher provided the context for discussion at our second meeting, the focus of the third team meeting was on the findings of the physical therapist and the occupational therapist, and the school counselor and I shared our information at the fourth meeting. However, it should be noted that the discussion at any given meeting was not limited to a specific domain of development. In fact, the conversation often turned to the ways in which the information being provided related to and diverged from other members' observations.

Implementation—Step Three: Selecting Alternatives

Step three required the systematic evaluation by the team of the strengths and weaknesses of the options proposed. Our team examined the appropriateness and effectiveness of all suggestion based on feasibility (Spencer & Coye, 1988).

Ultimately, the acceptance of suggestions as goals, objectives, or intervention strategies in special education is dependent on parent approval of the plan.

Therefore, when selecting options, we incorporated all the information we gathered from Katy's mother about her and her husband's perceptions of Katy and what areas they considered to be most critical to address. Additionally, we approached the annual IEP meeting as an additional phase or further refinement of alternative selection to continue to incorporate parent perceptions and preferences into the education plan.

Based on the information gathered, the team (including Katy's mother) came to the following conclusions:

- Katy's needs, at that point, were primarily in the areas of social/emotional and behavioral functioning.
- While some patterns in Katy's problem behaviors were apparent, her behavior was very erratic and the intensity and frequency of her problem behaviors were increasing.
- Katy was having tremendous difficulty identifying the frustrations in her environment and expressing her feelings.
- The recent transitions in Katy's life were compounding the issues.
- Katy's parents were very stressed by the increases in Katy's problem behaviors and were feeling overwhelmed by the demands of life at that point in time.
- Katy's social/emotional and behavioral needs must be addressed to focus on other areas of development.

Given the above list of issues identified, the team proposed the following options:

- develop Katy's ability to express herself appropriately
- increase Katy's peer-related social skills
- implement proactive measures to address identified problem situations
- increase Katy's ability to monitor her own behavior
- continue to work on skill development across all domains with Katy, taking into account her specific social and emotional needs
- provide Katy's parents with information and possible resources to support Katy's needs at home and address family stress
- have Katy evaluated for ADHD by the medical field

Steps Four and Five: Implementation and Monitoring

Implementation of the options identified by the team proceeded through both formal and informal channels. The formal implementation process involved developing goals and objectives for the IEP based on the team-identified options.

During the annual IEP meeting, the entire team developed the written goals and objectives. While the classroom staff was primarily responsible for the interventions designed, I remained formally committed to the implementation process since my services as a behavior consultant were written into the IEP on an "as-needed basis." On an informal basis, the school counselor and I remained committed to informal in-service activities related to managing problem behaviors for the school staff and Katy's family. These endeavors included mini-workshops for the staff and home visits with the family.

Monitoring the team-based decisions involved both group and individual activities. The team decided to meet on a monthly basis for the remainder of the school year to follow up on Katy's progress, address other issues as they emerged, and make changes when necessary. Individually, each team member agreed to monitor student progress through a variety of data collection procedures.

As the school psychologist, I committed to providing some methods and tools to facilitate the monitoring of student behavior. Additionally, I agreed to make biweekly observations of Katy in the classroom for two months. The school counselor took on the responsibility of following up with Katy's family. These activities included several meetings with the family to discuss strategies for addressing Katy's behaviors at home and following up on family attempts to access support resources in the community.

Disengagement

The collaborative effort presented in this case study focused on designing an effective educational environment for a child with many special needs. Developing and implementing programs for children with exceptionality is an ongoing process and, therefore, requires the team to continue its activities on some level over the course of at least one year (and often longer). Furthermore, given the dependence of collaborative teams on horizontal relationships (no one team member is more important than another), disengagement is likely to occur at the team level, not the individual level, when a student moves on to a new class or program. In this case, disengagement would coincide with one of two situations, Katy's social-emotional functioning reaching a level of stability at which mental health professionals are not vital to the team process or Katy no longer receiving services within my jurisdiction.

IMPLICATIONS FOR PRACTICE

Interdisciplinary school-based collaboration is a critical component of effectively meeting the educational needs of many children. The foundation of collaboration is shared goals, information, resources, and power (Rosin et al., 1996). This sharing of information, resources, and power allows the collaborative team to address multifaceted issues using a multidimensional approach. The case study presented in this chapter depicts collaborative efforts between school-based mental health services, education, and education-related therapeutic services to create a productive learning environment and education program for a school-age child with many special needs. The scenario provided illustrates ways in which disciplines and families can work together to meet goals.

While collaborative efforts and teamwork provide efficient means to important ends, the path to desired outcomes may not always be paved. Barriers to effective teaming occur at many levels and may involve individual team member characteristics, group characteristics, situational factors, group processes and outcomes (Spencer & Coye, 1988), or a combination of factors from each of these areas.

In this case study, the team process went relatively smoothly. However, there were several illustrations of difficulties that can arise during collaborative teaming.

For example, initially, the team members were hesitant about expressing their opinions and were concerned about offending their collaborators. Such situations often characterize teams in the early or formative stage of team development, particularly when the team members are not familiar with one another's working styles. Given that establishing a solid foundation for the group is an important aspect of team development, it is critical that team members enter a collaborative teaming situation with the understanding that time for establishing the team must be factored into the process. Collaborative teams that do not take time in the short run to address issues related to team processes may hurt attainment of their team goals in the long run. In addition to obstacles related to developing effective interaction and communication, the team experienced some turf-related issues, especially early on in the teaming process. Specific examples of turf issues included concerns between the school counselor and myself about overlapping areas of expertise and the occupational therapist taking offense with other team members making suggestions related to issues typically considered the province of her discipline. The first situation was one of dealing with the unknown (in this case, who would be responsible for certain aspects of information gathering). Such scenarios are unavoidable when the qualifications and skills of each team member are not yet established. The team facilitator correctly suggested that we address the unknown together. In this way, the school counselor and I were required to try to resolve any interpersonal issues without automatically involving the entire team. Had we been unable to come to some agreement, the full team would have been available as a resource.

The second situation is also one that teams encounter frequently and during all stages of team development. That is, comments are made that unintentionally put other team members on the defensive. In this case, several important actions took place. First, the classroom teacher realized that her comments about Katy's handwriting skills offended the occupational therapist and was able to provide some clarification for her reasoning. Second, the occupational therapist was asked to take responsibility for looking into alternative strategies for developing Katy's fine motor skills. Finally, the team acknowledged the importance of the skills in question to Katy's future functioning. Every member of a collaborative team needs to feel that the other team members value the expertise they bring to the situation.

Given the number of factors that may undermine the team process, it often seems easier to work alone. Despite the complexity involved in establishing productive collaborative teams, evidence suggests that even the most basic multidisciplinary team evaluations may be more accurate and comprehensive than determinations made by the most perceptive professional from a single discipline (Gashelis & McConnell, 1993).Therefore, it is in our best interest as professionals in service delivery fields to consider collaboration an integral part of our responsibilities.

Spencer and Coye (1988) identified basic elements necessary for productive collaborative teams. The first element is a common or overriding goal or philosophy. In the case presented here, the common goal was developing an effective program for Katy. In fact, one could say that all school-based interdisciplinary teams share the goal of promoting positive outcomes for children. The second dimension of effective collaboration is positive interdependence. It is important to keep in mind that positive interdependence is an element of collaboration that develops over time. Given a shared commitment to a goal or an outcome, positive interdependence should evolve from information sharing and mutual problem solving. In this case study, the systematic efforts to share information and explore the issues in the context of this shared information enabled the team members to see the importance of the shared experience. The third dimension of effective teaming is common commitment to the team concept. Examples of such commitments in this case study could be seen in the flexible approach team members took to scheduling meetings and the willingness of team members to share responsibilities across disciplines. The fourth element is accountability. In this case the team was accountable primarily to the child, the family, and the special education process. To increase the likelihood that the team was making the best decisions with the best information, the team chose to involve the family as much as possible in the decision-making process. By doing so, the team was able to incorporate the family in the process and increase the likelihood that the family would support team outcomes. Additionally, the team is held accountable for its decisions according to the IEP. The IEP is evaluated and rewritten annually and reviewed for appropriateness every six months. Thus, team members are held accountable for the efficacy of their decisions.

The final aspect of effective collaboration is leadership. In this case, team leadership was identified by group consensus; however there are many ways in which leadership can be determined. For example, the person with the most contact with the child or client may take the leadership role (Rosin et al., 1996). Leadership also may be appointed, elected, rotate among members (Spencer & Coye, 1988), or be shared between members. Additionally, in this case, team leadership was vital to maintaining focus on the team's purpose.

Specifically, the facilitator reminded the team of its goals at times when interpersonal and group characteristics threatened the team process. Such actions help team members move away from making decisions that reflect individual interests without feeling threatened. In short, this case study illustrates one way in which a school-based collaborative team evolves and progresses through the team processes while employing the critical elements of effective collaboration.

The case study presented in this chapter illustrates interdisciplinary school-based collaboration for a child receiving special education. However, the collaborative model is by no means limited to services for children with special needs. All children are multidimensional and deserve consideration and service that reflects this reality. Professional and professional-family collaboration provides a means to this end.

QUESTIONS FOR DISCUSSION AND REFLECTION

1. Identify the ways in which the team processes identified in this case study may be altered given the three team models (multidisciplinary, interdisciplinary, transdisciplinary) discussed in the chapter.

2. Discuss the potential impact (strengths and weaknesses) of the following group characteristics and situational factors on collaborative teaming: a. increased team size (more disciplines represented on the team) b. at least one very assertive team member c. a very soft-spoken team member d. rotating team leadership e. leadership appointed by administration outside the team f. team composed of members from separate agencies (not just separate disciplines)

3. How might time constraints, resource allocation, social and political climates, and administrative support (or lack thereof) affect collaboration? What steps could be taken to limit the negative influences of these variables on team functioning?

4. Identify additional ways in which the systematic sharing of information between team members may be facilitated.

5. Imagine that Katy's parents were resistant to the team process (they had a history of bad experiences with the professionals on teams). What are some steps the team may take to encourage family participation in collaboration?

6. Imagine you are working with a professional who does not think collaboration works. What steps could be taken to promote the value of collaboration with this individual?

7. Explore your own work style, values, and belief system and identify three personal attributes that are conducive to collaboration and three personal attributes that may serve as barriers to collaboration. What measures might be taken to build on your strengths and develop your areas of weakness?

8. Discuss ways in which cultural diversity among team members may influence collaborative efforts. What steps can be taken to ensure that diverse cultural perspectives are respected within the team process.

REFERENCES AND SUGGESTED READINGS

American Academy of Pediatrics (1986). *Project BRIDGE—decision making for early services: A team approach.* Elk Grove Village, IL: American Academy of Pediatrics.

Anderson-Butcher, D., & Ashton, D. (2004). Innovative models of collaboration to serve children, youths, families, and communities. *Children and Schools, 26*(1), Retrieved February 17, 2004 from Academic Search Premier.

Bailey, D. B.,& Wolery, M. (1992). *Teaching infants and preschoolers with disabilities* (2nd ed.). Englewood Cliffs, NJ: Prentice-Hall, Inc.

Bruder, M. B., & Bologna, T. (1993).Collaboration and service coordination for effective early intervention. In W. Brown, S. K. Thurman, & L. F. Pearl (Eds.), *Family-centered early intervention with infants and toddlers: Innovative cross-disciplinary approaches* (pp. 103–127). Baltimore: Paul H. Brookes.

Council for Exceptional Children (1988). *Early intervention for infants and toddlers: A team effort* (Eric Digest, No. 461). Reston, VA: Author.

Dougherty, A.M. (25). *Psychological consultation and collaboration in school and community settings.* (4ᵗʰ. Ed.). Belmont,CA: Wadsworth.

Foley, G.M.(1990).Portrait of arena evaluation: Assessment in the interdisciplinary approach. In E.D. Gibbs & D. M. Teti (Eds.), *Interdisciplinary assessment in infants: A guide for early intervention professionals* (pp. 271–286). Baltimore: Paul H. Brookes.

Friend, M.,& Cook, L. (1997). Student-centered teams in schools: Still in search of an identity. *Journal of Educational and Psychological Consultation, 8,* 3–20.

Gardner, S. (1999). *Beyond collaboration to results: Hard choice in the future of service to children and families.* Tempe and Fullerton: Arizona Prevention Resource Center and the Center for Collaboration for Children, California State University.

Gashelis, J.A.,& McConnell, S. R. (1993). Comparison of family needs assessed by mothers, individual professionals, and interdisciplinary teams. *Journal of Early Intervention, 17,* 36–49.

Hohmann, M.,& Weikart, D. P. (1995). *Educating young children :Active learning practices for preschool and child care programs.* Ypsilanti, MI: High/Scope Press.

Individuals with Disabilities Education Act (IDEA) of 1990, PL 101-476. (October 30, 1990).Title 20, USC 1400 et seq: *U.S. Statutes at Large, 104,* 1103–1151.

Kelley, M. F. (1996).Collaboration in early childhood education. *Journal of Educational and Psychological Consultation, 7,* 275–282.

Lawson, H.A., Anderson-Butcher, D., & Barkdull, C. (2000, September). *Evaluation of Colorado, Nevada, New Mexico, and Utah design teams.* Paper presented at the New Century child Welfare and Family support Conference, Snowbird, UT.

McWilliam, R.A. (2000). Recommended practices in interdisciplinary models. In S. Sandall, M. McLean, & B.J. Smith (Eds.): *DEC recommended practices in early intervention/early childhood special education* (pp.47-54). Longmont, CO: Sopris West.

Rosin, P., Whitehead, A.,Tuchman, L. I., Jesien, G., Begun, A. L., & Irwin, L. (1996). *Partnerships in family-centered care: A guide to collaborative early intervention.* Baltimore: Paul H. Brookes.

Smith, A.J., Armijo, E.J., & Stowitshek, J. (1997). Current approaches of case management in schools to improve children's readiness to learn. *Journal of Case Management, 6*(3), 107-115.

Spencer, P.A., & Coye, R.W. (1988). Project BRIDGE:A team approach to decision making for early services. *Infants and Young Children, 1*, 82–92.

Turnbull, A. P.,&Turnbull, R. H. (1997). *Families, professionals, and exceptionality: A special partnership.* Upper Saddle River, NJ: Prentice-Hall, Inc.

Tourse, R.W.C., & Surlick, J. (1999). The collaborative alliance: Supporting vulnerable children in school. In R.W.C. Tourse & J.F. Mooney (Eds.), *Collaborative practice: School and human service partnerships* (pp. 59-78). Westport, CT: Praeger.

Thomas, C.C., Correa, V. I., & Morsink, C.V. (1995). *Interactive teaming: Consultation and collaboration in special programs* (2nd ed.). Englewood Cliffs, NJ: Prentice-Hall, Inc.

PART V

Conclusions and Practice Cases

What do these cases suggest to us about the effective practice of consultation and collaboration? What messages can we glean from them to continue to develop the skill of reflecting on or practice of consultation and collaboration? In Chapter 11, I answer these questions.

In Chapter 12, I provide some additional cases for practice. These cases will help you enhance the skill of reflecting on situations peculiar to a case, teaching you to keep such situations in mind as you proceed.

11

Implications for Effective Practice

A. MICHAEL DOUGHERTY

T his chapter pulls together some of the main ideas that run throughout the cases described in Chapters 2 through 10. The cases presented demonstrate the importance of considering the stages in the consultation and collaboration processes. Consequently, I relate the implications of the issues and concepts derived from the cases to the general stages of consultation and collaboration. I first discuss topics gleaned from the case studies and then suggest possible implications for effective practice in each of the stages of consultation and collaboration. Because of its importance, I have supplemented the discussion on multicultural influences with additional material.

As you will recall from Chapter 1, there are four stages in the process of consultation and collaboration: entry, diagnosis, implementation, and disengagement.

The entry stage involves the general process by which the consultant or collaborator enters the system in which consultation or collaboration is going to occur and then creates relationships with consultees or fellow collaborators.

In the diagnosis stage, the consultant or collaborator gathers information, defines the problem based on that information, sets related goals, and generates possible interventions. Next, in the implementation stage, a plan is put into action and evaluated. In effect, the disengagement stage "winds down" what was started in the entry stage.

The issues and concepts discussed in this chapter include:

- Consultation and collaboration have many basic elements.
- The personal characteristics of the helper are most likely a critical factor related to success of consultation or collaboration.
- Multicultural influences need to be accounted for in consultation and collaboration.
- The consultee or fellow collaborators should be recognized as valuable assets in the process of trying to assist the client system.
- All consultation and collaboration occur in some organizational context.

COMMON-SENSE ELEMENTS

One conclusion we can draw about consultation and collaboration from the cases is that, in spite of their complexity, the difficulties in adequately defining them, and the permeability of their boundaries, they involve many basic elements.

In consultation and collaboration, the magic is that there is no magic! Like most other enterprises, successful consultation and collaboration involve a combination of effective planning and hard work.

Consultation and collaboration have many common-sense aspects. James, Addy, and Crews note the importance of the consultant's interpersonal and communication skills. Deck and Isenhour point out that effective planning will maximize the benefit received from consultation. Carrington Rotto corroborates this same point when she emphasizes the problem-solving nature of consultation.

Carrington Rotto also points to the importance of collaborating as a way to take into account the broader behavioral relationships across environments.

Deck and Isenhour as well as Carrington Rotto advocate the importance of formative evaluation. Many consultants do not evaluate their work in any manner. This is ethically questionable. Deck and Isenhour point out the importance of having a framework for approaching consultation and show that formative evaluation can be a useful tool for keeping consultants on track in the consultation relationship. James, Addy, and Crews make a strong case for the importance of summative evaluation of the consultation process. Carrington Rotto points to the importance of a relatively sophisticated evaluation design as a critical aspect of consultation. This same author also demonstrates the importance of proper assessment. Tack, Dougherty, and Morrow recommend that consultants point out to their consultees how they (the consultants) feel that the consultation could have been improved. Tack, Dougherty, and Morrow suggest that such an approach enhances the perceived genuineness of the consultant and models a nondefensive attitude for the consultee.

Tack, Dougherty, and Morrow highlight the notion of what parties-at-interest to involve at the preliminary exploration of organizational needs phase. They infer that all parties-at-interest be included in the preliminary phases of consultation as a safeguard against misunderstanding and confused expectations. Further, as Becker-Reems suggests, some parties-at-interest may well become consultees in the future. Tack and Morrow as well as Kottman point out the obvious, yet often unspoken, understanding that even an *experienced* professional or parent can benefit from consultation, and consultants themselves can benefit from ongoing professional development experiences. These same authors raise the issue of the difficulty in determining the appropriate number of sessions comprising a typical consultation relationship. Kottman raises the point that consultants need to be knowledgeable about the resources available to assist consultees in conceptualizing client concerns and making effective interventions. The same author discusses the importance of consultants being able to apply the model they are employing to organizational consultation and training situations.

DeEsch and Murphy recommend that all collaborators be involved from the outset of the team formation and that someone needs to be recognized as the team leader or facilitator. These same authors suggest that there can be a synergistic impact when all collaborators' evaluations are put together, yet each team member has a unique contribution to make. Boat and Boat point out in their case some basic elements for an effective collaborative team: a guiding philosophy, positive interdependence, common commitment to a team perspective, and accountability. These authors also suggest that shared goals, information resources, and power allow multifaceted issues to be approached effectively.

All of the authors of the case studies in this text either state or imply that *how* consultants and collaborators do what they do is as important as *what* they do. For example, how a consultant and consultee communicate is as important as the subject of their communication. James, Addy, and Crews demonstrate the importance of the consultant's ability to process the group dynamics occurring within a group of consultees. This ability to process the dynamics occurring in groups is related to effective entry and to coping with issues such as organizational politics during the consultation process. Tack, Dougherty, and Morrow stress the importance of strong process skills on the part of the consultant. By knowing not only how things are going but also what exactly is going on, consultants are in a position to make comments on the process at any point in a consultation session. By calling attention to process issues such as how a consultee is discussing a client, consultants may shed additional light on important issues related to consultation success.

Process issues are also critical in collaboration. Boat and Boat point out the importance of a variety of process events, such as positive interdependence, the commitment to a team concept, and team leadership. DeEsch and Murphy emphasize processes that enhance ownership and affiliation. These authors stress the process of continual monitoring and refining of team goals, roles, and functions, as well as team maintenance and development issues. DeEsch and Murphy also note the importance of setting ground rules for the inevitable conflict and controversy that teams encounter.

Entry

If you were a consultant or collaborator, what kind of things would it make sense for you to do during the entry stage? If you were internal to the organization, you would make sure appropriate parties were informed of your intentions and you would then begin to build appropriate relationships. If you were an external, you would explore, with the help of a representative of the organization, the possibilities of initiating a consultative or collaborative relationship; depending on the situation, you would be seeking assistance or prospective consultees or collaborators. Based on these explorations you would determine if consultation or collaboration was in order.

You would then negotiate a contract that was detailed enough to set clear expectations and yet broad enough to give the parties involved some latitude in behavior. You would be mindful of the psychological aspects of the contract as well as the formal aspects. You would try to make sure that your work site was in a neutral location and make a point to abide by the cultural norms of the workplace.

You would deliberately go about your work in such a way that you would be accepted by prospective consultees and collaborators as a person who is both helpful and trustworthy. You would most likely view resistance as a necessary thing among consultees and, on occasion, fellow collaborators. You would try to manage resistance by maintaining a strong rapport with the parties involved.

Diagnosis

There are many common-sense elements related to the diagnosis stage. As a consultant or collaborator you would make sure that there was an adequate plan for gathering information or data. You would determine who would be gathering the information and by what methods. You would try to use multiple information-gathering techniques while at the same time avoiding the pitfall of gathering an overabundance of information. For example, you might use teacher interviews and classroom observation to gather data on a student. Taking the information you and others gathered, you would analyze the data by first determining a frame of reference for analysis (such as the client's adaptation to school). You would also use methods (such as thematic analysis) to help define the problem. Once you had defined the problem to the satisfaction of the parties involved, you would make sure that effective goals were set in a manner that was not rushed. You would raise the question of methods to meet the goals. You would be creative in assisting the consultee or fellow collaborators to determine possible interventions by using brainstorming activities.

Implementation

Consultees and fellow collaborators often feel uncomfortable in having to choose between a possibly large number of apparently viable interventions. If you were a consultant or fellow collaborator in such a situation you might use your problem-solving skills by asking questions like, What are the potential negative consequences, risks, and potential payoffs of each of the interventions we have generated? By engaging the consultee or fellow collaborators with questions such as these, you would increase the probability that an effective intervention would be selected. To ensure that there was a good probability that the intervention would be followed through once it was fit into a plan, you would determine that the intervention was in line with the consultee's or fellow collaborator's perception of what needed to be done to solve the problem.

When formulating the plan, you would make sure that the plan had an articulated sequence with appropriate timelines. You would make sure that the what, the where, the when, the how, and the who of the plan were determined.

You would ensure that there was available the proverbial "Plan B," a contingency plan. While the consultee was implementing the plan you would provide any needed assistance. You would take the initiative in following up with how things were going during the implementation phase. As a collaborator, you would do your part to implement your part of the plan and be available to consult with fellow collaborators about their parts of the plan. You would make sure that the plan was evaluated in a proper way. You and the consultee or fellow collaborators would have agreed on an evaluation method prior to implementing the plan. Based on the outcome of the evaluation, you would determine to try another plan or proceed with the disengagement stage.

Disengagement

During the disengagement phase you would conduct an evaluation of the entire consultation process. You would have used formative evaluation procedures along the way. You would ask the parties involved to evaluate their satisfaction with your services. Aware that the consultee's contact with the client system would continue after you stopped your involvement with the case, you would help plan what needed to be accomplished after you disengaged from the case.

With fellow collaborators, you would plan what each of you needed to do after the collaboration team ended its formal meetings. Rather than quickly terminating after having been intensely involved with the consultee or collaboration team, you would have begun the process of reducing involvement once you saw that the client system was being adequately assisted. But you would follow up at your initiative on several occasions, particularly after postconsultation or postcollaboration planning had occurred. When you terminated the relationship or the collaboration team, you would do it in a personal yet professional manner (Dougherty, Tack, Fullam & Hammer, 1996). You would have a formal closure point and review what had transpired during the helping relationship.

PERSONAL CHARACTERISTICS OF THE HELPER

The cases suggest that the personal characteristics of professionals who consult and collaborate are critical factors in the successful outcomes of these professional services. Several of the authors directly illustrate the importance of the personal characteristics of professionals who consult and collaborate. Tack, Dougherty and Morrow note the need for objectivity as it relates to the professional's work. These same authors point out how important it is for the helpers who consult and collaborate to be open to feedback. Tack and Morrow suggest that it is very important for consultants to recognize their own issues, limits, and areas of expertise. They also note that it is imperative that consultants be clear about their own personal values.

Deck and Isenhour as well as James, Addy, and Crews suggest the importance of genuineness on the part of the consultant. Clearly, consultants need to possess a relatively high level of self-awareness to effectively conduct consultation.

Furthermore, professionals do not consult or collaborate *to* their consultees and fellow collaborators, but rather they consult or collaborate *with* them. When viewed in this light, the personal side of these helping relationships becomes as important as the professional side. Since consultation and collaboration are relationships between humans, they need to be conducted with a personal touch.

Consider the last time you developed a relationship with a person. If you are like most people, you probably started out engaging the other person in a somewhat superficial and guarded manner until you felt secure and safe with that person. People beginning professional relationships such as consultation or collaboration act much in the same way. Therefore, it is critical that consultants and collaborators possess attitudes that emphasize the use of interpersonal and communication skills related to creating an effective rapport with others. Further, many of the cases illustrate how important it is for the consultants and collaborators to value empathy, respect, and authenticity during the helping process.

Boat and Boat point to the importance of attitudes that foster interdependence of members of collaboration teams. DeEsch and Murphy point out the value of developing a climate of trust, respect, and openness when forming a collaboration team. These same authors as well as Boat and Boat discuss the fact that collaborators need an appreciation for conflict and controversy as natural aspects of the collaboration process. Carrington Rotto notes how important it is to be willing to integrate positive interpersonal skills with technical expertise to maximize consultant-consultee effectiveness. Deck and Isenhour as well as James, Addy, and Crews point out that consultants must have a sense of authenticity, which allows them to model the very behaviors they want their consultees to acquire. Such "walking the talk" demonstrates the consultant's trust in him- or herself and, at the same time, also shows the consultant's humanness.

Such modeling also provides an atmosphere in which consultees are more willing to try out new behaviors. The bottom line is, because consultation is an interpersonal relationship in which all parties have the opportunity to benefit, consultants need to be responsive to the human side of consultation if consultation is to be successful (Henning-Stout, 1994; Dougherty, 2005). The case described by Kottman, in which the consultant provides feedback to the consultee on the consultee's lifestyle, dramatically demonstrates the necessity for building a working alliance upon trust.

Entry

The cases in this text suggest some important points about the personal characteristics of professionals as they relate to the entry stage. First, consultants and collaborators will want to take the time necessary to create a rapport with their consultees. External consultants and collaborators may require more time to do this than internal professionals who provide these services. Internal consultants and collaborators, on the other hand, must exercise caution and remember that a rapport developed in the past will not necessarily transfer automatically into a new helping situation involving consultation or collaboration. Although empirical research on entry is limited, there is some evidence that consultees perceive the consultant's relationship activities as more important than the consultant's knowledge (Martens, Lewandowski, & Houk, 1989). Consequently, helpers should pay attention to relationship skills when initiating consultative and collaborative relationships. Kottman notes the importance of proceeding at the consultee's pace in creating the consultation relationship. Tack and Morrow show in their case how consultants can encounter sensitive issues and how they need to be aware of their values about these issues. These authors go on to point out that sensitive issues can extend the entry stage.

In developing contracts consultants and collaborators will want to recall that there is an aspect of contracting known as the "psychological contract." These psychological aspects refer to the expectations that the parties involved have for one another. These expectations govern the relationship. The more trust that the parties have for one another, and the stronger their rapport, the more the psychological aspects of the contract become secondary to the process of helping.

Some of the cases you have read involved professionals internal to the system in which the helping relationship occurred, while other cases involved professionals external to the system. Whether they are internal or external, helpers will have to gain psychological entry. Psychological entry refers the gradual acceptance of the helper by members of the organization in which consultation or collaboration is to occur. As the cases you have read illustrate, professionals who consult or collaborate need to deliberately focus on gaining psychological entry. An example of this would be how Deck and Isenhour spent some of their initial time with their consultees.

It is essential that human service professionals determine and define the boundaries of consultation or collaboration at the outset of the relationship. Tack and Morrow reflect a different aspect of the human side of the consultation relationship when they point out the difficulty in differentiating between a counseling and consultation relationship. When they discuss the self-care plan with which the consultant assisted the consultee, did this constitute a counseling relationship? Or was the consultant simply helping the consultee make a plan that would effectively benefit the consultee and her future clients? The answers to these questions are not clear, particularly in light of the fact that the consultant had referred the consultee to a counselor.

Diagnosis

When consultants or collaborators are seen as trustworthy, others working with them are more likely to share accurate and relevant information related to the situation at hand. For example, put yourself in the place of a consultee who is asking for help. You are now at the stage of the helping process in which the problem is to be identified. Perhaps you know that some of your own professional inadequacies are contributing to the problem you are having with the client system. Would you share this information willingly with a consultant or collaborator whom you didn't trust? Probably not.

It is useful for consultants and collaborators to be willing to take risks and be creative. James, Addy, and Crews point out the importance of these characteristics in generating possible interventions. Consultants frequently need to take the lead during the diagnosis stage because consultees have previously exhausted their own resources prior to asking for help. Consequently, the ability to look at events in a fresh light and the willingness to be patient are desirable personal characteristics for consultants and collaborators to possess.

Collaborators will need the ability to engage in perspective taking, or the ability to understand and respect others' views of events. Because collaboration involves mutual and reciprocal consultation among team members, it is essential for collaborators to be able to understand how other team members grasp a situation in order to assure that adequate data-gathering procedures are chosen and that appropriate goals are set. Both collaboration cases in this text accent this point.

Human service professionals, when they consult and collaborate, need to be thorough in the activities they engage in during the diagnosis stage. Such thoroughness will help the professional avoid hastily drawing conclusions due to time constraints within organizations. The school counselor, for example, will avoid the temptation to make a quick prescription to a teacher or parent about a child's behavior. The school or community psychologist will slow the team process down to more thoroughly review the problem at hand.

Given the nature of collaboration as a team activity, collaborators will need to view conflict as an opportunity to assist the team to move forward in helping the client systems. Conflicts can easily arise over selecting goals, determining interventions, and deciding who is going to do what.

Finally, the human service professional needs an action orientation during the diagnosis stage. The consultee or collaboration team wants assistance for a reason. There are many activities competing for people's time. Clearly, consultants and collaborators have to be reflective, thorough, and able to react in a timely fashion in order to have their services regarded as productive.

Implementation

The personal characteristics of human service professionals are also important in the implementation phase. Consultants and collaborators need to be flexible during the implementation phase. When choosing interventions, consultants and collaborators need to accommodate others' views about how to proceed. They also need to be aware of their own values about certain types of interventions. For example, a consultant who is biased against behavioral interventions may unknowingly act in ways that are counterproductive to a thorough review of possible intervention options.

Needless to say, collaborators have to view the relationship as a partnership if they are to facilitate successful implementation. They need to be able to take on their own interventions while allowing others to take on different interventions that are part of the plan. Consultants often need a collaborative orientation in order to insure that the best possible plan is developed and to make sure that the consultee is empowered. Clearly, a collaborative attitude among human service professionals can be a major asset in the endeavors related to consultation and collaboration.

Consultants and collaborators need to be aware of any control issues. This characteristic is particularly critical when the plan is being implemented. Consultants, for example, are typically "on call" during this phase. Since one of the goals of consultation is to enhance the independent problem-solving skills of consultees, clearly consultants need to be aware of and effectively manage issues related to controlling helping relationships. Collaborators also need to be aware of issues related to control. In collaboration, there are often several people responsible for part of a plan's implementation. In order for the implementation phase to work smoothly, all parties involved need to have the freedom to conduct their part of the implementation as they see fit while relying on other members of the collaboration team for assistance when needed. Further, collaboration controversy can be positive because it causes the team to reflect upon the processes in which they are engaging.

Part of the implementation stage is evaluating the plan that has been implemented.

Consultants and collaborators need to be objective. As you know, evaluating something to which you are connected can be unsettling. If you are responsible for part of a plan, then you naturally will want the plan to be successful.

Evaluation is a process that determines whether the plan, and the consultant, to some degree, were successful. If you are not objective, you might construe the evaluation data to meet your needs for being successful rather than consider them objectively relative to assisting the client system.

Disengagement

Consultants and collaborators need feedback from their consultees and fellow collaborators in order to enhance their own professional development. This professional growth orientation can be enhanced through actively soliciting feedback on one's performance. Here objectivity is just as essential as it is in evaluating the consultation or collaboration team plan. Without objectivity, the consultant or collaborator may fall prey to interpreting the evaluation data to meet their own needs.

Consultants and collaborators need to be risk takers when conducting evaluations of the helping process. Some consultants, for example, insist that every evaluation of each consultation they conduct include the question, What could the consultant have done to make this experience even more beneficial? Such a question sets up a response that suggests the consultant could have done even more. Feedback like this facilitates the professional growth of the consultant.

Dependency can be an issue in consultation, and to a lesser degree in collaboration. It is imperative for consultants and collaborators to be aware that dependency can not only lead to self-aggrandizing behavior on their part but also defeat one of the major goals of consultation and collaboration by not empowering the recipients of these services. Focusing on postconsultation and postcollaboration planning can minimize dependency issues. By its nature, planning for what the parties involved will be doing relative to the client system after the consultation or collaboration relationship is over helps reduce the possibility of dependency.

The consultant and collaborator need to be aware that terminating the helping relationship can be a source of anxiety for the parties involved. If they are aware of their feelings regarding termination, human service professionals can better prepare themselves for it. Consultants and collaborators need to be sensitive to their consultees' and fellow collaborators' feelings about terminating. For example, internal consultants and collaborators can begin discussing the possibility of future consultation and collaborations as a particular helping relationship is terminating.

ACCOUNTING FOR MULTICULTURAL INFLUENCES

We are living in an increasingly culturally diverse society. Consequently, consultants and collaborators will more often have contact with people with varying cultural backgrounds. When working with consultees or fellow collaborators who are culturally different, or with consultees or fellow collaborators whose clients are culturally different, consultants and collaborators have to demonstrate sensitivity to and respect for these differences. They also need to be aware of how their own cultural upbringing has affected them (Behring & Ingraham, 1998; Ingraham, 2000; Corey et al., 2003).

People from differing cultural, ethnic, or racial backgrounds can vary in their values, language patterns, and child rearing patterns (Thomas, Correa, & Morsink, 1995). Further, there can be differences within cultural groups regarding these same constructs, which makes generalization difficult (Tobias, 1993).

As a result, specific cultural characteristics may assist professionals in dealing with consultees, fellow collaborators, and their clients to the degree those people possess such characteristics (Correa & Tulbert, 1993). Nonetheless, working effectively with people from differing cultural backgrounds requires knowledge of and respect for the person's cultural heritage (Miranda, 1993) and life experiences such as gender (Henning-Stout, 1994).

If consultants or collaborators do not take such differences into account, they can inadvertently cause difficulties in the helping relationship, or even exploit individuals. When consultants or collaborators do not act with multicultural sensitivity, they often become frustrated while attempting to be of service, get locked into their "expert" role, and become more content (as opposed to process) oriented (Dougherty, 1996-97).There is some likelihood that the effectiveness of their communication will suffer.

The experiences of growing up in a different culture can create language patterns, learning styles, and ways of acting that differ from those of the majority culture. For example, speech in high-context cultures, such as Native American, relies heavily on nonverbal aspects of communication, whereas low-context cultures like those of the majority culture rely more heavily on the use of words (Miranda, 1993; Miranda 2002). It is easy to imagine a person from a low-context cultural background wanting a person from a high-context cultural background to think, act, and speak more concretely and quickly. The implications for consultation and collaboration are obvious.

Multicultural sensitivity and awareness of diversity have become essential qualities for all successful consultants and collaborators to possess. Consultants and collaborators have a professional and ethical obligation to be aware of the influence of their culture and gender on their work with people of different cultural identities. Consultants and collaborators need to be aware that their models are often deficient in the areas related to ethnic, racial, and cultural diversity (Jackson & Hayes, 1993; Ingraham, 2000). For an excellent resource on enhancing multicultural sensitivity and competence see Ortiz and Flanagan (2002) and Ramirez et al. (1998). For a culturally competent consultation, see Salzman (2002).

Entry

There can be differences between groups of differing cultural backgrounds in the way they approach the consultation relationship (Gibbs, 1980). For example, African Americans may be more concerned than the majority culture about the interpersonal orientation of a consultant, whereas a consultee from the majority culture may be more interested in determining whether or not the consultant is able to be of assistance (i.e., instrumentally competent) (Gibbs, 1980).

Clearly, consultants and collaborators will want to be knowledgeable about culturally different groups and take that knowledge into consideration as they initiate the helping relationship. In that way, they increase the probability of providing culturally sensitive services.

Some consultees or collaborators from culturally different backgrounds may defer to the consultant as an "expert." Consequently, consultants will have to determine whether they wish to enter the relationship in this context or aim for a more nonhierarchical, collaborative relationship. Whichever decision a consultant makes, there should be a clear acceptance of the resources the consultee possesses and an attempt to utilize those resources within the consultative relationship.

How consultants use their communication and interpersonal skills during consultation will, to a large extent, determine the success of consultation (Jackson & Hayes, 1993). One method consultants and collaborators can use to determine their suitability to work with consultees or fellow collaborators is to determine their level of comfort in dealing with any cultural or ethnic issues related to the problem at hand (Jackson & Hayes, 1993).Awareness of cultural differences and how they might impact the consultative relationship should be considered before contracting.

Diagnosis

Multicultural influences impact the diagnosis stage (Jackson & Hayes, 1993). For example, a consultee's or fellow collaborator's view of the methods used for data gathering may be influenced by cultural variables such as context. Consultees or fellow collaborators from high-context cultures may prefer interviewing or observational methods whereas those from low-context cultures may prefer methods such as reading documents or conducting surveys. Consultees of different cultural backgrounds may be more comfortable with more ambiguous definitions of the problem than the training of most consultants and collaborators suggests. When setting goals, there can be cultural differences related to perceptions of what needs to be accomplished. Whereas, for example, one collaborator may view the family as the focal point of the goals, another collaborator may view a particular member of the family as the focus. Cultural differences can play a part in determining what kinds of interventions are generated.

Consultees or fellow collaborators influenced by high cultural context may shy away from interventions that are time bound, perceived to be overly structured, or deal exclusively with authority figures.

Implementation

In choosing an implementation, cultural differences can impact the perception of the type of intervention selected. Based on the perspective of one's cultural view, interventions focusing on the use of groups may be preferred, and the time required to implement an intervention may not be considered an important factor. Whatever the case, the cultural views and expectations of the consultee or fellow collaborators should be taken into account when selecting an intervention (Jackson & Hayes, 1993).

When a plan is being formulated, there may be differences in opinion about the importance or necessity of a time frame for the plan's implementation. The parties involved may feel differently about whether the consultee should have exclusive responsibility for carrying out the plan. In fact, it is reasonable to assume that people with some cultural backgrounds would prefer collaboration to consultation based on their views of interdependence. In cases such as these, even collaborators will want to make sure that the team keeps a team approach to the implementation and doesn't attempt to "divvy" out the responsibility for various aspects to individuals.

In terms of evaluation of the plan, input from consultees or fellow collaborators is essential if the perspectives of different cultures are present. People from high-context cultures, for example, may approach evaluation of the plan in a quite different manner, relying more on a constructivist model. For example," efficiency," a must in a typical low-context culture, may not be of particular interest to a person from a high-context culture. Similarly, whether or not the plan was executed in a timely fashion may not be nearly as relevant as the social impact of the plan. The preferred model of evaluation itself may be built on a social consensus, constructivist model rather than the traditional positivist, empirical model.

Disengagement

Multicultural influences can have a strong impact on the evaluation of the consultation process. The cultural experiences of some consultees may suggest that the evaluation be guided by general questions, therefore bringing into question the suitability of questionnaires designed to assess consultee satisfaction with the consultant. Just as in evaluating the consultation plan, consultants should be cautious about assuming what kind of evaluation process is to be conducted. When it comes to postconsultation and postcollaboration planning, there can be cultural differences related to perceptions of what needs to be accomplished.

Whereas, for example, the consultant may see this as time to begin the withdrawal process from the relationship, the consultee may see this time as one of increased collaborative activity for putting the finishing touches on the case.

Consultants and collaborators will want to involve consultees and fellow collaborators in the planning process and observe the same cautions about planning that were mentioned in the discussion of planning in the implementation stage.

Follow-up can take on additional significance depending on the cultural experiences of the parties involved. For example, some fellow collaborators may desire frequent follow-up contacts, not due to dependency, but due to the person's view of social professional relationships. The critical nature of termination in consultation and collaboration becomes even more apparent when cultural experiences are taken into account. Termination is "saying good-bye" in a personal yet professional manner. Depending on one's cultural experiences, the termination process may be rather drawn out. For example, a consultant who terminates with a "Well that's it, I think we've met our goals and I hope you enjoyed it as much as I have" approach is in risk of jeopardizing the relationship as well future consultations.

Clearly, multicultural influences need to be taken into account when providing consultative and collaborative services. I believe what Axelson (1993) says about counselors is also true for consultants and collaborators: namely, they should possess an awareness and comprehension of their own cultural group and the cultural group of their consultees and fellow collaborators. They should also have perceptual sensitivity toward one's own personal values and beliefs as well as those of consultees and fellow collaborators. And they should have a comprehension of the impact of the experiences of the mainstream culture on the parties involved in the helping process.

THE VALUE OF THE PARTIES INVOLVED IN THE PROCESS

Consultants and collaborators do not operate in a vacuum when providing their services. They are influenced directly by the consultee and fellow collaborators and indirectly by the client system. Consultants can use the consultee as a resource in the consultation process and probably should do so. Carrington Rotto as well as Kottman point out the importance of involving parents and teachers as resource people in working with children. The case described by Kottman points out the importance of consultee input in the diagnosis stage.

Deck and Isenhour discuss the importance of acknowledging the professionalism and expertise of adult learners and suggest that it is presumptuous to ignore the training and background of consultees. James, Addy, and Crews dramatically illustrate this point when they describe riding with their police consultees on Friday evening shifts. These same authors point out the increasing importance of consultants' knowledge of group process and group dynamics skills. Tack, Dougherty, and Morrow echo this.

Tack, Dougherty, and Morrow note that a consultant can do an even better job of consulting when they have their consultees "be the teacher." Becker-Reems suggests that consultants take time during the consultation process to discuss what they are learning with their consultees so as to maximize learning in the consultee and increase the probability of success in consultation. The authors of each case either directly or indirectly emphasize the importance of collaboration.

Indeed, consultants seem to be well advised to take on roles, when appropriate, that maximize the use of consultees in the consultation process. In their cases, DeEsch and Murphy as well as Boat and Boat point out the obvious: by its nature, collaboration attempts to utilize the resources of all team members in helping the client system.

Entry

Resistance is the failure of the consultee or a fellow collaborator to participate constructively in the relationship. Although resistance in consultation or collaboration can take place in any stage, it is most likely to occur during the entry stage. By utilizing the resources of consultees and fellow collaborators at the outset of the helping relationship, consultants and collaborators decrease the probability of resistance.

By engaging in a "we," not an "I" or "you," mind-set, consultees and fellow collaborators feel invited to share their ideas and skills that relate to helping the client system. Since consultees and fellow collaborators can be quite familiar with the client system, their input can be valuable in making an initial exploration of the problem as well as in setting a foundation for a collaborative relationship.

Adopting a posture that validates and respects the professionalism of consultees and fellow collaborators can expedite psychological entry and thus the entire helping process.

There are strong implications for contracting when the resources of others are taken into consideration. To avoid confusion, verbal and written contracts need to be explicit about who is to do what. When the resources of consultees or fellow collaborators are employed, the psychological elements of the contract, such as the expectations of the parties involved, take on new significance.

When consultees, for example, understand that they will be active participants in the problem-solving aspects of the consultation process, their expectations about their behavior during consultation will be different than their expectations in a consultation relationship where they give the problem away to the consultant. Clearly, the involvement of consultees early in the consultation relationship is essential in order to set the expectations for the nature of their contributions.

Diagnosis

Because consultees and fellow collaborators are close to the problem at hand, they can be valuable resources during the diagnosis stage. Different members of the collaboration team, for example, may have direct access to different aspects of the client system. A school teacher may have unique information about a child's learning styles and achievement. A counselor may have a view of the child's family life. A school psychologist may have insights into the child's psychological functioning. Clearly, the potential of multiple, varied sources of information can add to the quality of information necessary to define the problem.

Consultees, also, are "on line" with their client systems. This familiarity can allow for a range and depth of information that can be invaluable.

Just as consultees and members of the collaboration team have valuable information concerning the client system, they can also provide insight in determining the nature of the problem to be dealt with. Defining the problem is a critical phase in that, once the problem is defined, this definition guides the remainder of the consultation or collaboration process. Consultees and fellow collaborators can provide input to make sure that the problem is reasonably well

defined, practical, and agreed with by the parties involved. For example, a mental health collaboration team working with clients from a group home reaches a consensus on the problem to be dealt with through a process of providing multiple perspectives on the information pertaining to the client system. Through a process of give and take, the team agrees upon a definition of the problem.

The expertise and perspectives of consultees and fellow collaborators can allow for creative goal setting. Many of the suggested techniques for effective goal setting, such as brainstorming, divergent thinking, scenario writing, and fantasy are obviously more likely to be successful when there are multiple inputs.

Consider, for example, the concept of "piggybacking" in brainstorming. In piggybacking, one person's idea stimulates a related idea in another person.

In generating possible interventions to meet designated goals, creativity can be enhanced through using the input of consultees or team members. Just as in goal setting, brainstorming can be an effective tool to generate possible interventions.

The familiarity the consultee or team members have with the client system can allow for concrete and practical interventions that are directly tailored to the needs of the client system. In addition, consultees and team members are most likely to generate interventions with which they are most knowledgeable and comfortable, thus increasing the probability that they will follow through on interventions.

Implementation

When choosing an intervention, consultees or members of the collaboration team often have a good sense of what will or will not work with a given client system. A psychologist on a collaboration team might be very aware of a client's resistance to experiential approaches to counseling. A family therapist on the same team may have insights about what might be effective based on the client's participation in family counseling. Consultees and team members can provide valuable information about potential positive and negative factors related to possible interventions.

In formulating a plan based on the intervention selected, consultees and members of collaboration teams can identify and gather the appropriate resources that can dramatically increase the probability of successful outcomes.

They can participate in the creation of a checklist that is designed to avoid the pitfalls of inadequate planning, provide their perspectives in a force field analysis about prospective plans, and take responsibility for developing contingency plans. A consultee who is a therapist, for example, may be able to generate a variety of positive consequences to, what appears on the surface to be, a simple and perhaps superficial plan.

In most consultation procedures, the consultee implements the plan with the consultant being "on call." The understanding is that the consultees retain responsibility for the case even though they are seeking assistance with it. A mental health consultant may provide assistance to a substance abuse counselor, but that counselor will carry out the agreed-upon plan. Things are quite different in collaboration. In collaboration, each team member carries out a part of the plan and at the same time is "on call" to assist other team members who may need assistance with their parts of the plan. For example, an activity therapist may work with a client on social leisure activities while a group therapist helps the client develop social skills in an assertive training group.

Consultees often have a sense of what did or did not work as a plan was being implemented. They can be valuable resources in ascertaining the degree that a plan was effectively implemented. Evaluation of the plan is more complex in collaboration because the parts of the plan are implemented by more than one person.

Clearly, it is critical for consultants and collaboration teams to have a design in place for evaluating plans. In that way, the consultant and consultee and collaboration team can use this design to guide their evaluation procedures effectively.

Disengagement

The resources of consultees and fellow collaborators can be used effectively during the disengagement phase. Evaluation can help determine the effects of a given consultation or collaboration experience and assist in providing accountability in service. The use of the resources of consultees and fellow collaborators allows for increased objectivity and multiple perspectives in the evaluation process.

When planning postconsultation and postcollaboration matters, the input of consultees and team members is essential. They are, after all, most familiar with the system in which they have contact with the client system. Consequently, consultees and team members will most likely have a good sense of what needs to be accomplished after consultation is over or after the collaboration team has disbanded or moved on to another client. Ownership by consultees and fellow collaboration team members of what needs to be accomplished at this point is critical to follow-through.

ORGANIZATIONAL CONTEXT

The organizations in which consultation occurs have powerful forces that influence the consultation process." Smart" consultants take these forces into consideration when providing services. Kottman points out the importance of having consultation sanctioned by the top administrator in the organization in which consultation is occurring to ensure that members of the organization view consultation as a normal professional development activity. James, Addy, and Crews note the importance of having the top administrators of the organization committed to and involved in the consultation process. These same authors recommend the importance of creating, in different subsystems of organizations, the mind-set that consultation will create beneficial results for all parties involved. Tack, Dougherty, and Morrow suggest the helpfulness of knowing the system in which consultation is occurring. These same authors point out some of the advantages and disadvantages, from an organizational perspective, of being a part of the same system that is receiving consultation.

Consultants will want to bear in mind that there are a variety of forces in organizations of any kind, such as the organization's culture, that influence the nature of consultation. When the consultant and other parties involved account for these forces, they can be used to affect success in consultation. Becker-Reems points out the importance of organizational dynamics as they relate to confidentiality and also demonstrates the importance of recognizing that not all consultees willingly take part in consultation. Boat and Boat stress the need for accountability in collaboration due in part to the varying missions representatives from organizations often have. By holding the team itself accountable for its actions, the influence of any one organization on the team's processes is limited.

DeEsch and Murphy discuss the necessity of training potential collaboration team members in collaborative procedures prior to establishing teams. In addition, these same authors suggest the importance of taking organizational factors into account when attempting to establish collaboration teams in any setting. For example, in organizations that stress hierarchical and mechanistic ways for services to be implemented, collaborative services must be sold before they will be accepted by the organization.

Entry

Consider yourself a teacher in a school in which consultation services were perceived by members of the organization to be remedial interventions for personnel "not quite up to snuff." Would you be overly zealous in seeking out consultation services? Probably not. Consider yourself a therapist in a mental health center in which consultation services were promoted from the top down as professional development experiences designed to enhance professional skills.

People who engaged in consultation were actually rewarded in their performance evaluations for their participation. Would you be likely to seek out consultative services when you felt you could benefit from them? Most likely. As you can see, the organizational factors such as how the organization views consultation services can strongly influence how those services are implemented and utilized. Therefore, professionals who wish to provide consultation and collaboration must make every attempt to work with top-level administrators to ensure the consultation will be a desirable professional development activity for all members of the organization.

External consultants in particular will need to spend additional time studying the organization in order to accomplish entry adequately. There is perhaps no better way to do this than by visiting the organization and meeting with parties-at- interest for extended periods of time. Understanding how to gain credibility in organizations is critical for effective entry. Recall that in the James, Addy, and Crews case, the consultants rode with police officers on the night shift to learn what they faced every time a mental disturbance call came over the radio.

In making contracts, consultants and collaborators will want to take the norms and mores of the organization into account. For example, even internal consultants may want to use written contracts if the organization values a "write everything down" attitude. When negotiating the contract, consultants and collaborators will have to take into account whether the organization will have a "give the problem away to the specialist" attitude when collaboration or consultation is sought. If this is true, then effective collaboration is unlikely to occur and most consultation will end up being a purchase of expertise type that does not provide professional growth experiences for the consultee.

Physical entry takes on significance in light of organizational forces. Is it prestigious or stigmatic for the consultant or a collaborator to be housed near the administrative office in an organization? This will be determined by the culture of the organization, which is molded by the forces within that organization.

Consultants and collaborators who work smart will ascertain the importance of office location and act accordingly. Organizational forces also affect psychological entry. How does upper management perceive consultation and collaboration in the organization? What is the reputation of consultation and collaboration services within the organization? What is the current state of morale within the organization? Factors such as these can exert powerful forces on the processes of consultation and collaboration and therefore need to be considered.

Diagnosis

Forces within the organization often determine the "depth" of diagnosis, that is, they determine the degree to which consultants and collaborators can define problems or change issues. For example, in one organization a consultant may be able to deal with morale issues, while in another only case consultation is permitted.

Collaboration teams in one setting may be allowed to focus on the quality of work life, while in another deal only with identified clients. As you might be sensing, the more consultation or collaboration moves toward changing the organization rather than individuals, the more likely organizational forces can be a factor. Organizational factors can influence which methods are used in gathering information. Time constraints, for example, may prohibit the use of interviews. Attitudes in the organization toward surveys and questionnaires can influence return rates and the frequency of additional comments made. Some teachers may not want observation used as a method for gathering information about a student due to concerns about how other professionals may react to the observational data.

Organizational forces can influence how the problem is defined. In some schools, consultants and collaborators may be expected to define the problem only in terms of the client system. Defining the problem in terms of the professional development of consultees or fellow collaborators may be frowned upon.

The organization's culture and ways of doing things all heavily influence the setting of goals and the generation of possible interventions. The goal of assisting a student to be more assertive with school personnel may be unacceptable in one school, while in another it may be considered part of character education.

Forces within the organization can either facilitate or inhibit the range of possible interventions that are generated. A bias toward one style of dealing with the client system can automatically eliminate a large array of possible interventions.

Implementation

Assume you work as a professional in a group home for adolescents and are asked to consult with the home's activity therapist. The group home is run on a behavior modification system. As a consultant you want to suggest some experiential activities that are related to one of the group home member's adjustment to the home. You know if you make such suggestions, the activity therapist will most likely remind you that your suggestions go against the grain of the program now in place. Biases within organizations can not only restrict the range of possible effective interventions but can also determine which interventions are chosen. Consider one organization in which the treatment of choice is family therapy and another organization with a similar mission whose focus is individual counseling and psychotherapy. Chances are that the forces in the organization will determine to a large degree the intervention chosen irrespective of the selection process.

Organizational forces will likely determine the who, what, when, where, and how of planning. Let's consider the following example: in some schools there is a bias toward consultation; in others, toward collaboration. Biases such as these are more than just differences in terminology. In a school with a bias toward consultation, there will be pressure on the recipients of consultation to maintain responsibility for helping the client system. In schools with a bias for collaboration, on the other hand, there will be a bias to spread the responsibility over a collaboration team. Forces within the organization dictate who is ultimately responsible for helping the client system. These forces, then, directly affect the planning process.

Forces within the organization probably have less effect on how plans are put into practice than on what plans are selected in the first place. One exception is a major change in the organization once the plan is underway, such as a cut in funding or the addition of new staff. Imagine a situation where a mental health center receives funding for an adolescent substance abuse unit. A collaboration team within the center is dealing with an adolescent substance abuser, a recidivist who is likely to be a long-term client. You can see how changes within the organization may impact a plan that is in the process of being implemented.

Or consider an example using consultation: you are a counselor or psychologist in a school setting providing consultative services to a teacher. Due to an increased enrollment in the school, the teacher's class size grows by four students. The amount of time the teacher now has to dedicate to the student concerning the consultation plan has been radically decreased. Chances are that the plan will need some adjusting.

In evaluating the plan, organizational forces will dictate the amount of time and attention paid to evaluation of the plan. Such forces will impact the decision concerning ways to measure the plan's effectiveness and with whom the results should be shared.

Disengagement

In high-accountability environments, there will be a greater expectation for consultants and collaborators to have their services evaluated. Consultants and collaborators have to look beyond the evaluation of the plan and examine the entire helping process, including satisfaction of consultees and fellow collaborators.

In low-accountability environments, on the other hand, there may be little incentive, beyond the professionalism of consultants and collaborators, to conduct an evaluation. Effective evaluation procedures can take time. Organizations that view service delivery as more valuable than accountability may well deemphasize evaluation procedures.

Organizational forces most likely have little to do with reducing involvement and follow-up, since these are typically considered a prerogative of a professional. It is hard to imagine an organization having a dictum that says, "Don't touch base with your consultees or fellow collaborators to see how things are going." On the other hand, organizations that have informal expectations about the duration of consultative or collaborative relationships may indirectly affect the timing of the onset of reduced involvement.

Organizational forces can have a strong impact on how a relationship is terminated. Recall the case by Becker-Reems. In her termination with Larry, they discussed rather personally the amount of pressure Larry had been under to receive consultation and the fact that he felt like his behavior was under a microscope during consultation. Yet they also discussed the possibility of future consultative contact. On the other hand, the case by Tack and Morrow illustrates another professional way of terminating in which the goals of consultation were reviewed and the relationship ended.

This chapter has attempted to pull together some basic ideas related to effective practices in consultation and collaboration as they relate to the stages of these helping relationships. The information in this chapter will help you face the real-life challenges of developing consultation and collaboration programs in your professional work setting.

REFERENCES AND SUGGESTED READINGS

Axelson, J.A. (1993). *Counseling and development in a multicultural society* (2nd ed.). Pacific Grove, CA: Brooks/Cole.

Behring, R. K.,& Murphy, J. J. (1998). *Journal of Educational and Psychological Education, 9,* 57–72.

Block, P. (2000). *Flawless consulting.* (2nd ed.). San Francisco, CA: Jossey Bass.

Bramlett, R. K.,& Murphy, J. J. (1998). School psychology perspectives on consultation: Key contributions to the field. *Journal of Educational and Psychological Education, 9,* 29–55.

Corey, G., Corey, M. S., & Callanan, P. (2003). *Issues and ethics in the helping professions* (6th ed.). Pacific Grove, CA: Brooks/Cole.

Correa, V. I., & Tulbert, B. (1993). Collaboration between school personnel in special education and Hispanic families. *Journal of Educational and Psychological Consultation, 4,* 253–265.

Dougherty, A.M. (Fall/Winter 1996-97).The importance of effective communication in consultation. *The Consulting Edge, 8(2)*, 1–2, 4–7.

Dougherty, A.M. (2005). *Psychological consultation and collaboration in school and community settings.* (4th ed.). Belmont, CA: Wadsworth.

Dougherty, A. M., Henderson, B. B., Tack, F. E., Deck, M.D., Worley, V.,& Page, J. R. (1997).The relation of level of facilitative conditions, consultant experience, and stage of consultation to consultees' perceptions of the use of direct confrontation. *Journal of Educational and Psychological Consultation, 8,* 21–40.

Dougherty, A.M., Tack, F. E., Fullam, C. B., & Hammer, L.A. (1996). Disengagement: A neglected aspect of the consultation process. *Journal of Educational and Psychological Consultation, 7,* 259–274.

Gibbs, J.T. (1980).The interpersonal orientation in mental health consultation: Towards a model of ethnic variations in consultation. *Journal of Community Psychology, 8,* 195–207.

Henning-Stout, M. (1994). Consultation and connected knowing: What we know is determined by the questions we ask. *Journal of Educational and Psychological Consultation, 5,* 5–21.

Herlihy, B.,& Corey, G. (1997). *Boundary issues in counseling.* Alexandria,VA: American Association for Counseling and Development.

Ingraham, C. L. (2000). Consultation through a multicultural lens: Multicultural and cross-cultural consultation in schools. *School Psychology Review, 29,* 320–343.

Jackson, D.N.,& Hayes, D. H. (1993).Multicultural issues in consultation. *Journal of Counseling and Development, 72,* 144–147.

Keys, S.G., Bemack, F., Carpenter, S. L.,& King-Sears, M. E. (1998). Collaborative consultant: A new role for counselors serving at-risk youths. *Journal of Counseling and Development, 76,* 123–133.

Martens, B. K., Lewandowski, L. J.,& Houk, J. L. (1989).The effects of two sequential- request strategies on teachers' acceptability and use of a classroom intervention. *Professional Psychology: Research and Practice, 20,* 334–339.

Miranda, A. H. (1993).Consultation with culturally diverse families. *Journal of Educational and Psychological Consultation, 4,* 89–93.

Miranda, A. H. (2002). Best practices in increasing cross-cultural competence. In A. Thomas and J. Grimes (Eds.), *Best practices in school psychology* (4th ed., pp 353-362). Bethesda, MD: National Association of School Psychologists.

Ortiz, S. O., & Flanagan, D. P. (2002). Best practices in working with culturally diverse children and families. In A. Thomas and J. Grimes (Eds.), *Best practices in school psychology* (4th ed., pp 337-351). Bethesda, MD: National Association of School Psychologists.

Ramirez, S. Z., Lepage, K. M., Kratochwill, T. R., & Duffy, J. L. (1998). Multicultural issues in school-based consultation: Conceptual and research considerations. *Journal of School Psychology, 36,* 479-509.

Ross, G. J. (1993). Peter Block's flawless consulting and the homunculus theory: Within each person is a perfect consultant. *Journal of Counseling and Development, 71,* 639–641.

Salzman, M. B. (2002). A culturally congruent consultation at a Bureau of Indian Affairsboarding school. *Journal of Individual Psychology, 58,* 132-147.

Steward, R. J. (1996).Training consulting psychologists to be sensitive to multicultural issues in organizational consultation. *Consulting Psychology Journal, 48,* 180–189.

Thomas, C.C., Correa, V. I., & Morsink, C.V. (1995). *Interactive teaming.* Englewood Cliffs, NJ: Prentice-Hall.

Tobias, R. (1993).Underlying cultural issues that effect sound consultant/ school collaborations in developing multicultural programs. *Journal of Educational and Psychological Consultation, 4,* 237–251.

12

Cases for Further Practice

A. MICHAEL DOUGHERTY

This chapter provides you with nine brief practice cases that allow you to apply some of the concepts of consultation and collaboration to lifelike situations. I have designed the cases to include dilemmas that have no "pat" answers. Reflect upon the cases and determine how you might proceed in managing each of them. The ideas you have gleaned from reading the other cases in this text should provide you with a wealth of strategies to use in dealing with the cases that follow. For each case, you will want to pay special attention to the section entitled "Additional Information."

CASE 1: A SCHOOL-BASED CONSULTANT ASSISTS A TEACHER

A middle school teacher asks a school-based consultant for assistance with a boy in one of the teacher's classes. The boy's father is dying of a terminal illness. The teacher notices the stress that the father's illness is placing on the boy. The student's academic work has deteriorated significantly over the duration of the father's illness. At the last report card time the student failed the two subjects he takes from the teacher. The teacher is concerned about the impact of the failures on the student's psychological well-being. The teacher wants help in determining what he can do to help the child cope with the failures.

Additional Information

1. The child was counseled by the counselor during a previous school year.

2. The teacher lost one of his own parents through death only a year before.

3. Some of the boy's teachers are concerned that the boy may be using the father's illness as an excuse not to perform academically.

4. The academic areas in which the child failed were math and science.

5. The student's family belongs to a fundamentalist religious sect that had been the subject of investigative journalism into alleged "mind control" by a national television news show.

With these facts in mind, how would you proceed with this case?

CASE 2: A SCHOOL-BASED CONSULTANT WORKS WITH PARENTS

Two parents approached an elementary-school-based consultant regarding a child's "school reluctance." The child was fearful that his parents were going to suffer some type of harm or even death. This fear was causing the child (in his parents' minds) to be reluctant about going to school. When the child was taken to school and left there against his will by the parents, he became very anxious during the school day. The theme of harm to his parents permeated much of the child's work and play at school. The child, the younger of two children, was a "late arrival" in the family. The older sibling was now pursuing studies at a university far from the family's hometown, thus making the child in effect an only child. Both parents were psychiatrists by training and consequently they were both very insightful into the dynamics of their family. The father termed his son's diagnosis as school reluctance, whereas the mother felt that the child was definitely school phobic. The parents decided that they were too close to the situation to help their son with this concern.

Additional Information

1. The parents were estranged from their older child who was at college.

2. The parents worked together in a private-practice setting.

3. The school-based consultant was very experienced in cases such as these but was intimidated by the credentials of the parents.

4. When the child was younger, he had been placed in three different preschool programs before the parents were satisfied with the "quality" of the setting.

5. The child would wander to the window several times during the school day reporting that he was making sure that his parents were not out in the street hurt somewhere.

With these facts in mind, how would you proceed with this case?

CASE 3: A CONSULTANT AIDS A THERAPIST AT A COMMUNITY MENTAL HEALTH CENTER

A psychologist was under contract to provide consultation services to counselors at a community mental health center. One of the therapists asked the consultant for assistance with a case involving a client suffering from a terminal illness. The therapist was having difficulties because the client was denying her terminal situation. In spite of the gentle but direct encountering by the therapist, the client continued to use denial or resistance to maneuver the sessions in other directions. Yet, the client did ask for assistance in important areas such as managing finances and learning coping strategies for the pain she was experiencing.

Additional Information

1. The therapist had never lost a significant other in her life through death.
2. The client saw the therapy sessions as meeting some of her social needs.
3. The consultant was approaching retirement age and had dealt with several bouts with cancer.
4. The therapist did not have strong religious values; the consultant had no religious values.
5. The therapist had completed eight sessions with the client. Supervisors at the mental health center actively discouraged long-term therapy.

Given the information above, how might you proceed with this case?

CASE 4: A MEMBER OF A UNIVERSITY COUNSELING CENTER CONSULTS WITH A UNIVERSITY'S DIRECTOR OF STUDENT DEVELOPMENT

The Director of Student Development of a medium-sized university seeks out consultation because of increasing conflict among several of the university's fraternities.

She reports that some fraternities have taken it upon themselves to "crash" other fraternities' parties. This type of behavior has led to physical violence among members of several fraternities. The director notes that she believes that some of the conflict is racial in nature. Many students have reported being afraid to walk or bike down "Greek Street" for fear of being accosted or caught in the middle of some conflict. The director reports that she is considering placing several of the fraternities on disciplinary probation but would like to try something as a last resort to create some positive momentum for getting the problems solved in a constructive manner. She asks the consultant to help her determine how to proceed.

Additional Information

1. The consultant is a graduate of a private university that did not permit fraternities.

2. Neither the consultant nor the director is a member of the dominant culture.

3. The director is actively seeking a position at another university.

4. The counseling center does not actively encourage its staff to engage in consultation.

5. There are four weeks left until the end of the academic year.

Given the information above, how might you proceed with this case?

CASE 5:A HUMAN SERVICES CONSULTANT PROVIDES SERVICES TO A MIDLEVEL MANAGER IN AN INDUSTRIAL SETTING

A midlevel manager in a tire manufacturing plant has contacted a human service consultant in private practice. As part of its emphasis on total quality, the company is involved in enhancing bottom-up communication within the organization.

The manager reports that this emphasis is backfiring in his unit. He notes that the line supervisors charged with relaying information to the manager are distorting the information provided by their subordinates to gain more power for themselves in the manager's unit. For example, the manager notes that inquiries regarding flexible scheduling are distorted into demands for allowing supervisors to grant flexible work schedules without the manager's input or approval. The manager suggests that the consultant observe a series of meetings between the manager and the line supervisors.

Additional Information

1. The consultant and the manager are former college roommates.

2. The manager is the only college graduate in the primarily blue-collar unit. The unit is marked by cultural diversity.

3. The quality management movement in the company has been in existence for six months. The manager has been trained in quality management; the line supervisors have not.

4. There has been a history of substance abuse among the members of the unit.

5. There is talk of the tire company merging with a Japanese firm.

Bearing these facts in mind, how would you proceed with this case?

CASE 6: A MEMBER OF A UNIVERSITY COUNSELING CENTER COLLABORATES WITH A FACULTY MEMBER WHO SPONSORS A SORORITY

A faculty member who sponsors a sorority at a prestigious liberal arts college and one of the two counselors assigned to the school's counseling and psychological services center have met and agreed to collaborate regarding the image of one of the college's sororities. During their first meeting the sponsor lamented the shallow and glib image of the sorority in the eyes of many on the campus. She related that the president of the institution had mentioned to some of the sponsor's friends that the sorority was not living up to the institution's standards of excellence. The counselor noted that the typical grade point average of the sisters of the sorority was significantly lower than that of other sororities.

Both were aware that during rush the sisters sought out students they thought would be great "partiers." Yet, at the same time, the sorority was among the top of the Greek organizations in engaging in philanthropic efforts. The counselor and sponsor decided to work together to enhance the sorority's image in the eyes of both the campus community and the members themselves.

Additional Information

1. The officers of the sorority were pleased with the way things were. They didn't believe that the sorority had an image problem.
2. The faculty member had sponsored the sorority for the past 12 years and frequently taught honors courses.
3. There was a history of tension between the sponsor and the various officers of the sorority over the years.
4. The sponsor received credit for sponsoring the sorority through a stipend and "points" for providing service to the institution.
5. The counselor, a person of color, had a daughter who was a member of a sorority at a nearby state university. The daughter was having difficulties with her "sisters." Given this information, how might you, as the collaborating specialist, approach this case?

CASE 7: AN EMPLOYEE ASSISTANCE PROGRAM COORDINATOR COLLABORATES WITH A VICE PRESIDENT OF A TELEPHONE COMPANY

The vice president of a telephone company has asked the coordinator of the company's employee assistance program (EAP) to help her deal with a morale problem her department is having with employees in the field. A spring tornado recently destroyed a large number of telephone lines only a couple of months after a winter storm called the "Storm of the Century" caused a tremendous number of lines to need repair in extreme weather. The vice president is concerned that there is a morale problem due to a disagreement between the managers and the field workers over how much stress the field workers have been experiencing due to work demands. The managers feel that, because the field workers are being paid overtime, the storm has provided them a windfall. The workers, on the other hand, see the work demands as stretching them as thin as the last storm did, and they want more work concessions than just overtime for their efforts. The vice president and the EAP coordinator agree to work together and be mutually responsible for developing a plan to improve morale.

Additional Information

1. The company is currently undergoing the beginnings of reorganization.

The vice president's unit is affected by the reorganization plan.

2. Part of the reorganization includes a downsizing plan. The EAP coordinator is aware of the downsizing plan because of his unit's likely involvement in outplacement.

3. There is a rumor going around the organization that the vice president is looking for a new position.

4. Workers at the company, as well as those at other companies owned by the parent company, went on strike for increased benefits five years ago.

5. The EAP coordinator has been with the company for only one year.

Considering these facts, how would you, as the collaborating specialist, approach this case?

CASE 8: A COLLABORATION TEAM ATTEMPTS TO HELP AN AGGRESSIVE STUDENT

A secondary school had a school-based interactive collaboration team designed to deal with behavior concerns of the school's students. The team consisted of a school psychologist, a school counselor, and four teachers. The team agreed to a referral from the school's principal. The referred student was a sophomore who had frequently been in trouble for fighting at school. Both the school psychologist and the school counselor were new to the school. The leadership of the team rotated on an annual basis, and it was the psychologist's turn to be the leader. The teachers were doubtful that any team effort would be productive due to the nature of the family "system" in which the child lived. Nonetheless, the team members agreed to meet to find ways to help the boy decrease his fighting behavior and learn more constructive ways of behaving at school.

Additional Information

1. The team members came from a variety of cultural backgrounds.

2. The child in question was the nephew of one of the collaborating professionals.

3. The team system used by the school was not working very well.

4. The faculty resented the school's principal for being a "drill sergeant" type.

5. The child's parents prided themselves on being "free thinkers" and encouraged their children to rebel against any organized authority.

Given these circumstances, how would you as either the school counselor or school psychologist approach this case?

CASE 9: A SCHOOL PSYCHOLOGIST CONSULTS TO IMPLEMENT A POSITIVE BEHAVIORAL SUPPORT PROGRAM

The school psychologists and counselors in a school system have been asked to consult with the leadership teams in their schools to assist with the implementation of school-wide positive behavior support program. The goal is to create a program applicable to the school, classroom, and individual levels. Strategies included developing clearly stated purpose for the program, a set of positively stated expectations for behavior, procedures for teaching school-wide expectations. The consultants were also asked to ensure that their school developed a continuum of procedures for encouraging students to engage in expected behaviors and discouraged from violating school wide expectations. Finally, they were asked to assist with the development of a method for monitoring and evaluating the program. The school psychologist at Mountainview Elementary School was preparing to meet with the school's leadership team.

Additional Information

1. The existing school discipline program used a "pink slip" method that lead to defined consequences.

2. Most teachers in the school were not well versed in positive behavior support.

3. Ninety percent of the students in the school were eligible for free or reduced lunch.

4. The school's principal was a former school counselor.

5. The school has grades kindergarten through eighth grade with approximately 675 students in its student body.

Considering these facts, how would you, as the school psychologist, approach this case?

A PARTING THOUGHT

Developing a personal consultation and collaboration style is a lifelong process based on your professional and personal experiences. For your consideration, here are some suggestions to assist you in forging your personal style when delivering these services: continue to strive to know your values and what you stand for in life; attempt to be genuinely aware of your personal and professional limitations; seek out as much training and experience in consultation and collaboration as possible; and continually assess the needs of the organizations and the people with whom you are working. Taken together, these will provide a cognitive map to guide your practice and help you develop the art of providing effective assistance.

About the Author
and Contributors

THE AUTHOR

A. Michael Dougherty (Ph.D., Indiana State University) is Dean of the College of Education and Allied Professions and Professor of Counseling at Western Carolina University in Cullowhee, North Carolina. He is author of *Psychological Consultation and Collaboration in School and Community Settings* (Fourth Edition), also published by Brooks/Cole-Wadsworth Publishing Company. In addition to fulfilling his duties as Dean, he teaches graduate-level courses in consultation, theories of counseling, and counseling children. He has consulted, taught courses, and made presentations in a variety of international settings including Barbados, Colombia, Cypress, El Salvador, Germany, Great Britain, Guatemala, Honduras, Jamaica, and Jordan.

THE CONTRIBUTORS

Catherine Addy, M.S. NCC, is a student at the University of Memphis completing her doctorate in Community Agency Counseling, specializing in crisis intervention. Formerly she was a manager in Air Traffic Services with FedEx Corporation, responsible for the movement of aircraft in four major hubs. Additionally she directed the design of the crisis preparedness planning which included business continuation and disaster recovery for the company.

Elizabeth D. Becker-Reems is a partner in The Asheville Group, a management consulting firm.   She provides planning, organization development, project management, process redesign, executive coaching, and leadership development services.   She is the co-author of *Testing the Limits of Teams* (1998) and author of *Self-Managed Work Teams in Healthcare Organizations* (1994), has taught Information Management and Organization Development at the graduate level, and has published numerous articles on management topics.   Elizabeth has a Certificate in Executive Leadership from Wake Forest University's Babcock Graduate School of Management and a Master's of Science degree in Human Resource Development from Western Carolina University.

Barbara Walling Boat, Ph.D., is an associate professor in the Department of Psychiatry at the University of Cincinnati and Children's Hospital Medical Center, and Executive Director of The Childhood Trust, Cincinnati, Ohio. Dr. Boat received her doctoral degree in clinical psychology from Case Western Reserve University. She is internationally recognized for her scholarly and clinical activities in the areas of childhood trauma and maltreatment and currently is investigating the relationship among child abuse, animal abuse, and domestic violence.

Mary Barbara Boat, Ph.D. is an assistant professor of early childhood education at the University of Cincinnati.   Dr. Boat received her doctoral degree from the University of Minnesota in educational psychology with a focus in special education. She has taught persons ages 3 to 21 with a variety of exceptionalities.   Dr. Boat's teaching and research emphases are in early childhood special education and early education.   She is the co-principal investigator of a Head Start outcomes research grant and has been involved in research and publication related to the assessment of young children, behavior concerns in young children, early intervention policy, and mastery motivation in young children with and without disabilities.   Dr. Boat is the co-editor of a forthcoming book on the assessment of young children.

Pamela Carrington Rotto, Ph.D., is a psychologist at the Child Development Center at Riley Hospital for Children in Indianapolis, Indiana. She also holds a position as Adjunct Professor in the Department of Educational Psychology at the University of Nebraska–Lincoln. Dr. Carrington Rotto received her doctorate in school psychology from the University of Wisconsin–Madison in 1993. Dr. Carrington Rotto has professional experience in the schools both as a school psychologist and special education teacher. Her research interests include behavioral consultation, parent training, and systems of care for children with emotional and behavioral needs and training. She has coordinated a federally funded research project examining the effects of an intervention program that integrated the principles and procedures of behavioral case consultation and competency-based parent training.

Walter Crews has an M.S. in Community Agency Counseling from the University of Memphis. He is former director of the Memphis Police Department. He is presently executive director of Memphis Crime Stoppers.

Mary Deck is Professor of Counselor Education in the Department of Human Services at Western Carolina University. She holds a Ph.D. in counselor education from the University of Virginia and prior to her tenure at Western Carolina she was on the faculty at the University of Alabama. She holds membership in the American Counseling Association, American School Counselor Association, and Association for Counselor Education and Supervision, as well as in regional and state associations. She has been a school counselor and a teacher of special education.

Jesse B. DeEsch is an Associate Professor in the Counseling Services Program at Rider University in Lawrenceville, New Jersey. He is a consultant with school districts in New Jersey and southeastern Pennsylvania and with the New Jersey Administrative Offices of the Courts. The school consultations are primarily for creating comprehensive developmental school counseling services, creating developmental classroom management systems, and increasing the school counselor's consultative and collaborative functions. With co-author Jim Murphy, he is developing a collaborative graduate training model involving counselors, school psychologists, school administrators, and reading and language arts teachers. This evolving collaboration model has been presented at national, state, and local levels. He is an active member of the Association for Specialists in Group Work and a recipient of an ASGW Fellowship. He is also active in the New Jersey Counseling Association and has served as its president.

Glenda E. Isenhour, Ph.D., L.P.C., is Vice President of Student Affairs at the University of Montevallo, in Montevallo, Alabama. She has presented programs at national, regional, and state professional conferences and has conducted numerous in-service training programs in both mental health and school settings. She is a past president of the American Mental Health Counselors Association and serves on the Alabama Board of Licensed Professional Counselors.

Richard James Ph. D. NCC,NCSC, is an Earl Crader professor of counseling at the University of Memphis. He is a licensed professional counselor in Tennessee and a licensed psychologist. He has written books in theories of counseling and crisis intervention. He is a former director of a Title III ESEA nationally validated program for socially maladjusted and emotionally disturbed children in Illinois. He has consulted with numerous police departments across the country in implementing programs to deal with the mentally ill.

Terry Kottman, Ph.D., is the Director of The Encouragement Zone in Cedar Falls, IA. She is a licensed mental health counselor and a registered play therapist-supervisor. She has a small private practice, focusing on life coaching and play therapy supervision. Dr. Kottman's most recent book is *Partners in Play: An Adlerian Approach to Play Therapy* (American Counseling Association, 2003). Other books are *Play therapy: Basics and beyond* (American Counseling Association, 2001), *Adventures in guidance: How to integrate fun into your guidance program* (with Jeff Ashby and Don DeGraaf) (American Counseling Association, 2001), Play *Therapy in Action* (with Charles Schaefer) and *Guidance and Counseling in the Elementary and Middle Schools* (with James Muro). Dr. Kottman developed Adlerian play therapy, an approach to working with children that combines the concepts and strategies of Individual Psychology with the techniques of play therapy. Dr. Kottman has been a university professor, a school counselor, and a special education teacher.

Deana F. Morrow, PhD, LPC, LCSW, ACSW, is an Associate Professor and BSW Program Director in the Department of Social Work at the University of North Carolina at Charlotte. She received her doctorate in Counselor Education from North Carolina State University, the Master of Social Work Degree from The University of Georgia, and a Master's Degree in Counseling from Western Carolina University. Dr. Morrow teaches clinical practice courses at both the graduate and undergraduate levels. Her practice background is in clinical counseling and clinical social work in the fields of mental health, aging, and healthcare. And her research focus is principally centered in clinical practice with sexual minority populations. She is a Licensed Professional Counselor and a Licensed Clinical Social Worker in the state of North Carolina, and a member of the Academy of Certified Social Workers at the national level. She holds memberships in the National Association of Social Workers, the Social Work Baccalaureate Program Directors Association, and the Council on Social Work Education where she holds an appointment to the Commission on Sexual Orientation and Gender Expression.

James Murphy coordinates the Counseling Services Program at Rider University in Lawrenceville, New Jersey. He has practiced as a school psychologist in public and private school settings for over 20 years, serving on many collaborative and "not so collaborative" teams during that period. He currently teaches courses in consultation and school counseling that emphasize a systematic, collaborative model of student services delivery. With co-author Jesse DeEsch, he has presented papers and conducted workshops on effective collaboration at the national, state, and local levels. In his private work, he has consulted with national nonprofit agencies on team building, organizational culture and leadership.

Frances E. Tack, M.S., L.P.C., C.C.A.S., N.C.C. is the clinical unit supervisor for CASCADE, a Mecklenburg County, North Carolina substance abuse treatment program serving peri-natal, maternal, homeless and Family Drug Court involved women. She is also an adjunct instructor in the Department of Social Work at the University of North Carolina at Charlotte where she teaches substance abuse courses in the graduate program. She received her Master's degree in community counseling from Western Carolina University and has worked in detoxification, intensive outpatient and day treatment substance abuse programs and in outpatient mental health. Ms. Tack is a Licensed Professional Counselor and Certified Clinical Addictions Specialist.

If you are interested in contributing a case study to a subsequent edition of this text, please contact the author, A. Michael Dougherty, c/o Brooks/Cole- Wadsworth Publishing Company, 511 Forest Lodge Road, Pacific Grove, CA 93950-5098.